Between the Lines
THE AUTOBIOGRAPHY

VICTORIA PENDLETON

WITH DONALD MCRAE

Between the Lines

THE AUTOBIOGRAPHY

HarperSport

An Imprint of HarperCollins*Publishers*

HarperSport
an imprint of HarperCollins*Publishers*
77–85 Fulham Palace Road,
Hammersmith, London W6 8JB

www.harpercollins.co.uk

First published by HarperSport 2012

1 3 5 7 9 10 8 6 4 2

A catalogue record of this book is
available from the British Library

HB ISBN 978-0-00-732752-2
TPB ISBN 978-0-00-747653-4

Printed and bound in Great Britain by
Clays Ltd, St Ives plc

MIX
Paper from
responsible sources
FSC™ C007454

FSC™ is a non-profit international organisation established to promote
the responsible management of the world's forests. Products carrying the
FSC label are independently certified to assure consumers that they come
from forests that are managed to meet the social, economic and
ecological needs of present and future generations,
and other controlled sources.

Find out more about HarperCollins and the environment at
www.harpercollins.co.uk/green

For Scott

CONTENTS

PROLOGUE: TODAY ...

Laoshan Velodrome, Beijing, Tuesday 19 August 2008

I'm going nowhere fast. On a set of whirling rollers, with my head down, it feels as if I'm flying without moving. The bike below me shudders a little from side to side but it never moves forward. It just spins on the gleaming drums, the wheels of an otherwise stationary machine whirring endlessly. My whole life shrinks down to these surreal moments. I try not to think about it now; but I can't help it. I'm just one race away from becoming an Olympic champion.

A new song in my head starts prettily, lilting and yearning in headphones that are meant to shut out the madness and tension around me in the pits. As I get ready to return to the wooden track in another ten minutes, I look up and think of Scott. This song binds us together. I can sense him nearby, even if I can't see him. He has to become invisible to me between my races, just as we have had to keep each other secret from the world these last few months. Maybe the furtive nature of our relationship should make me feel guilty; but it doesn't. I allow myself the smallest of smiles, on the inside, behind my racing face.

1

On a steamy Tuesday evening in Beijing, a long way from home, the opening words to 'Today', by The Smashing Pumpkins, ring through me. They tell me that today is the greatest day I've ever known.

Today should become the greatest day of my life. In the final of the individual sprint I'm already a race up on Anna Meares, my old rival, the Australian rider who so often tries to bully and intimidate me. Meares is a formidable competitor but I'll never forget how she once smashed her bike straight into mine to stop me winning. Scott, who is also an Australian, used to be part of the team that helped make Meares an Olympic champion four years ago in Athens. She won the 500m time trial while, at those same Games, I endured one of the most miserable experiences of my life. I cried like I'd never cried before.

Everything should be different now. Everything should be fantastic.

As I keep myself warm on the rollers the song begins to change in my head. I can now hear The Pumpkins' Billy Corgan singing, with a muffled yelp, of burning his eyes out and tearing his heart out. I know the feeling. Racing, especially the tactical nightmare of an individual sprint, sometimes makes me want to scream. It can feel like torture.

Today, however, is different. Today I seem untouchable.

I can hardly feel my legs turning beneath me. I can see them pumping and pedalling, in a blur of bony knees and fastened feet, but it's almost as if my legs have disappeared from the rest of my body. Usually, in competition, my legs are in a permanent state of fatigue. A nagging weariness runs through them, telling me how often they have gone up and down, round and round, in ceaseless circles. But during these long weeks in Beijing my legs have been unbelievably quiet. They lead down to my feet, touching the pedals, and I pump them effortlessly, hard and fast, up and down, round and round. There is no ache.

In the first race against Meares these legs of mine were unstoppable. I beat her without really extending myself, winning the first in a possible series of three sprints. If I win the next race I'll have won Olympic gold – the only medal that I came all this way to take. It will be all over then, the waiting and the fretting, and I can go and find Scott. We can drink champagne and maybe even come out in the open. Then, and this rises up like an image of bliss on my static rollers, we can fly home happily.

I am going to win this race. I feel the certainty coursing through me. That arrogance goes against every neurotic bone in my body. Normally, I'm a seething tangle of doubt and insecurity. I question myself, and my ability, every pedal of the way. But not now, not today, not with The Smashing Pumpkins on a resounding loop; and not with my legs feeling so strong.

It's taken my whole life to reach this point. The little girl trying desperately to stay in sight of her dad, pedalling up a hill until it seemed her heart might burst, would not believe we'd end up here. There were no Olympic dreams then. That small girl, me in a different world, just wanted Dad to slow down or look back to see that I was all right. But turning the pedals on the rollers, I can now imagine Dad driving me on, never glancing over his shoulder while I struggled to keep up with him. Dad would climb away from me on the long hills, a great amateur cyclist who would have loved to have had the chances I had, a father who didn't often reassure me. I just wanted Dad to love me, and be proud of me, and so this is where I've ended up.

I'm riding this one for you, Dad, despite everything, because you, more than anyone, made me who I am – this racer going somewhere, chasing something that would make you very proud.

And this one is also for you, Mum, because you're so different. You never wanted me to be anything but myself. You'll

3

love me just the same – whether I come home with a gold medal or, instead, I just give up and slip off this bike forever. I'll be the same Lou to you. It might not make me a champion but I feel happy knowing I'm still Lou to Mum.

My name is Victoria Louise Pendleton. Alex, my twin brother, against whom I used to race so hard and so often when we were small, called me Lou-Lou for years. Our big sister, Nicola, was Nicky. And so, when Mum yelled up the stairs for one of us to get a move on, 'Nicky' and 'Vicky' sounded too similar. So Mum switched to Lou for me. Nicky, meanwhile, still sometimes calls me Scooby.

Scooby Lou might be starting to spin out but for the fact that I've been here before. There's little time left and this is not a place for songs or families. This is race time. It's the moment I've thought about so often. I've even dreaded it, especially these last few weeks as my need to win has intensified. We're at the end of the Olympic track cycling programme in Beijing and I've sat and watched at a distance as one British gold medal after another has been won. I've not even been allowed at the velodrome; to keep my legs in their springy shape, I've been made to rest at the Olympic village.

In a small room, on Chinese television, I've seen my team-mates win six gold medals so far. Chris Hoy, my equivalent in the men's sprint, has already won two golds and looks a certainty for a third a few minutes after my race. It's been a British procession, the culmination of years of work and planning, but I've just sat and watched. Sometimes I've hugged a pillow to myself, while staring at the screen alone, thinking, 'Shit, shit, shit … if I don't win I'm not going to be part of this team. Shit, shit, shit … I have to win to be part of this story. I need to win.'

Now, before I slide the mask across my face, the mask that tells Meares I'm going to blitz her, I allow myself to think once more of Scott. On the rollers I remember his last love letter to me. I cherish the fact that it was handwritten on a sheet of blue squared paper. Scott had also cut out some photographs of me winning World Cups and World Championships – just to remind me that I'm pretty good at riding fast. He wanted me to remember that I'm the world sprint champion and I've beaten Anna Meares often enough. I can beat her again.

Scott's words resonate in my head. I linger over his suggestion that I put myself through this trauma for three reasons. I endure the pain and strife because I'm doing this for the people who have loved and supported me so long. I'm doing this for my family, my friends, my coaches and, of course, for Scott. I also go through the ringer, from the rollers to the track, just for myself. I'm twenty-seven years old. I've poured my whole adult life into preparing for this moment. So I'm out to win gold for the people who love me and, yes, I want it for me too.

The third and more shadowy group are now in my mind. I will soon blank every single one of them and home in on Meares. But Scott told me, in his beautiful letter, that I should also go out there and push myself to the edge of my ability so that I can show all those people who didn't believe in me during the long and lonely years. They doubted me. They dismissed me. They hurt me. It's time I show them how wrong they were about me. It's time I make them change their minds forever about me.

Suddenly, I see Frédéric Magné, the coach who made me cry so hard in Athens. Fred, whom I liked and respected so much when I worked with him for eighteen months at his sprint academy in Aigle, walks around the pits. He's training the Chinese girls now and, specifically, another great rival of mine, Guo Shuang, who has just won the bronze medal race. Fred keeps drifting in and out of my eye-line but, now, I hold him in my gaze. He looks at me, getting ready to go out and seize Olympic gold.

I look right through him as if he's not even there.

I can feel the resentment surging inside me. Staring through Fred, it's as if I'm looking beyond him to that moment when he tore into me in Athens. His words cut me far deeper than my own knife had done. He seemed to have no awareness of the pain he caused me.

On the rollers my legs keep turning, moving faster and faster. My face is utterly impassive. I am not the same frightened and confused girl I was in Switzerland. I am not the same girl who took a Swiss army knife and used it on herself because the cutting was less hurtful than the darker pain inside. Who would have thought it? Who would believe that distressed girl, who harmed herself, would make it all the way to an Olympic final?

The Smashing Pumpkins, singing of pink ribbon scars and cleansed regret, remind me of that past confusion.

Away from Fred I see another man who ripped into me. Martin Barras, a French-Canadian who is now Australia's sprint coach, ridiculed me when he held a similar position within British cycling. He took just one look at me when I joined the sprint programme in Manchester in 2001 and decided I was far too slender and girly and weak to ever make it in the world of professional cycling. 'Miss Victoria,' he said, 'I'm going to find you very annoying.'

Well, Martin, here I am, seven years later. I'm one up on your girl, Anna Meares. She has the squat and powerful physique that you believe is a pre-requisite for success on the sprint track. Anna looks like she could flatten me with just one swipe of a killer thigh. She's got the force, too, in her backside to make someone like Martin think she should smash a frail and vulnerable little girly like me every time.

I feel like I am about to start growling on the rollers as my gaze switches from Fred to Martin, from one doubter to another. My uncomplaining legs pump just a little harder as the darkness descends. I'm going to show you, Fred, I swear to myself. I'm going to show you, Martin, I swear again.

I'm not just going to beat Martin's big hope, Anna Meares. I am going to crush her. I want to annihilate her not just by winning the Olympic final but by demolishing her by an entire straight. I want to obliterate her hopes with the fastest time a woman has ever ridden in a sprint match.

I've never felt like this before. It's an incredible emotion. I turn tingly with excitement. Adrenalin courses through me. There is so much tension and expectation in these last minutes. It seems like I've been touched by fate.

I think to myself: 'God, this is going to happen. I am going to become the new Olympic champion.'

On the rollers, of course, I have no idea of the terrible pain and disappointment that will soon follow. I just know that victory, in this race, is mine. I start to lose myself to the sprint. I turn as powerfully blank as my pumping legs.

I feel ready. I feel like, at last, I'm going somewhere fast ...

1 | THE GIRL ON A HILL

Dad rode away from me as we climbed the hill on a cold and drizzly Sunday morning in Bedfordshire. 'He doesn't love me,' I said to myself as I tried to keep up with the distant figure of my father. 'He doesn't love me. He doesn't love me ...'

I repeated the words over and over again as, never lifting my gaze from the unbreakable man on the bike climbing the steep hill, I turned my legs as fast as I could. I had to hang onto Dad. I was sure that if I lost sight of him I would lose hold of his love.

The drizzle hardened into rain. Dad still didn't look back. He sped away from me, up towards the clouds rolling down from the top of the hill. Dad looked more ghostly then.

I was fifteen. I had grown used to the ritual of chasing my father as he sped ahead of me. Dad dealt in clear and simple truths. He never told you that you were better than you were – even to boost you at your most vulnerable. Dad just expected you to do your best every single day. He was tough but, when I pleased him, I felt radiant with happiness. I knew how much it meant when Dad said he was proud of me.

The rain trickled down my face. It might have looked like I was crying, but I wasn't. I was just concentrating and pedalling, pedalling and concentrating. But I was so tired and freezing I could no longer feel my hands on the handlebars or my feet on the pedals. I held on, numb to the finger-tips, pushing down with my churning legs and deadened feet. The gap between us might have widened but I would not let myself lose Dad. I clung onto the blurry image of him up ahead. An invisible twine must have bound his bike to mine.

Dad was strong; I was skinny. He was a really fit man, who had been cycling for decades, while I was a puny little girl with stick-like legs and a serious face. Max Pendleton was a star amateur rider. I was a worried waif. But Dad must have sensed I had a huge heart because he never made it easy for me. He pushed me every single mile, especially on those gruelling hills where he was such a deadly climber.

Days and climbs such as these, Dad said, were 'character-building.' That old-fashioned phrase covered everything that was mean and testing, because what didn't kill you made you stronger. But I didn't care about building my character. I just wanted Dad to slow down and show me that he loved me.

The rain kept on; but, somehow, so did I. The cold bit deeper into my bones but, still, I wouldn't surrender. I wouldn't let Dad escape. My gaze held him and I rode even harder.

I would survive the cruel climb, as long as I made it to the top with Dad. I could taste my tenacity now. I could push myself some more.

My face felt shiny and wet. I could imagine how pale I looked against the dark grey sky. I lifted myself out of the saddle and heard my rasping breath. Coming from the back of my throat, it framed the space between Dad and me.

Yet the pain eased because, slowly, I realized that Dad was no longer getting away from me.

I was catching him. Out of my seat, and up in the air, I was catching my dad.

I kept pedalling. I kept riding. I kept climbing, higher and higher.

* * *

I am a twin. But my brother, Alex, always liked to remind me that he was an hour older than me. When you're a child, an hour between twins seems important. I adored Alex, but I knew we were different.

When we were four years old that difference almost became terminal. I nearly lost Alex then. He was so ill with leukemia that I went and stayed with my grandparents for a few weeks. Alex was in and out of hospital and it was simpler that I was looked after by my mum's parents – Alf and Mabel Viney.

Rather than being scared of the terrible disease that had invaded Alex, life with Alf and Mabel felt like a summer holiday. My nanna was just like Mum in making me feel like a four-year-old grown-up. She tied an apron under my armpits and handed me a plastic knife so I could pretend I was peeling new potatoes as I stood on a stool next to her at the sink. Granddad was just as lovely. He made me feel very important when letting me help him with his gardening.

Mum and Dad came to see me at least once a day. They always told me that Alex was going to be all right. He had lost all his hair and his head looked very shiny. But we would soon be back together again. They hugged me. And when they left I ran back to the kitchen or the garden, or just carried on dusting the front room with Nanna. I was content. I felt safe.

But maybe some deeper doubt uncurled inside me. Almost randomly, I started to pray every evening. I must have seen the pretty scene on television for I was fascinated by an image of praying, in a time of need on bended knees, at the bedside. Every evening I prayed, in my jim-jams, my hands clasped together neatly and a list of requests falling politely from my mouth – as I asked Jesus to help Alex get better and to look after Mummy, Daddy, Nicola, Nanna, Granddad and me. I did not understand the extent of Alex's illness but I knew it was serious and that we needed help.

It might have worked because Alex survived. He was lucky that our GP had diagnosed his leukemia very early; and that chemotherapy had been so successful. The staff at Great Ormond Street Hospital also looked after him with great care. Alex began to recover and, eventually, we became a proper family again. To welcome Alex home, Mum and Dad allowed him to choose a special present. He asked for a rabbit. Alex called him Peter; and the name stuck even when we were finally told that Peter was actually a girl. It was hard to tell with rabbits.

Mum, Dad, Nicola, Alex and me lived in Stotfold, which was then a large village, rather than the town it is now, in Bedfordshire, not far from Stevenage. There wasn't a lot to do in Stotfold but I was happy. Alex grew bored with the rabbit and I took over and looked after Peter. I was a busy girl – especially when it came to competing for attention. Mum and Dad still kept a close watch on Alex, just to make sure that there was no dark sign of the returning illness. I sometimes I had to fight to get noticed as much; but, mostly, life felt sweet and good.

I also loved having a big sister who, besides being five years older, was much more creative and expressive than me. Nicky was a gifted musician and she was willing to break out on her own. Far more than me, praying on bended knees, Nicola became religious. She started to go to church with her friends.

I was still little, and so she allowed me to tag along with her. I liked Sunday mornings because Nicola let me use her roller skates on the way to church. It was an ordinary Church of England service but, even when I wasn't skating behind her, I liked hanging out with Nicky. I was impressed that, on her own, she decided to get herself christened and confirmed.

Our parents were atheists which, Mum explained, meant they didn't believe in God. But they found it amusing that Mum's middle name is Mary and Dad's is Joseph. Neither Alex nor I looked like the baby Jesus. But Mum and Dad were relaxed about Nicola's religious discovery. They were happy for us to think for ourselves.

'Enjoy yourselves, girls,' Mum said every Sunday morning as, with me rolling along the cracked pavement on Nicky's old skates, we weaved our way to church.

I followed Nicky cheerfully when she decided to switch to the Baptist church for a change of scenery. The Baptist service was a bit happy-clappy but we loved singing. We felt uplifted.

It was only when we went to the Sunshine Club in our school holidays that we became slightly less enthusiastic about church. On the day we learnt about the feeding of the five thousand we were also given cold fish fingers and white bread for our lunch. The club didn't seem so sunshiney after that and, when I was six or seven, I swapped Sunday mornings at church for time with Dad on his tandem.

We'd go riding with his cycling friends, Andy and Gordon, and Dad would chat away to them all morning – only occasionally turning to ask if I was alright on the back. But I liked riding the tandem with Dad, on our own special bike for two, even though part of me wished I was still at home with Mum.

I liked doing everything Mum did on a Sunday morning when Dad was out on his bike. I liked cleaning the house with her. I liked sewing and baking and cooking. Most of all, every Sunday morning at home would revolve around Mum preparing our traditional roast which, just like her mother before her, she would serve to the family at half past one. I could have quite easily whiled away each Sunday with Mum, peeling vegetables, laying the table and getting everything ready for our meal together. But Mum never made me feel guilty for going out instead with Dad on the bike. 'Have fun, Lou,' she'd say.

Dad had loved riding his bike as long as he could remember. I began to understand that, for him, it was both part of his family past and his own personal escape from the world. His parents used to go out for weekend cycle rides when they were young, in groups of forty or more people. Cycling was a social event and, having moved from Kegworth in Leicestershire, where Dad was born, they loved the easy terrain around their corner of Bedfordshire, where they would pass through small villages on their relaxed Sunday rides with friends. It was perfect for bike riding.

Cycling became more solitary and personal for Dad. He always thought that, between him and his sister, he was the less favoured child and so, as a boy, my dad would find refuge from those feelings on his bike. He would ride further and further every weekend and his fitness and ability became increasingly evident.

By the time that Mum and Dad met, through work at the same company, he was serious about cycling. Max Pendleton was twenty-four; Pauline Viney was twenty-two. They were married within six months of meeting. Max and Pauline Pendleton, of course, went on a cycling honeymoon. There is a photograph of my mother in a family photo album which shows her having a break on top of a hill somewhere. She looks red and very puffed. I could relate to the exhausted look of Mum in that photograph. I knew better than anyone what it was like to go for a long ride with Dad. He never slowed down for anyone.

It felt as if the only way I could hold Dad's attention was if I did what he liked to do most – ride a bike. Alex was a boy and, even if he had once been a very sick little boy, it seemed as if Dad went riding more with my brother than me. At St Mary's Primary School in Stotfold I wrote a poem about my dad. It was heartfelt. The poem began with a line which said, 'My dad's got dark brown hair and he's good at DIY.' It wasn't very punchy but in the last line I wrote, more yearningly, that I wished Dad took me out on my bike as often as he did with Alex.

Max Pendleton was still a name, and a rider, to strike fear into the hearts of amateur cyclists across England. He was a winner. I remember going to track meetings with Dad when I'd hear other riders groan out loud and say, 'Oh no, I can't believe he's here.' They all knew that Max Pendleton would clean up. He'd win, pick up the prize money and go home.

Tough and aggressive, Dad was always the rider who attacked when everyone else was suffering. He would wait as long as it took for everyone else to start to wilt and then, showing no mercy, he would turn on the burners. I thought my dad was incredible.

Max Pendleton was good enough to make the black-and-white cover of *Cycling Weekly* – because he had been successful at national championship level. It made me proud to be his daughter. Secretly, I wanted to impress people like Max Pendleton did. I wanted to be really good at something; even if I didn't know then what that 'something' might be or even how I might turn that feeling into words.

Something unusual began to take shape on a grass track in Fordham, a small village near Colchester in Essex. Alex and I stood next to our shiny new race bikes. We fiddled awkwardly with our helmets. It felt like a big block of polystyrene, covered by stretchy red, white and blue fabric, had been shoved on top of our heads. We looked ludicrous, and we knew it. We had just turned nine.

Nicola, who was fourteen, called her helmet a piss-pot. We all thought that was hysterical – and it took Nicky's mind off cycling because she was far more interested in music. Nicky would have been happier performing a solo in the school orchestra, a challenge that would have scared me half to death. I felt safer on my bike, even with a massive piss-pot sliding off my head.

Dad never wore a helmet. He always rode hard and free. But we couldn't escape the piss-pots. That year, in 1989, it had just been made legally binding for children to wear helmets in a race.

The Pendleton twins had their photo taken before our first-ever race in Fordham. Alex and I felt even more ridiculous, posing alongside our bikes. Our skinny arms stuck out of our baggy jumpers and our tiny legs looked strangely white beneath our black shorts. We were the only riders in the junior race that day. It was enough for me. I just wanted to beat Alex. Nothing else really mattered.

I felt amazingly close to Alex but I found it infuriating that, just because he was a boy, he was naturally stronger and faster than me. He was also much less fearful than me and had ridden his BMX far longer and more daringly than I had done on my bike. Years earlier, long before I felt confident enough to do so, Alex had asked for his stabilizers to be removed. I was more worried that I would fall off and hurt myself.

Alex was just better and braver than me. It wasn't fair; and I was always trying to prove that I finally could match my twin for speed, endurance, efficiency, courage, tidiness, you name it. We all had the urge to beat each other. Even Nicola, when it came to war over Monopoly, was determined to win. It got very messy during board games. But, on our bikes, it was different. Alex still wanted to win but he was not as obsessed as me. He usually beat me but, on those rare occasions when I won while we were racing for fun at home, Alex just shrugged it off. I was much more like Dad. It felt important that I rode faster than Alex.

No more than thirty spectators stood around the track in Fordham. Most of them knew Dad and they must have been amused that his twins were the only two riders in the children's race.

A Pendleton vs V Pendleton. A twin brother versus his twin sister. A boy against a girl.

I held the handlebars tight as we waited for the gun. The piss-pot felt heavy and unsteady on my head but I stared straight down the length of the grassy track. I could sense Alex at my side. He knew how much I wanted to beat him and so neither of us uttered a word.

Alex got away quicker than me, as usual, and he picked up speed down the long straight. I peddled as fast as I could but the track was bumpy. Every time we hit another little mound of earth my helmet wobbled and slid down over my eyes. By the time I was about to take the first corner I was blinded by the piss-pot. I had to take a hand off the steering wheel and push the helmet back up my forehead. Alex had done the same. Our helmets were more likely to kill us than save us.

In between the bumps and the blinding moments I struggled to keep up with Alex in our one-lap race. Four hundred meters were just not long enough for me to haul my brother in – especially not with a piss-pot on my head. He won our first proper race. It was one-up to Alex, one for the boys.

I didn't cry. I knew I'd be better next time. I would beat Alex one day in a proper race.

Dad was a man of achievement. He made things happen, often with his hands or the sheer force of his will. Dad might have made me feel bad some of the time but, still, I placed him high on a pedestal I built in my mind. I loved the fact that he was so practical and that he knew so much about everything. When he and Mum decided we needed to build an extension to the house, Dad did it himself. He learnt all he needed about the electrics and the plumbing; and he set about his work with drive and precision.

I liked helping Dad, and so I would pile up bricks in the wheelbarrow and move them to exactly where they were needed. Dad was cheerful. He even let me lay some of the bricks as he built our solid new extension. He taught me a lot and I could soon identify and hand him a jubilee clip. I was that sort of girl.

When Dad was in a good mood, no-one else in the whole wide world came close to being as much fun as him. I loved the fact that Dad still made us laugh uncontrollably and squeal when he took us out to fly our kites. We had many great days with Dad.

He could also be kind. Sometimes, when we were in the car, and driving to school or a race, and I felt nervous, Dad would lean across and squeeze my hand. He didn't waste words but so much was packed into that gesture it felt as if he had steeled me for the trial ahead. At primary school, I hated being in the embarrassing group given extra maths and reading work while the rest of the class went off to assembly. But Dad always thought I was smart. And he knew I worked hard. Dad thought I would be alright because life was less about books and studying than living and learning out in the real world.

He and Mum took us on some wonderful holidays – with our bikes of course – to the Peak District and the Lake District. We also went cycling abroad, to stunningly beautiful places like the Pyrenees, and stayed in youth hostels where we met some intriguing people. Dad was happy that, through cycling, we were opening our minds. He also concentrated on his own distinct way of educating us.

It meant that, in the car, we had some traumatic clashes – usually over a map. Dad was fanatical about maps. He thought we should all learn how to read a map. And so, whenever we went somewhere new, and it was just me and Dad in the car, I would be the designated map-reader.

'Where are you taking us?' Dad would finally ask when my confused directions gave way to puzzled silence.

'I don't know where we are,' I would admit.

'Well, Victoria,' Dad would reply, sighing with strained patience, 'look at the map.'

'I don't understand the map,' I'd say.

'It's all there – right in front of you,' Dad snapped.

Even when I had sent us the wrong way, Dad would not turn back. That was impossible. We had to press ahead until I found a new way out of the mess I had made. Dad put a lot of pressure on me but, in the end, I learnt how to read a map.

I understood, deep down, that his unyielding way had been embedded into him during his childhood. He had been caned regularly at school and he remained a man who believed more in the proverbial old stick than the sweet and tasty carrot. Dad never smacked me but he did frighten me when he used his shouty voice. He was a very powerful figure and if I had to describe the dad of my girlhood years in one word I would say 'extreme'. Dad either made me very happy or pretty miserable. There was not much bland stuff in between those extreme emotions.

Alex was smarter than me in dealing with Dad. Even when Dad got frustrated with him, Alex remained relaxed. 'Oh Dad,' he'd say, 'it'll be fine.' Alex, in the end, was granted much more leeway than Nicky and me. We were indecisive and susceptible to Dad's moods and whims. He steered us in directions that Alex avoided.

I couldn't help but notice that Alex was cleverer than me at school, and much more popular. It didn't upset me because I loved Alex. He deserved to be popular because he was so easy to be around. Alex helped me all through childhood – so much so that, on our first day of school, I'd been bewildered when so many kids burst into tears after their mothers left. I didn't feel like crying. Why would I? At Etonbury Middle School in Stotfold I had Alex at my side. Even if I didn't have many friends, I never felt lonely with Alex around. We were always in the same class and I worked hard.

As we prepared to move on to senior school, at the age of thirteen, I had caught up with Alex. But it was obvious that, unlike me, my brother could sail through our classes and exams. I could have followed Nicola to Bedford Girls – a public school where she did well academically and musically. Dad and Mum were willing to make the necessary sacrifice to pay for my and Alex's senior education. But Alex was happy with an ordinary comprehensive and I preferred to stay with my twin. We moved together to Fearnhill School, in Letchworth, north Hertfordshire, just under four miles from where we lived in Stotfold.

Life became trickier. All the girls I knew at Brownies had mutated into ultra-cool teenagers who wouldn't be seen dead with a bony runt like me. I was innocent and boring. At Fearnhill, I was consigned to the losers' list. None of the cool girls wanted to do what I did – which was to play sport and listen to grungy, depressing music. They liked wearing make-up and learning how to smoke and pick up boys.

I much preferred playing hockey, where I suddenly became a very competitive girl, and riding on my bike with Dad and Alex every Sunday morning. Of course I was confused. I wished I could become both stronger and more feminine. But I drew pride from the fact that we rode so far with Dad every Sunday.

We racked up some big rides together. I remember telling my teacher at Fearnhill on a Monday morning that I had ridden fifty miles the previous day. 'Fifteen!' she said, as if I needed to be corrected. 'No,' I said quietly. 'Fifty. Five-oh.' I don't think she believed me, even though she knew I was not a girl who usually lied. But Dad, Alex and I had really ridden fifty miles. We had stopped for a break in the middle but, still, fifty miles for a thirteen-year-old girl felt like an achievement.

Alex and I also won lots of little trophies at grass-track meetings around the Home Counties. They felt more like picnics than anything serious and we enjoyed racing each other and some of the same kids that popped up all over the place. The grass-tracks developed our bike-handling skills and, allied to the stamina we'd forged on our Sunday morning marathons with Dad, Alex and I began to win regularly. We'd come home and say to Mum: 'Look what we won! Ta-dah!' And we'd wave our small cups and plinths of bronze cyclists in the air.

Over the previous year, I had grown taller than Alex. Maturing more quickly than my brother, I no longer trailed behind him in speed and fitness. I also raced more often than Alex did in grass-track meetings because, so keen to please Dad, I hardly missed a competition. Alex was different. He didn't feel compelled to go to the track every time with Dad.

Early in the summer of 1994, when we were thirteen-and-a-half, Alex and I went with Dad to the world's oldest grass-track meeting. Heckington, for English amateur riders like Dad, was significant. Deep in Lincolnshire, at the famous Heckington Agricultural Show, national grass-track titles were decided on a narrow track where the turns were tight and the sidelines were crammed with spectators.

Dad was realistic about the limitations of amateur cycling. He always knew he would have to work either in accountancy or property management for a living. Cycling could never be more than a consuming hobby. But Dad loved winning at tracks like Heckington where there was more prestige at stake.

This time only Alex and I went to Heckington with Dad. Nicola, at eighteen, was physically talented and rode well, but she was far more intent on working towards her A-levels and Grade Eight exams in the piano and flute. Nicky had seen her chance to escape and she took it. But Dad's cycling hooks had dug deep into Alex and, especially, me.

We raced at Heckington in a handicap for riders between the ages of nine and sixteen. I didn't expect that, even in a handicap, I could beat boys of fifteen and sixteen. Victory for me would be racing faster than Alex. But I knew it was going to be difficult. As I had raced so much more than him that year, I was handicapped harder than Alex. I started behind him which meant I'd have to race considerably faster than my twin to overtake him.

On the start line I was determined and ready. I wore a more modern kind of piss-pot on my head. A properly fitting helmet meant that there were no moments of being blinded every time I hit a bump. It was just me and my bike – up against Alex and his bike. We knew we could beat the other kids.

My mind went blank at the gun and I pedalled hard. The grass track became a green blur beneath my tyres. Raising my head, I locked onto the flying figure of my twin. I knew I could catch him and, soon, the distance between us shrunk. It seemed much easier chasing Alex round a flat track than it did trying to haul in Dad on an unforgiving hill.

I caught and then passed Alex on the final bend. I powered away from him down the last straight. Dad watched silently as someone shouted out to him. 'Gosh, Max,' the man said, 'your girl was phenomenal.'

Dad didn't want to make a big fuss of me in front of Alex; but he then heard a more understated voice: 'Pretty impressive ...'

'Yes,' Dad said. 'It was ...'

He told me as much later, when we were on our own. I shrugged him off. Dad tried again. He thought I could become a special cyclist if I put my mind to it and tried hard. It looked as if I had real talent and a lovely, smooth style of riding. 'Yeah, Dad, thanks,' I said, thinking a duty-bound father was obliged to say such words. Strangely, in that rare moment between us, I simply forgot how difficult it was to win Dad's praise. I just assumed he was going out of his way to be kind to me because I had won. It was only years later that I understood how, alongside the grass track at Heckington, Dad really did believe he had seen something magical in me. Dad began to imagine a life for me that he might have wished for himself.

The complications between me and Dad, perhaps as a consequence of Heckington, became more tangled. A familiar ritual, a mostly silent showdown, played out between us at home in Stotfold a year later. I had been invited to the movies by two of my friends. We all knew I was hardly inundated by bosom buddies and so such invitations carried real meaning and novelty inside their simple appeal. It was not the first time, but the opportunities for me to go the movies or even parties on a Saturday night with some friends were rare enough to be exciting. Mum and Dad reacted in typically contrasting ways.

As always, Mum was pleased. She thought it would be good for me to go out and enjoy myself. 'You deserve some fun with your friends, Lou,' Mum said.

Dad was different. Mum had already said it would be fine, but I felt the old dark pull towards him. Dad just grunted when I asked if it would be alright to go to the movies that evening. I repeated the question. Dad answered me finally but, with just two words, his response became more clouded.

'Suit yourself …' he said with a shrug.

That shrug said so much more than his words. The shrug spoke of the fact that I was meant to be riding with Dad the following day. That shrug reminded me how tired I would be in the morning if I went out on Saturday night. That shrug implied that there was nothing Dad could do if I couldn't be bothered to ride properly on Sunday – our special day together. The shrug was a small masterpiece of emotional blackmail.

How could I suit myself when, so plainly, my going out didn't suit Dad?

Dad would not reassure me. He had his plans for the weekend and it was up to me whether I fitted in with him. If I chose not to go riding he wouldn't say anything. He would just get up early and go out on his bike on his own. But we both knew how disappointed Dad would be if I let him down. He probably wouldn't speak to me much all weekend.

The mute pressure Dad exerted on me felt heavier than usual. Alex, having just turned fifteen with me on 24 September 1995, had opted out of cycling. Just like Nicky before me, he saw his chance and took it. Alex knew I wasn't going to give up. I needed Dad's approval too much to abandon my bike. I was in for the long haul. There was no need for Alex to force himself down the same tortuous path. Dad would be happy if he had just one of us, me, to ride with him every Sunday morning. Alex quietly gave up his bike. He had other interests to explore.

'It's just you now, Vic,' I said to myself. 'Just you.'

I felt more responsible than ever for Dad's weekend mood. I couldn't disappoint him. And, over the prospect of an ordinary night at the movies, it felt like I had hurt him to the core.

Rather than looking forward to a modest teenage night out I felt consumed by guilt. I was letting Dad down by even thinking of me and my friends before him and the bike. Dad, without really saying anything, made me feel terrible. I also knew he was right. I would be utterly rubbish on my bike if I woke up tired on Sunday morning. It was enough of a strain hanging onto Dad racing up a hill when I had slept well and felt fresh. So, as Dad stalked off to let me think about my decision, I crumbled inside.

I went to find Mum. She was sweet and generous. We all knew what Dad was like so I should do whatever made me happy. If I fancied the pictures, I should go with my friends. Grumpy old Dad would survive.

Those sensible words were difficult to follow. The old teeming emotions rose up inside me. Dad was very good at making me feel very bad. He left me in a tight little world of fear and guilt. It was not a great place to be, not at fifteen, and so I gave in to the inevitable.

I didn't tell Dad but, quietly, almost furtively, I disappeared upstairs to call my friends. I was sorry, I said, but I couldn't make it to the movies after all. I'd forgotten that I had to go training with my dad in the morning. They were mystified; but they also knew I had ridden my bike every Sunday morning for so long. I felt grim, of course, for letting them down. That seemed worse to me than the fact that I was the one who would miss out on the movies and a few hours of fun.

The only good thing, after putting down the phone, was knowing that I would have felt much worse if I had gone out with my friends. Dad would have really given me the silent treatment then.

Instead, later, as I went off to bed, he sounded almost cheerful. 'See you in the morning, Vic,' he called out. 'Early start for us …'

I knew my place. I would be on my bike again in the morning. I would be the girl on the hill, chasing the fleeing and distant figure of her father.

''Night, Mum,' I said as I turned to climb the stairs to my room. ''Night, Dad …'

Alex and I began to fight more, which was normal, but horrible for me as a teenage girl. It took a long time for me to forgive him after he read my diary one night and, the next morning, waltzed straight up to a boy in our class to blurt out that I fancied him. I could have curled up and died in a dark hole but, as that option wasn't available, I just turned the most embarrassing shade of red and seethed inside. How could boys, especially my twin brother, be so unspeakably cruel?

I survived the diary humiliation. Yet the whole world, for a while, became a desolate place. I felt unloved and misunderstood – especially at school. I really did feel like kill-ing myself. Of course I was never going to do anything so drastic. I was far too guilty a person to seriously contemplate anything as selfish as suicide – but I harboured grim fantasies and became more withdrawn.

Most other girls in my class, at the ages of fifteen and sixteen, were going out, getting drunk and talking about boys. A few of them were already having sex. I was different. I just wanted to play sport and look a little prettier and much less skinny. It wasn't much to ask.

I also wanted to be a germ-free girl; and so I washed my hands incessantly. It was one way of keeping the world at bay and, I guess, trying to rid myself of the stain I felt on the inside. I didn't want to walk around and spread my germs to everyone else. At the same time I already knew that the world had enough germs of its own. So even if I was scrupulous about not passing on my bugs it became increasingly important that I did not pick up anyone else's germs. Every time I had to open a door it became a real issue. It was impossible to use my hands, for fear of either spreading old germs or catching new germs, and so I had to stick out a foot, lean down with an elbow or, more self-consciously, use my bum to push open a door. I got into a right old state if the door could only be opened by swinging it towards me. In those difficult encounters I preferred to hang around until someone opened the door from the other side.

My hands were still exposed. They were germ-breeders and germ-magnets. The only solution was to wash them repeatedly. I scrubbed them with soap and held them under hot water until they looked red and raw. They were not so pretty, then, but at least I knew they were clean. Well, they were clean for a while until, naturally, they felt germ-ridden again.

The compulsive washing of my hands drove Dad mad. 'That's enough!' he would shout. 'Stop it.'

I got it under control after a while but, well, the germ paranoia never really went away. A grubby door handle and a public loo still unsettled me. I would do anything to avoid them. The hand-washing, however, dried up. Dad wasn't going to allow me to get away with that for long.

It also helped that, finally, I began to make some real friends. We had little in common – apart from the obvious fact that we were the waifs and strays, the misfits left loitering far from the cool kids. We also tended to work hard and get irritated that most of our teachers seemed unable to quell the unruly mob that caused havoc in class. Those kids didn't care about learning or working, but we did – which automatically made us even weirder to everyone else. Our weirdness bound us together.

We were just a small group at first – Cassie, Katie, Ruth, Anna, Helen and me – but by the time we reached the sixth form we had grown in confidence and numbers. Ten or eleven of us hung out together at lunchtime. We did well in class and began to feel that, rather than being the crazy outsiders, maybe we were the normal kids. Perhaps the cool kids were really the weird losers after all.

I also began to challenge Dad. At sixteen I started to question his authority just a little. I even managed, wonder of wonders, to go out on some Saturday evenings with my friends. It was never anything more outrageous than visiting the village pubs with some girls and boys, and I'd fret terribly if I missed my 10pm curfew by a few minutes. I still went riding on my bike with Dad the following morning; but life had begun to open up.

Cycling also became more successful for me. I won lots of competitions on the grass tracks of southeast England and started to enjoy the limited amount of prize money I was given after each victorious race.

Dad kept telling me that I was improving at an extraordinary rate. He thought I had the potential to be an amazing cyclist. Dad said I might be good enough to become a world champion one day.

'Yeah, yeah, Dad,' I said. But I was happy Dad was happy. I stopped washing my hands more than three or four times a day. They looked pale and slender again, rather than raw and puffy.

Mum still wouldn't allow me to race on hard tracks, in case I fell and injured myself, but Dad and I dreamed up a devious plan. He was racing on the cement at Welwyn Garden City and we decided between us that I'd also have a crack at the junior event. We did not dare tell Mum. So we sneaked my bike into the boot of the car and covered it with a blanket. Mum thought I was just going to watch Dad race when we set off for Welwyn. She had no idea that I was about to make my cement-track debut.

The track at Welwyn was organized by some very officious people – in particular a grumpy woman who was furious that I climbed onto my bike from the wrong side. Even though the track was relatively flat, and without any steep inclines, she made me get off and walk around to the apparently safe side of my bike.

'That's how you get on your bike at Welwyn,' she said cuttingly.

I couldn't believe it. I was going to show her and all her sniggering cyclists. The girl who got on her bike the wrong way would destroy the field.

And I did. I won the junior race, beating boys and girls, with ridiculous ease. I made a point of getting off my bike the wrong way. I did it the grass-track way, rather than the Welwyn way.

I was getting noticed – and by more thoughtful people than just surly ladies in Welwyn. All my results, and victories, were printed in the back pages of *Cycling Weekly* and, incredibly, attention was being paid to my progress; and not just by Dad.

After Welwyn I started to ride against men, in handicap races. Dad and I would turn up and they would take one look at my skinny legs and my puppy-dog face and the handicapper would decide to push all the men a few more metres back. How could a puny sixteen-year-old girl hold off the muscly hulks? They were expected to hunt me down. Most of them couldn't. At the finish line I would still be ahead. I would go up to the presentation table, collect my trophy and prize-money, smile demurely for the local photographer and go home, to Mum, where I would say, as usual, 'Ta-Dah!' and show her my booty.

Yet, when it came, the telephone call just about knocked me sideways. I could tell that Dad thought it was important because he looked flushed when he handed me the phone.

'Hello?' I said, not guessing for a moment that my life was about to change forever. I still thought of myself as the guilty and frightened girl on the hill, chasing after Dad as hard as her spindly legs could pedal. I could not believe that anyone, seri-ously, thought of me in a positive way.

Marshall Thomas sounded gentle and kind. He explained that he was the assistant coach of the national track team. I was amazed that we even had a British track team – let alone a coach who had actually heard of me. Marshall had been following my results. He had even seen the details of my win in Welwyn.

I didn't tell him that I was the girl who climbed on her bike the wrong way. Too stunned to really speak, I waited for him to continue.

'We'd like to invite you up to Manchester,' Marshall said, 'if you fancy having a ride at the velodrome.'

'I'll pass you over to my dad,' I said helplessly, but remem-bering to thank him for calling.

I had no idea there was even a velodrome in Manchester; but Dad knew. His eyes shone and he smiled when he put down the phone. He looked so proud of me. The girl on the hill, the girl who once couldn't read a map and kept washing her hands, had made her father so happy.

'I knew it,' he said quietly as he pulled me towards him. 'I knew you were good ...'

2 | VELODROMES AND CAMPER-VANS

My bed turned into a fairground ride. I lay in the dark and clutched the mattress as I seemed to tilt up and down, round and round, in an endless loop of blurring movement. There were moments when I wanted to laugh out loud, or even say '*woooaaahhh!*' as the room rocked.

'God,' I whispered to myself, 'this is crazy shit ...'

I didn't take drugs, and I hardly drank, but an afternoon at the Manchester Velodrome left me tripping round the dizzying curves of the wooden track. Six hours had passed since I had slipped off my bike, but the wild rollercoaster ride would not leave the leaping pit of my stomach or the lurching whir of my mind. I could feel the same rolling sensations climbing high inside me, creeping up towards my buzzing brain, before racing back down again as if I was still on the bike and careering along the sharply banked track.

At first, because he was careful not to scare me, Marshall Thomas made sure I did not really notice the dizzying gradient of the velodrome. Speaking in the same quiet voice I remembered from our phone conversation, he concentrated on making me feel comfortable in this jolting new environment. I was a flat grass-track girl, with just a gritty smattering of experience on the hard cement at Welwyn Garden City.

Yet Marshall made me feel at home. He was much younger than I had expected – in his early thirties – and more low-key than Dad in his approach to cycling. He was also obviously intelligent and I liked the relaxed way in which he introduced me to the surrounding track.

The Manchester Velodrome belonged to another world. It looked strange, even beautiful, as Marshall slowly led me round the curved wooden bowl on my fixed-wheel bike. Marshall explained that the structure of the roof was based on a 122-metre, 200-tonne arch which provided unrestricted viewing for spectators. The roof was covered in aluminum, and weighed around 600 tonnes. But Marshall, like me, was more interested in the track.

The wood looked very shiny under the bright lights. Marshall said the 250m track was Britain's first purpose-built indoor velodrome and that the wood flashing beneath us was the finest Siberian pine. Back then, in my teenage innocence, I had no idea that those smooth and gorgeous boards could tear chunks of flesh off your legs or arms as easily as a butcher might skin a rabbit.

I might have fainted if I had seen the sight I witnessed on this same track fifteen years later when, in a World Cup keirin race in 2011, the Malaysian rider Azizulhasni Awang stared in horror at his leg after a crash. Twenty centimeters of pure velodrome wood ran through his calf, like a meaty kebab stick, with the pointed ends jutting out on each side. The pain of being skewered must have been terrible. A day later, surgery removed that huge splinter in a clean excision from Awang's calf.

Fortunately, as a sixteen-year-old schoolgirl, I was spared such grisly visions of the future. I was also blissfully unaware that Jason Queally would suffer a similar fate later that same year, in 1996. He crashed on his bike, while circling the track at 35mph, and a large chunk of wood lodged in his back. Chris

Hoy revealed later that it was eighteen inches long and two inches wide. Suggesting it was 'more like a fence post than a splinter', Chris quipped in his dry way that, 'Jason's scream of "I've got half the fucking track in my back" was not unreasonable in the circumstances.' It took almost 100 stitches to close the wound. I was far too naïve to imagine that splintering trauma.

Marshall skirted the dangers of the track by explaining that, as we cruised along the blue band running round the base of the circuit, we would ride at a steady pace. I followed him, my front wheel holding a perfect line with his back wheel, as Marshall led us round and round. After all my years of trailing Dad, I knew how to follow a wheel, and so I began to settle. It helped that Marshall was so warm and engaging. He kept telling me just to enjoy myself. There was no pressure or expectation on me.

Gradually, Marshall took me further up the track. By the time we had reached the upper banking it felt almost ordinary as we went round in high circles. After so many years on the road and the grass, I felt comfortable on the wooden boards.

Then, seamlessly, we began. Marshall's bike banked to the left and, carefully at first, he steered us down the sheer gradient to the bottom. After another half-lap, he pulled us up towards the right and we began to climb back again to the top. We repeated the procedure again and again, and each time we seemed to gather speed as we zipped down the sumptuously curvy circuit. Up and down, round and round we went, faster and faster, until it really did begin to feel like a fairground ride. Towards the end we hurtled along the boards, my bike tracking his, as we flew down the banks with an exhilarating whoosh. The sensations were sharpened by the fact that, like all track bikes, there was only one gear and no brakes.

I loved the giddy contrasts and rollicking speed of the velodrome. Marshall must have sensed my passion because we rode together for over an hour – more than long enough for the sensations to still be unfolding inside me late that night. Yet it was only after our ride, when he walked me round the top of the track, that I appreciated the height of the velodrome.

Marshall explained that the steepest part of the track rises to 42½ degrees. Towards the bottom it dips down to a shallower 12½ degrees. Clutching an iron railing, I suddenly noticed how scary it looked from the top. The geometry of the design, Marshall said, helped maximize the speed of the riders. The angle of our exit from the bankings, so much sharper than our entry, explained why it felt like we were being catapulted along the straights – as if we were riding downhill.

Alone in bed, in the dark, I closed my eyes. I saw all the piney patterns and deeper shadows of the track. I heard the distinctive sounds of the velodrome in my head and, most of all, I felt the surreal excitement of riding a fast and beautifully geometric track. I knew I'd be back, and the thought sent a thrill rippling through me. Sleep was elusive; but I didn't mind. In my head, I was riding round and round, up and down, dreaming of the next time. I was happy in the fairground.

No-one in the Pendleton family had ever been to university; but I resolved to break the mould. Nicola, my big sister, was always much brighter than me. I was certain she would have been suited to university life had she broken free from Dad's pragmatic grip. But, like me, Nicky found it hard to step away from our father. Dad, in his straightforward way, did not really see the point of university. Why study some more, after all those years at school, when you could go straight into the real world and earn money in a proper job? Life would always teach you much more than university – and at least you would be paid for it at the same time. Dad's logic was unshakeable.

As an accountant it made sense to Max Pendleton that his eldest daughter should follow him into the same career. Nicky was intelligent and artistic; and she did not feel any compulsion to enter the dazzling world of accountancy. But it was hard for her being the eldest. Dad had only mellowed a little by the time, five years later, it was the turn of Alex and me to make our career choices.

My sister, as Dad decreed, worked in an office and studied, at the same time, at an accountancy college. Nicky has done remarkably well and now runs her own small accountancy business – and lives a good life. But it's easy to see Dad's influence over her working life.

Alex, as always, was more independent than his sisters. He decided early on that he would go to art college and become a graphic designer. Dad could see commercial merit in that choice and so there was no big drama around Alex. His future would follow a much less intense path than mine.

By the time we were in the upper sixth, and I was taking my three A-levels in Chemistry, Biology and Geography, I knew I wanted to go to university. The idea that a track cyclist, especially a woman, might make money out of riding round in circles, was too ludicrous to consider. I needed a university education to help me forge a decent career.

I could handle Dad by then, and convinced him that I needed to stick to my instinct when it came to choosing university over an ordinary job straight out of school. But I still tussled with wider uncertainties. I wanted to be exceptional at whatever I did – even if it drove Dad halfway round the bend when I couldn't tell him what that work might be one day.

It was enough for me that, in my last year of school, I was happy. After all the lonely trauma of senior school it seemed striking that I suddenly found contentment at the very end. I had my gang of girls; and we were cool enough in our own heads. I also had a boyfriend and cycling.

My bike world remained a mystery to everyone else at school. Even though my boyfriend and my closest girls knew I had been approached by British Cycling, it was such an esoteric activity I rarely spoke about it. I liked it that way. It felt good to have something that belonged to me alone. At home, it was different. Cycling was Dad's domain. He was fascinated by the training programmes Marshall Thomas sent through the post and, much more than me, he was excited by my prospects in the sport he loved.

Marshall's emotional intelligence made him very different to most men in professional cycling; and he instinctively recognized my vulnerability and always tried to reassure me. Whenever he suggested a new training routine, Marshall stressed I should only attempt anything that suited me and my schooling. If a more dogmatic coach had tried to take hold of me at seventeen, and forced his will onto me, I would have given up cycling even before I really started.

For a guilt-stricken girl, Marshall's compassionate and easy manner resembled the sweetest of gifts. I discovered that I loved training. I was happier than ever on my bike and it felt natural to fulfil all Marshall's programmes.

The order and discipline of training matched the intricately planned revision timetable I set myself – and so my last months of school flew past. I began to understand myself more clearly. My appetite for hard work, and my ambition to succeed, were obvious. The demons of teenage doubt were pushed down further as, in my exams and on my bike, I hurtled towards the future.

Soon after I arrived in September 1999 at the University of Northumbria in Newcastle, one of my lecturers sat me down and said, as an aspiring athlete, I could only fulfil two of the three options available to me. Those possibilities consisted of obtaining a good BSc degree in Sports Science, training hard in my chosen sport and having a great social life. One objective would have to be surrendered to ensure the success of the two remaining aims. I knew he was right and, for me, it was not a difficult choice.

I felt certain my social life would expand in later years but, back then, I was committed only to my degree and to cycling. Life at Northumbria consisted of an agreeably Spartan existence. I went to my lectures and worked hard. And, when I wasn't studying, I tucked myself away in the gym – where, as some kind of indulgence, there was a television to watch while I pummelled my body. I didn't have a TV in my room and so my exercise routine also offered escapism.

Training mostly with the runners, as there were no serious cyclists at university, I made some new friends. We soon became a tight-knit group. In the gym I also learnt how to use weights – as I set about trying to build strength into my slight frame. At the same time, while I was not especially scientific, I was interested in an analytical and statistical approach to sport. Despite remaining a real chatterer, I liked the rigour of work and training. I felt both purposeful and serious in Newcastle.

Significantly, I also felt liberated from Dad, especially the arguing and the long painful silences of my adolescence. We'd had many good moments towards the end of school – and I loved the fact that Dad bought me a toolbox for my eighteenth birthday – but it was hard to escape some of the old struggles. I was tired of Dad making me feel guilty and I wanted to shape my own decisions.

Our relationship improved when I was living away from him. I felt less sapped by our battles, and it was good to tell him how my training was progressing. But whenever I phoned home I spoke mostly to Mum. We'd natter away easily because nothing had changed between us. Mum was less concerned with my training schedule than hearing about what I was eating and wearing, who I was hanging out with, and when next I planned a trip down south to see them again. It was only at the end of our long and breezy conversations that Mum would invariably shout out: 'Max, do you want to say hello to Lou?'

Dad would come on the line but it was noticeable that we hardly spoke about anything but cycling. The bike remained our only real connection. I didn't believe him but Dad seemed more certain than ever that I was on my way to becoming a world champion.

Mum, of course, was an unchanging source of comfort and common sense. She always would tell me that I could only do my best. It was very simple advice, but the wisest set of words anyone ever gave to me.

Her dad, my old granddad Alf, straddled the difference between my parents. He was much more passionate than Mum about sport, and he loved hearing how well I was doing on the track, but his way of boosting me was more humorous than Dad. For years Granddad had been telling me that I should strut around and tell everyone to call me 'Champ' – as they had better get used to me being a champion. I just smiled and said, 'Granddad – no!' He would then regale me with another story of how he used to drive Mabel, his wife and my nanna, crazy by always being the last on the team bus when he played football.

'If you're good enough, Mabel,' he would say, 'they'll always wait for you ...'

Alf Viney was an amusing and kind man; and he survived the death of Mabel by keeping active. Every lunchtime Granddad made the short walk down the back alley behind his house to the Irish Social where, without fail, he would drink his pint-and-a-half of beer while remembering the days he'd also played cricket and football and table-tennis for the county.

Granddad told me that a pint-and-a-half a day kept him strong. It helped him play golf until the age of ninety-two and he was always trying to get me to taste his beer. 'It's good for you, Victoria,' he'd say when I scrunched up my face at the taste, before reminding me again that everyone should call me 'Champ'. Granddad always made me laugh.

My relationship with Nicola and Alex also improved once we were living apart from each other. In our teenage years the typical strains between siblings had been evident. But now, leading new lives away from home, our old closeness re-emerged. Everything had begun to gel – family, university and, increasingly, cycling.

At the start of a new century, during the spring of 2001, I discovered a different world in a battered and stationary old camper van. For seven weeks, in the parking lot outside the Manchester Velodrome, I fell into exhausted sleep every night. It was a bizarre way to gain my first sustained taste of professional cycling but, having turned twenty the previous September, I loved my camper van experience.

Phil Hayes, my personal tutor, and Marshall Thomas helped shape that profound change. Marshall had also studied at Northumbria and he was receptive when Phil, who worked with elite athletes at the university, approached him to see if he might help me find a work placement. Deep into the second year of my degree, Marshall arranged a seven-week-long work secondment for me in the World Class Performance Plan offices of British Cycling. Apart from giving me the chance to work in a sports office, my weeks on site allowed me to train regularly. Every lunchtime, and after work each evening, I could take my bike out on the gleaming boards that had so entranced me on my first afternoon at the velodrome. It was a unique opportunity for me to improve with consistent training.

My record was still modest. I was best known for having won three national grass-track titles over 800m. In 1999, on the track, I had finished third in the national sprint championships over 500m. Those results look better now than they felt then. There was only one other British woman sprint cyclist of note – Wendy Everson. She had finished fourth in the 1994 Commonwealth Games and had ridden in a couple of World Championships without coming close to any medals. Everson didn't make the Great Britain Olympic squad in Sydney in 2000 and, fifteen years older than me, she would not receive any funding from the new lottery-based scheme. But at least she had some experience. I had nothing on an indoor track.

The pursuit events were different. Yvonne McGregor had won a bronze medal at the Olympic Games in Sydney in 2000. She had also won gold that same year at the World Championships.

On my first day at the velodrome, having carefully parked the old camper van Mum and Dad had driven up to Manchester for me, I was excited to be in the same building as Yvonne and the male cyclists who had won medals at the Sydney Olympics. I had watched transfixed when Jason Queally won gold in the men's kilo – the one kilometre time trial. Jason's victory had marked a turning point in my life.

In the summer of 2000 it had been a huge moment when, in the stark setting of a motorway service station, I had stood alongside my parents and a small but whooping crowd as we watched Jason race on the other side of the world. Mum and Dad were in the midst of taking me back up north when, luckily, we stopped off for a break just as the climax of the kilo was reached in the Olympics. The images beamed down from the service station television meant all the more to me because it was the first time I had actually seen live track cycling. Jason's triumph made me tingle with the realization that I had ridden at the very velodrome where he trained in Manchester. Track cycling, from that point on, became as tangible as it was thrilling.

Twelve years earlier I had been too young to notice the significance of Chris Boardman's gold medal in the individual pursuit at the Barcelona Olympics. But I realized that Jason would change perceptions of cycling in this country. His extraordinary achievement, alongside Yvonne's bronze, was bolstered by two further British medals in Sydney.

Riding with Chris Hoy and Craig MacLean, Jason also won silver in the men's team sprint. And then, in the team pursuit, Paul Manning, Chris Newton, Bryan Steele and a young Bradley Wiggins won bronze. Bradley, born in April 1980, was just six months older than me – but he moved in a more rarefied world. Never imagining then that I would be in contention for an Olympic medal myself, I looked up to riders like Bradley, Craig and, especially, Chris and Jason. They were gods of the track to me.

I was too shy to really talk to them and, instead, I usually waited for them to leave the track before I went out on my bike. A morning of filing, photocopying, checking stock, writing the occasional letter and cheerfully making tea and coffee for everyone suited me and the level of my track proficiency. I would have felt an utter fraud if I had been in the way of medal-winning Olympians.

But Marshall and Peter Keen, the performance director at British Cycling, were generous men. They wanted me to make the most of my stint at the velodrome. And so there were times when, to my amazement, I did share the track with the men. I kept my head down and tried hard not to be noticed.

Four years earlier, in 1997, Peter had shocked many people when he had stood up at the sport's national convention and expressed his intention to turn British Cycling into an international powerhouse. It seemed an absurd ambition for a minority sport in Britain. Sniggers echoed round the room as he reached the culmination of his snazzy PowerPoint presentation. Peter, however, had the vision to match his ambition. He also knew that young riders like Bradley and Chris, in their respective pursuit and sprint events, had the potential to become World and Olympic champions if the economic limitations were overcome.

Peter would no longer accept a situation where a talented sprinter like Chris did not even have his own skinsuit when he made his international debut in the European Under-23s in 1996. Chris was loaned a GB skinsuit which, once the championships were over, he had to return so that it could be used the following year.

That same year, without any funding or the appropriate facilities, Peter used his own bathroom in an attempt to create the heat and humidity Yvonne McGregor would face at the Atlanta Olympics. He always joked that he had a very tolerant wife because, working with Yvonne, the bathroom carpet went out, the rectal probe went in, the bike-on-rollers started whirring and the heater was switched to 30 degrees. With hot water running out of the bath and shower until a humidity level of 90% was reached, Yvonne could then train in the appropriate conditions.

Pete always used to say, with a light laugh, 'We cooked her.' After an hour there would be a line of oil and sweat and bike-dirt going up the door, across the ceiling and down the wall because Yvonne would have lost two litres of sweat. Her perspiration hit the rollers and was flicked around the room – in apparent defiance of the fact there was neither lottery funding nor elite programmes at the velodrome then.

In 1998, when Peter secured a £6 million sponsorship scheme, funded by the National Lottery, he reinvented British Cycling in a profound way. Bradley, who had just won the World Junior Championships, was called into Peter's office and offered the chance to become the first rider on British

Cycling's world-class performance plan. Chris went through the door next as a cycling dynasty was laid out in meticulous detail. The first achievements of that plan emerged in those four Olympic medals in Sydney.

Despite the lack of a women's sprint programme, Peter and Marshall encouraged me to chase a place on a junior scheme called the England Potential Plan. They believed that, with sustained training, I had the ability to make the designated qualification time for the sprint. I had never before had a chance to really practise the line and grow used to the velodrome – and I was amazed how quickly I improved.

There was much to motivate me as I worked in the administrative office of British Cycling, rode hard on the track and ate my meals and slept in the camper van. Most nights, in the deserted but guarded car park, I relished the quiet. My only problem was that, unlike in training for competition, there was no tapering down of my programme. I attacked the track with abandon. I wanted to eat up as much time as I could on the wooden circuit – especially as most of my sessions were free.

Unfamiliar with the rigours of riding twice a day, seven days a week, I was wearily unsurprised when I just missed the qualifying mark. Peter and Marshall invited me to try again a few weeks later.

After some rest back in Northumbria, I returned to Manchester early the following month. There was a freshness to my legs, and a vigour to my riding, as I smashed the qualifying time at my first attempt. Peter and Marshall smiled and confirmed that I had made it onto the England Potential Plan – the lowest rung on the ladder of elite British cycling.

Before I left Manchester they presented me with my kit. As an increasingly fashionable girl, I tried hard to conceal my amazement at the terrible canary yellow colour they had chosen. Instead, I thanked them both for believing in me so much.

'I'll do my best not to let you down,' I promised.

'We know that,' Marshall said as he patted my shoulder. 'You're going to be just fine ...'

I was still dazzled whenever I returned to the velodrome for training during my time away from university. I gazed in wonder at Chris Hoy and Jason Queally, trying to work out what they did to become such exceptional sprinters. Cycling has always been a masculine environment. I was used to the dominance of alpha males, especially with a dad like Max Pendleton, and riding against men as a junior. But Queally, Hoy, MacLean, Wiggins and the rest of the men's elite squad were remarkable riders. I felt it was a sham for me to be training alongside them.

It was also odd for them. I think they were all slightly disconcerted and despairing of me. I would turn up to training in a GB top matched with a mini-skirt and sparkly sandals. The boys never said anything out loud to me but I did see the odd eye-roll and I could imagine them all saying, 'Oh my gosh, this girl cannot be serious.' But I was deadly serious. I wanted to get better and become more like them on my bike. The distinction, however, was obvious. I did not want to try and look like them or act like them off the bike. It felt essential that I should keep on looking like a girl, and acting like a girl, even as I tried to turn myself into a rigorously committed cyclist.

None of the men on the squad believed that competitive racing and femininity worked together. It was almost as if one concept automatically cancelled the other. I set out, in my own way, to prove that it really was possible to both be a very girly girl and an imposing cyclist. It was hard because, in cycling, I had no-one I could look towards. And only a few women athletes inspired me. Denise Lewis had won gold in the heptathlon at the Sydney Olympics and she was strikingly beautiful and graceful. She was a formidable athlete; and a gorgeous woman. I was neither; but Denise gave me the template to which I would aspire over the next decade. Grit and glamour did not have to be mutually exclusive.

At the velodrome I probably just seemed ridiculous. I had a very girly voice and a very girly laugh. I also appeared as a waif on my bike next to Chris Hoy – who had thighs almost as big as my torso and muscles that rippled with the explosive power a great sprinter needs. I was small and slight with thin legs and a small bum. It seemed unlikely I would find the force to generate a natural jump – the acceleration that distinguishes a good sprinter.

Yet all those Sunday mornings, chasing Dad's wheel, had instilled conviction in me. I would not surrender easily. I might have appeared vulnerable but, deep inside, I was a fighter. I also knew that, when I concentrated my mind, I was capable of surprising people. I was not quite as delicate or as silly as some had decided. I was ready to shock a few cynics.

Martin Barras was top of my hit-list. In the midst of an eighteen-month stint at British Cycling in Manchester, Martin (or Mar-tain, to use the correct pronunciation of his name) took an instant dislike to me. 'Miss Victoria,' he said on the day we first met at the velodrome, 'I'm going to find you very annoying ...'

He might as well have slapped me in the face. Martin had never seen me ride my bike and we had not said more than 'hello' to each other when he declared his disdain for me. I was cut to the core and rendered speechless – a trait with which I'm not readily associated.

It soon became clear why Martin was so vehemently dismissive of me. He had specific ideas in regard to the physiological and psychological make-up of the ideal sprinter. I was far too puny, in Martin's view, to generate any raw power. There was no beef or muscle on me – and Martin simply could not see where I would find the strength to overcome my physical frailty. He also took one look at me and decided I lacked the swagger and killer instinct of a supreme sprinter. Martin mistook my diffidence for weakness.

I don't think he meant to be cruel. He just spoke with, in his opinion, blunt honesty. He could dismiss me physically but I was outraged he could deride my character within a minute of meeting me. Alongside my buried anger, I was shaken by his mockery. It made me wonder if he had seen some intrinsic flaw in me. All the confidence that had begun to flow through me since Marshall spotted me, and Peter Keen endorsed his belief, threatened to curdle over one snide sentence.

Privately, I resolved to prove Martin wrong. Yet, when training dipped or I was tired, I felt wounded all over again. I would have ridden well if I felt he respected or even liked me. But, to Martin, I was a source of pesky irritation. He set me back.

I summoned the courage to mention my problem to Chris Hoy and Craig MacLean – who both tried to reassure me that I had 'got Martin all wrong'. Chris was convinced that Martin would be too professional not to give me a chance to prove myself. I nodded quietly, but Martin had made it plain that I would never become a decent sprinter. My only slim hope would be to switch to endurance events on the track.

Fortunately, Marshall, Peter and Heiko Salzwedel, the new German-born manager of the sprint squad, believed in me. In July 2001, and still only a twenty-year-old student, I was startled to be selected to ride for Great Britain in the European Championships. The team would be managed by Marshall and, as the Europeans were then limited to riders under the age of twenty-three, Olympic medallists like Queally, Hoy and McGregor were not included. I was still daunted that two of the three other members of the team had been on the Olympic podium less than a year earlier. Bradley Wiggins would race in the individual pursuit while Craig would triple up in the individual sprint, the 500m time trial and the omnium. Steve Cummings, another talented rider, would compete alongside Brad in the individual pursuit.

They were all much more accomplished competitors than me, and each of them was chasing victory in the Europeans as a win would secure automatic qualification for the World Championships in Antwerp later that year. Riding in the women's sprint and 500m time trial I wasn't thinking of winning anything. I was just hoping I wouldn't fall off my bike and look a complete idiot.

The Europeans were held in the city of Brno, which we all pronounced Bruno, in the newly independent Czech Republic. I arrived at the airport in my GB tracksuit, brimming with pride and tripping over with nerves, while the boys managed to look outrageously laidback. I liked them all. Craig showed the first signs of interest in my future – in a way which would eventually help transform my approach to cycling – while Brad was the quirkiest guy in the national squad.

Brad was amusing and charismatic and I felt lucky to sit next to him on the flight across Europe. I also felt hopelessly out of my depth. Brad seemed to know everything about cycling while I knew nothing. He was intensely passionate about the sport, both on the road and the track, and he didn't seem to mind that I was so ignorant. Brad answered my fascinated questions generously and enthusiastically. I was certain he was on his way to becoming a legendary cyclist – while it was more obvious than ever that I had fallen into a strange new world by pure chance.

When we arrived in Brno, I was in a room on my own and immediately felt disorientated. The boys teamed up naturally and, as the only girl, I was unintentionally sidelined while they met up to chat or watch a film. I sat alone in my room fretting about whether they'd said we would meet at 6.30 or 7.30 for a meal. So down I went to the hotel lobby at 6.25. When no-one appeared for twenty minutes I returned to my room – having worked out that they must have said 7.30.

I should have spoken to Marshall but I was worried about looking worried. I was soon paranoid about looking paranoid. The boys, of course, were all lovely when we did meet up for dinner and I calmed myself down. It was much better than sitting alone in my room, obsessing about the coming races.

There was little serenity in the Brno Velodrome. Whenever I saw another female sprinter I thought of Martin Barras. The women all had meaty thighs and big behinds. Their upper bodies were squat and powerful and their haircuts, for the most part, appeared equally severe. Mullets were still cool in sprint cycling. The Russian women, in particular, looked brutally strong. Martin would have loved to have exchanged me for one of them.

It soon emerged that my lack of physicality mattered far less than my hapless tactical knowledge. I realized how unprepared I was for the strategic minefield of the individual sprint. Unlike in the pursuit, where riders start at opposite ends of the track, two sprinters begin from the same point in a three-lap race. I was still learning the intricacies of the sprint.

Luck of the draw dictates which cyclist is drawn for the role of the lead-out rider – with the second sprinter having the potential advantage of, at high speed, expending less effort if they manage to use the draft behind the first rider to reduce the physical toll. On the last lap they can zip out of the trailing slipstream and, with gathering momentum, rocket past the lead-out rider. The element of surprise is vital to any attack.

Lead-out riders were far from helpless; even if the need to constantly look over their shoulders, to monitor the sprinter following them, suggested vulnerability. In their own way, the lead sprinter could dictate the slow pace of the first two laps and settle on the line of the ride. The first sprinter often will lead the trailing rider up the steep bank where they can pin them against the barrier and so force the second cyclist to overtake and assume the lead-out role. Some riders are brilliant at bringing their bikes to a complete halt on the curved bank by standing up and balancing with both feet motionless on the pedals and their front wheel at an angle. If they can hold this position, a 'track stand' or 'standstill', long enough, the second rider will be forced to start pedalling again and take over the lead role. But the first rider can also outwit his or her rival by accelerating earlier than expected and opening up a sufficiently wide margin to deny the second cyclist a chance to benefit from racing in the slipstream.

The old cliché of a cat toying with a mouse felt especially vivid and true as I watched the cruel psychology of the sprint in Brno. I definitely fell into the mouse-trap and my defeat was swift and almost merciful. There wasn't even time for me to confront the tortuous tactical struggle. I got so confused in the slow ride around the track before the flying last lap and a half that I actually lost count. I even asked myself, at one bemused point, 'Is this lap two or lap three?' I was that bad.

I was finally classified a lowly eighth – both in the sprint and the 500m time trial. Unlike Bradley Wiggins, it did not seem like I was on my way to becoming a promising young maverick on the track. I just looked like a lost young girl, who hadn't quite mastered the art of counting to three.

During my final year at university I reached an understanding with Phil Hayes, my tutor, and Marshall Thomas that I would spend one week out of every month training in Manchester. It would keep me in touch with the track as I tried to qualify for the Commonwealth Games in the summer of 2002. Supported by my university's Elite Athlete programme, and by Sport Newcastle, I could just about afford my train tickets to and from Manchester.

I often struggled to Newcastle station, as I lived a kilometre away in the city, with the frame of my track bike over my shoulder, a wheel in one hand and my bag in the other. Taking my bike apart meant I wouldn't be charged extra for it on the train – and I just had to worry about racing down the platform in Manchester shouting ''scuse me, 'scuse me, can I have my bike!' as it would be stored in the far carriage. I always worried about losing it as, without a sponsor, I was responsible for all my own equipment. To that end I also supplied my own tools. As a way of reducing the weight, my dad had sawn down a spanner and made it so small the velodrome mechanics joked that it looked as if I worked on my wheels with a tea spoon. It was all part of my canny plan to travel light and cheap.

At Manchester Piccadilly I would walk another kilometre to the bus station. It sometimes felt like hard work, especially when it was cold and rainy, as I trudged down the road with my bike and heavy bag. I would then have to wait for a blue bus because it only charged 50p for a fare to Clayton. The two other different coloured buses cost £1.15 – and my saved 65p would go towards my tea that evening.

From Clayton it was only a short walk to the crack house on Ilk Street. We rather lovingly called it the 'crack house' because there was not much glamour or luxury about a place where you could stay for £10 a night. It belonged to the parents of Peter Jacques, a former sprint cyclist, and it was an open house for all cyclists affiliated to the national team. You could walk across the street and reach the velodrome through the back entrance, and for your ten quid you knew the house would be stocked with cereal, milk, butter and pasta. There was also a little corner shop where you could buy a jar of pesto or a loaf of bread.

The accommodation in Ilk Street was just as basic – as befitting one of only three houses on the road that had yet to be demolished. There were six bunk-beds in a large room and another all on its own in a very small room. I always opted for the small room. Sometimes the front door opened and a guy I had never seen before appeared. I couldn't really ask if he was a cyclist because I wondered if I should have already recognized him. And, to make myself feel just a little safer at night, I would wedge a chair underneath the door handle in my bedroom at the back of the slightly scary crack house.

On 13 May 2002, I handed in my final assignment at the University of Northumbria. I was on course to graduate later that year with a 2:1 in my BSc Honours degree. My student life had flashed past in a sprinter's blur. The following morning I left Newcastle for Manchester, to begin a journey that would consume the next ten years and three months of my life.

Martin Barras, much to my relief, had taken his leave of British Cycling and returned to Australia where I knew he would be much happier working with the strapping Meares sisters, Kerrie and Anna, than a lightweight girly like me. There would be further changes as Marshall Thomas was moving out of cycling and into photography. Peter Keen remained at the helm of British Cycling, at least for a short while longer. The introduction of lottery funding also enabled him to recruit Dave Brailsford, who had been a key adviser in obtaining that injection of public money, as the new programme director of British Cycling.

Dave was young and enthusiastic, with a degree in Sports Science just like me, and full of certainty that the country's elite cyclists were just waiting to be galvanized. He believed in 'the science of human excellence' and in finding ways to allow riders to unleash the very best in themselves. Dave spoke in smooth sentences which sounded like they had been inspired by the books on management that he had read. In later years, words like 'the aggregation of marginal gains', which sounded so bizarre when you first heard them, would become seamless catchphrases that defined the attention to detail paid by the leaders of British Cycling. Dave and Peter were convinced that if every single facet of a cyclist's performance was improved by even a couple of percentage points, the combined impact would transform the rider into a world-beating winner. It made such perfect sense that you wondered why no-one else had thought of it before Dave.

He carried the personal disappointment of not having achieved success as a road cyclist – and this just intensified Dave's determination to succeed in a managerial role. Slowly, the evolution of British Cycling gathered pace. Further impetus was added by Manchester's hosting of the 2002 Commonwealth Games.

I was selected to ride for England in the Games – my first senior international competition. Peter and Dave also confirmed I would be moved on from the England Potential Plan if I based myself in Manchester and committed myself to cycling. There would not be much money at first – but enough to pay for the monthly rent of a room and my living expenses while allowing a little pocket money. More significantly, I could train full-time and prepare myself for a life in professional cycling.

The Commonwealths were an unexpected prelude to those long-term plans. It was not the easiest of experiences as the only other girl I really knew on the British squad was Denise Hampson. At the Commonwealths she represented Wales and so Denise and I were in different parts of the village. I shared a room with an endurance rider I had barely met and always had the anxiety of looking for someone I could sit with in the food hall at every meal. Those little quirks unsettled me.

I was also shocked by the electrifying atmosphere inside the velodrome. As an unseeded rider, I was allocated the very first ride on the very first night of competition – in the 500m time trial. I could hardly believe it when I looked up from the pits, ten minutes before my bike was wheeled onto the track, and saw that the velodrome was crammed with enthusiastic spectators. The enormity of attention made my spindly legs feel just a little wobbly.

The arena went deadly silent when, supported upright on my lonely bike, I waited for the five-beep countdown. At the sound of the fifth and last beep, signalling the start of my timed race around two laps of the track, the velodrome erupted. The crowd had reacted before me and so, for a second, I remained static on my bike, stunned by the explosion of noise. I managed to start turning my legs just in time and, as I sped around the wooden boards, the roar of the crowd surged through me. The noise seemed to invade my very being. After I crossed the line, and looked down at my wrists as I circled the track in a warm-down lap, I could see that little goosebumps had formed on my skin.

I finished fifth in the time trial, missing a medal, but I was confused once more in the sprint. The tactical vagaries were as mysterious as ever – especially as I had never ridden the event on the velodrome's 250m of shimmering pine. Struggling again to keep count of the strategically slow laps, I won my first heat against Melanie Szubrycht, my England team-mate from Sheffield, but I was still immersed in the tactical head-fuck of trying not to be outwitted by my opponent. In the semi-final, Kerrie Meares, of Australia, introduced me to the rougher end of professional cycling. I didn't expect to beat her, but I thought I'd give Kerrie a little run for the line. But she went out of her way to intimidate me.

Even though she knew she had much more power and speed, she took me right up the bank and used her bike to flick me against the barrier. The crowd booed Meares vociferously. Even the briefest of glances made it plain that, comparing Meares's physique to mine, she had the clear beating of me if

53

we raced in a straight line. It seemed bizarre that she should feel the need to intimidate me.

It was illuminating to watch the final between Meares and Canada's Lori-Ann Muenzer. 'Suddenly the Friendly Games were wearing a scowl,' Eddie Butler wrote in the *Observer* as he moonlighted from commentating and writing about rugby to cover an obscure sport like cycling. 'Meares won the first of three sprints, but was disqualified for what the judges called "intending to cause her opponent to slow down". In other words, it seemed to this novice spectator, she tried to drive poor Lori-Ann up and over the cliff of the north curve. And what's more, she seemed to do exactly the same thing in the second leg. The crowd was just building up to a growl of disapproval when a judge fired a gun twice. Presumably this was to halt the race, but in terms of keeping the atmosphere wholesome it was most effective, if slightly draconian. Meares was not disqualified this time, which seemed a bit iffy to me, but it did not cause a flutter among more knowledgeable onlookers. They restarted leg two, which Meares won in legit style. As she did the decider. All very thrilling; she won by half a spoke on the line.'

I could see how the brutal riding and bullish physique of the Meares sisters, Kerrie and Anna, chimed with the perspective of their new coach. Australia, the Meares girls and Martin Barras were dominant. But the British squad, split into four countries at the Commonwealth Games, was growing stronger by the month. I already knew that, for Chris Hoy and Bradley Wiggins, a glittering future loomed. My own life, both on and off the bike, was less certain.

*   *   *

It took just weeks for the next twist. I was invited to race for Great Britain in my first World Cup event in Kunming, China. Even the name, Kunming, sounded deeply mysterious in early August 2002. Mum drove me to the airport and we met Shane Sutton for the first time. I found him a little frightening, and Mum admitted later that she felt mildly concerned leaving me in the company of such an intense Australian.

Shane had won a gold medal alongside his brother Gary in the team pursuit at the 1978 Commonwealth Games, and he'd eventually moved to Britain in 1984 to continue racing. Three years later, he had ridden the Tour de France. Since his retirement he had become the national track cycling coach in Wales and, in 2002, Shane had joined the GB programme. We were both new to the squad but there was little doubt that the grizzled Aussie was coping better than me.

Shane must have recognized my uncertainty, for he did much to try and help me settle. Beneath the gruff exterior there was, clearly, a paternal streak in him towards me. I was overwhelmed. Soon after we touched down, and feeling dazzled after so many hours in the air, I was shocked by a different culture. Walking to the airport toilet I sidestepped a few phlegm-ridden tracers of spit as old women simply cleared their throats and shot the snotty contents onto the concourse floor. I was even more taken aback by the sight of women leaving their toilet doors wide open as they did their personal business over an open hole. Feeling very prim and proper, I closed the door to my own cubicle. I was not quite ready to embrace all the customs of Chinese culture.

Our hotel, however, was beautiful, with huge ornamental gardens where hedges were shaped into Chinese dragons. I was even more fascinated by the contrast that was evident from the back window of my lavish room. In the slum behind the hotel, lines of corrugated iron and tarpaulin could not hide the seething life as people washed their hair, squabbled and shouted while children went to the loo in full view on the side of the jumbled streets.

Kunming was the capital of Yunnan province and the track was a two-hour drive away from the city. In a crammed mini-bus, Bradley Wiggins, Tony Gibb, Kieran Page, Shane and I sat alongside riders from other countries. I usually perched next to a slightly older and kind Czech sprint cyclist, Pavel Buran. My eyes must have looked huge as I gazed at everything around us. We had already been offered suckling pig at a welcome banquet at our hotel, which I firmly declined, but I was still shocked to see two half-pigs stuck on a spike on the back of a motorbike. A couple of kids were perched upfront on the bike, with their dad behind them, and I thought they would have been amazed to hear that, when I was a girl, I loved pigs so much that my pencil case at school was covered in pictures of them. I was not quite ready to see so many butch-ered animals covered by flies as they flashed past our bus.

Once we had escaped the clogged heart of Kunming we hit some bumpy road which took us deep into rural China. Women and elderly men could be seen on the land, doing the work of farm machinery with their hands, as we raced through the dust and the heat towards my first World Cup event.

The brand new outdoor track, found at the base of the Himalayas, was hidden behind a big cast-iron gate which swung open slowly to reveal a mysterious sight. It was the first time I had seen a 330m track. We mostly raced at night, so it looked even more surreal under floodlights as giant moths flew around our heads. They were around two inches in length, and half-an-inch wide, and they looked scary – especially when their furry wingspan spread to three inches. I did my best to duck under them and also to avoid riding over the splattered remnants of squashed moth on the track.

Li Na, from China, won the women's sprint. I finished fifth – amazed to have completed my first World Cup. I also felt like a freak-show star for, along with a blonde German cyclist, Christine Müller, I was stopped continually by Chinese people who wanted to take a photograph. Christine and I looked as unusual to the rural Chinese as the teeming slums and spiked pigs had seemed to me.

Shane Sutton still watched over me and, on the long trip home, we stopped off in transit in Bangkok. It was a nine-hour wait and Shane arranged for all of us to take a tour of the city. In a night market in downtown Bangkok, eating ravenously while watching some sumptuous Thai dancing, I melted into another experience. If these were the kind of strange, new places where cycling could take me I was ready for so much more. I was ready to see the world.

3 | LOST IN THE MOUNTAINS

I lost myself, for a long while, in a place of breath-stealing beauty. I cried and I bled high up in the Swiss Alps, above the small and pretty town of Aigle, and it took me years to heal the wound. Even now, a decade later, it's hard for me to return there in my head. It's a place and a time of tangled darkness and, slowly, I need to unravel it in an attempt to understand why and how everything happened.

At the far end of Lake Geneva, just eight miles southeast of Montreux, and twelve miles further from Lausanne, it took a funicular train forty minutes to travel up the alpine cliff, leading from Aigle at the base of the Alps to an idyllic setting in the mountains. I was smitten by the way the shimmering water was made to look deeper and more mysterious by the steepling trees and mountains overhead. Absorbing the view at the top, I remembered that Aigle means 'eagle' in French.

At that spectacular retreat above Aigle, the International Cycling Union's sprint academy was run by Frédéric Magné. An inspirational Frenchman who had won seven World Championships on the track, Fred Magné's most recent gold medal, and his third in the keirin, came in 2000. Two years on, in November 2002, when I left England for Switzerland, Fred

58

had swapped success on the track for a life of coaching sprint cyclists from around the world.

The departure of Martin Barras had filled me with relief – but it left all the sprinters at the Manchester Velodrome without a coach. Jason Queally, Chris Hoy and Craig MacLean shrugged off the loss. Quick-thinking and sure of their ability, they knew they could manage together until another specialist coach was appointed.

I had just turned twenty-two and, without any other woman sprinters on the team, I followed a lonelier path into the unknown. And then, out of nowhere, salvation was offered to me in the Swiss Alps.

Two months earlier, in late September 2002, at my first World Championships, in Copenhagen, a birthday cake began the transformation. On 24 September, the day I turned twenty-two, the lights in the restaurant of our team hotel dimmed after the evening meal. A beautiful chocolate cake was then brought to my table while everyone broke into spontaneous song. 'Happy birthday to you,' they sang, 'happy birthday, dear Vicky, happy birthday to you ...'

Those twelve sweetly familiar words sounded strangely resonant. Rather than being clichéd or twee, they were rich and warm. As the whole squad boomed out, just for me, I felt as if I belonged. It had taken six months but, finally, I was part of the team. All my uncertainty melted away in the candlelight. I blew out all twenty-two little flames as the boys whooped. They even threw in a few more hip-hip-hoorays for me.

I knew, then, that I was on my way to Switzerland – less in farewell to the team than with the certainty that I would eventually return to Manchester as an improved cyclist after a year of being trained by Magné. The opportunity arose unexpectedly, and I heard about it soon after I ended up in an ambulance racing towards a German hospital. I had just been knocked out, literally, during the European Under-23 Track Championships.

In the sprint, against Tamilla Abassova, the Russian rider, I was sent crashing head-first into the wooden track. She turned her wheel right into mine in the midst of our race and down I went. I heard later that a doctor was on the brink of trying to resuscitate me when I opened my eyes and tried to move. But I only became fully conscious in the ambulance – where a kindly German paramedic, a large man with soft eyes, had soothed me while I moaned 'Where am I? Where am I?' over and over again.

Abassova powered her way to the European sprint title and my sore head was eased by the consoling words of Heiko Salzwedel, our team manager. He revealed that, before my accident, he had discussed my potential with Fred Magné. Heiko, Peter Keen and Shane Sutton were determined to push me on and, in Fred and his new sprint school, they identified a way forward. Fred recognized my raw talent and he agreed to their request. British cycling would pay for me to work with Fred – and the option was thrilling.

A chance to commit myself fully to the track encouraged me to believe my future might be shaped by cycling. My subsequent selection for the World Championships, topped off by birthday wishes the day before competition began, boosted me even more. I was on my way.

In the Worlds, however, I lost in the first heat to Svetlana Grankovskaya; and I wasn't exactly mortified when Kerrie Meares was beaten in the final by Natallia Tsylinskaya, a multiple world champion from Belarus.

The men, meanwhile, won three gold medals. Chris Hoy became world champion in the kilo – and then, with Craig MacLean and Jamie Staff, he helped GB win the team sprint. Chris Newton also won the points race in magnificent style.

Australia, as usual, headed the table with thirteen medals. Great Britain finished second, with a tally of five. We were eight medals down on the Aussies but, significantly, they had won just one more gold.

There was a gathering sense that British cycling was closing the gap. Our men looked increasingly imposing; and, even if I cut a stick-like figure amongst the hulking women from Eastern Europe and Australia, I was determined to become fitter and faster. I was now an accepted member of the national team and about to embark on a life-changing adventure in Switzerland.

In November 2002, I arrived in Geneva with Ross Edgar, from the men's sprint squad. Ross was lovely company and it helped that he had already spent a sustained period at Fred's school. It was also obvious that Fred, who met us at the airport, loved Ross. He might have been born in England but Ross's mum was French and his dad was a Scot. Ross chose to represent his father's country – and in that year's Commonwealth Games he had won the team sprint with Hoy and MacLean. But Fred was most enamoured by Ross's French heritage and his capacity for hard work.

At the academy, Ross had lowered his personal best for the 200m from 10.7 to 10.1 seconds. He had been a full-time rider before joining Fred but Ross had since grafted discipline onto his training. He told me it was important I showed the same application. I relished such seriousness. There would be no danger of me giving anything less than my very best to the academy.

Ross, in his laidback style, didn't fuss over me. Later, when we went out together for a while, he admitted wryly that he might have done more to help me settle in Aigle. But Fred was charming and the regimented routine occupied most of our time. I soon learnt that, for example, we had to line up in a queue early every Wednesday so we could collect our clean sheets. We'd make our beds by 7am sharp.

Based in a hotel, which we shared with an international hotel school, the UCI cyclists lived in a series of rooms that stretched down a long corridor. The numbers fluctuated but, generally, there were between twelve and fifteen riders working under Fred. In contrast, almost two hundred students were registered on a course of hotel management and hospitality. We lived a different life to the aspiring hoteliers.

Every morning we caught a 7:30am train to our language lessons. We studied French while the other nationalities, including the Chinese girls, Li Na and Guo Shuang, were taught English. As we had to walk to the station, and did not dare miss the train, we set off early from the hotel, grabbing a quick breakfast on our way out. Snow had already fallen in November. I learnt quickly to rug up warmly, pull on my snow boots and make the slow trudge to the station. On the train we would vegetate for forty minutes, dozing or staring out of the window at the beautifully snowy landscape that flashed past in a blur.

At least Swiss French was spoken more slowly. I found it much simpler than ordinary French, which I had studied at school, and in the ninety-minute lessons our teachers concentrated on our conversational skills. I became braver the more I spoke in class. We were pushed hard to talk and I loved that rigorous cultural start to our day.

By 10 o'clock we were deep in a gruelling session of training, either on the track or in the gym. We were driven relentlessly and lunch came as some relief. The time-bound rituals then demanded that we would all take a communal sleep together after lunch. In the *Salle de Repose*, a large room in which Fred had ensured that mattresses were laid on the floor in the stark style of a Japanese dormitory, we were all expected to sleep like babies. I found it difficult when there were some loud snorers in the room and, even when I did fall asleep, I always felt terrible when we were woken at 2.30. It was like I had been shot with a tranquillizer gun. By 3pm, feeling jaded, we'd be back on our bikes. Each weekday was the same; and then every Saturday morning we all took a two-hour ride on the road.

Even here there were strict regulations. On the road you were only allowed to use the bottom three, smallest gears, irrespective of the speed of the group. I'd be pedalling flat out, knowing how much easier it would be if I could change gears. Fred, however, was usually around and he'd keep watch with regal scrutiny. Occasionally, at the back of the group, I'd sneak in a gear change just to taste the sweet relief.

My body was not accustomed to such intense training. It went into a state of shock during my first month in Aigle. I had never seen such big black bags under my eyes – which felt like they had sunk right into the back of my head. Luckily, we were allowed home for Christmas and I had a couple of weeks to recover.

Ross and I returned in early January. The snow lay thick on the ground and the cold up in the mountains began to bite. I worked hard and tried to keep warm as the temperatures dropped as low as minus 12. During training on the road, my face would be entirely covered as I huddled deeper into one of the red fleecy snoods Mum had knitted for me. It stretched over my nose while my eyes were hidden by shades that could not quite prevent ice crystals forming on my eyelashes. I also wore a thick headband and my helmet but, still, it felt as if the bitter cold had begun to eat away chunks of my face.

I felt anxious whenever we rode along the river and the path turned into a flat sheet of ice. We cycled in a straight line, in pairs, side-by-side, and we were fine as long as no-one braked or suddenly turned. Even a twitch of a wheel at the front could bring the whole pack of us down like a box of dominoes being spilled across the hard and clattering ice. Some of the Chinese cyclists were not as used to the road as me; and so I was always far happier when it was my turn at the front.

On the track, I struggled to match the pace of riders who were more accomplished and better drilled than me. Li and Guo were both incredibly strong. They were faster than me on the track and much more powerful in the gym. A few months earlier, at the World Championships, Li had won the keirin. Riding daily against a world champion, and having my times compared after every session to hers, was sobering.

I was used to training as a lone woman sprinter in Manchester but, in Aigle, I was surrounded. Apart from the Chinese girls, I raced against Canada's Lori-Ann Muenzer, who had won two World Championship silver medals, and the American Jennie Reed, a recent World Cup bronze medallist.

Yvonne Hijgenaar was my age, twenty-two, but she was ahead of me. Apart from being the Dutch national sprint champion she had also reached the podium in the 500m at the previous summer's European Championships – where I had ended up, instead, in the back of an ambulance. Hijgenaar was part of the Dutch squad that used Fred's school as a training camp. Her compatriot, Theo Bos, had won three medals at those same championships and he strutted around Aigle with the certainty of a future multiple world champion. Teun Mulder, the third Dutch rider, had picked up a couple of medals at the Europeans and was also on his way to various future World Championship victories.

At different times there were riders from Belarus, Cuba, Japan, Korea, Malaysia, Russia, South Africa and Venezuela and I loved the mix of cultures and personalities. I became close to three male cyclists: Josiah Ng from Malaysia, Tsubasa Kitatsuru from Japan and Chung Yun-Hee from South Korea. I always enjoyed it when they showed me their magazines of popular culture, aimed at guys in the Far East, and we soon developed our own private code as we adapted to the rigours of Fred's serious regime. Fred had once told Tsubasa that he was 'stupid, stupid, stupid!' and so we resorted to saying things in triplicate. Someone would say, 'Ah, Tsubasa … is so stupid, stupid, stupid!' and we'd fall around amid much hilarity. And if someone was feeling emotionally or physically weary they would resort to a similar quip as they said, 'Today, me no power! No power! No power!' The boys were fun and interesting to be around and helped me feel a little less lonely.

I also had daily banter at lunch with the Frenchman behind the counter in the canteen. He regularly tried to trick me into eating rabbit or veal – even though I always reminded him that, for me, both were off limits, alongside horse meat. I enjoyed French cuisine but I was an ardent animal-lover.

He thought this was hysterical and would point to another deep and steaming dish. '*Poulet*,' he'd say with a sly grin.

His chicken looked suspiciously like rabbit. '*Lapin?*' I said.

He smiled mysteriously at me, and then shook his head.

'*Cheval?*' I asked more pointedly.

'*Non!*' he would exclaim innocently. '*Poulet!*'

Every lunchtime we had a similar conversation and I'd end up laughing alongside him and choosing a safer option – which I would then eat happily alongside my new friends at Fred's school. I would often look around and feel fortunate to be in such a beautiful setting, with so many diverse professional riders in a cosmopolitan environment. I also thought Fred was great and I ate up the work he gave me with enthusiasm and, gradually, resilience.

I was motivated by a need to try and keep up with the other women. Every time we went out on the track our individual times would be logged in the book, and compared by the whole group that same day. There were no secrets. Everyone knew who was flying and who was battling. I was always at the back of the battlers, clinging on for dear life to the rest of them. It felt as if they were miles ahead of me. In the gym it was even more clear-cut. I could not lift the weights most of the women hoisted effortlessly.

My only advantage on the track lay in my superior leg-speed, while on the road I was more efficient and grittier during longer rides. All those years of chasing Dad had, at last, given me some benefit.

The months slipped past and I remained at the bottom of the timed track efforts. My lack of confidence was apparent. I was disappointed not to qualify in the sprint in my first two World Cups as an Aigle student riding in GB colours. Travelling full of hope from Switzerland, I would then arrive at a competition feeling suddenly weary and edgy. My qualifying times were never quite quick enough. I felt deflated; but the excellence of Fred's coaching team and his managerial skills meant that I still savoured the training.

Gradually I could feel a new strength coursing through me, even if my results did not yet reflect that sense. Tangible proof only emerged during extended training races on the track. My slight build offered some reward here. I tired much less quickly than the bigger girls whose bulkier muscle-mass made them more subject to fatigue over distances exceeding 500m. Small victories in training provided reassurance that, slowly, I was moving forwards.

As late winter turned into a gorgeous spring in Switzerland, the daily routine barely shifted. But, deep inside the same pattern, I concentrated on developing my qualifying speed. My times on the track quickened. Something was stirring. I kept working.

The 2003 World Championships were held in Stuttgart that summer. I took a huge step forward, finishing fourth in the sprint behind the winner Svetlana Grankovskaya, Natallia

Tsylinskaya and Mexico's Nancy Contreras. Outside of the tight-knit training circle in Aigle, and my GB camp, everyone else in track cycling was astonished by my apparently sudden leap into the final four.

William Fotheringham, in the *Guardian*, was a more generous observer. Already looking ahead to the following summer's Olympic Games in Athens, Fotheringham suggested, on Monday 4 August 2003, that 'these World Championships, which finished yesterday, are merely the beginning, not an end in themselves … Perhaps the most encouraging portent for Athens was the surprise emergence of a world-class woman sprinter, Victoria Pendleton, who was narrowly beaten yesterday by Nancy Contreras in the ride-off for the bronze medal in only the fourth sprint series of her career. She has spent this year at the International Cycling Union's track racing academy in Aigle, Switzerland, and has clearly proved an able pupil.'

More suspicious glances were shot my way, and dark mutterings were mouthed, by those who knew little of my work with Frédéric Magné. To them, the only answer for my improvement had to be found in doping. It didn't bother me. The veiled innuendos told me how well I had done.

I had nothing to fear, being utterly clean, and so I peed cheerfully into every drug-tester's little vial. I knew that none of the testers or the doubters had seen the journey I had taken over the last nine months.

They had not seen me rise from my bed early every morning. They had not seen me work hard as I tried my heart out against superior and more experienced riders like Li Na – who successfully defended her keirin world title. They had not seen me riding alongside Theo Bos in the build-up to him arriving in Stuttgart, where he won bronze in the kilo behind Arnaud Tournant of France and Chris Hoy.

Great Britain gained a second gold medal when Brad Wiggins swept to victory in the individual pursuit. The men won two more medals in the team pursuit and sprint events – and we finished fourth in the table. Russia were first, with four golds, but we had won one more than Australia and the Meares sisters who, for once, were not seen on the podium.

I smiled demurely when I handed my last warm specimen of urine to the waiting dope tester. If this was the kind of rigmarole foisted onto the world's fourth-best sprinter, I could get used to it.

'*Danke schoen*,' I said in my very best Swiss-German accent.

My hard-won progress had been noted by Dave Brailsford and Shane Sutton. They knew Fred Magné was keen for me to stay on in Aigle for another year; and British cycling was prepared to fund an extended stay at a sprinting academy that might inspire me to a realistic tilt at an Olympic medal in Athens.

If it was difficult for me to think of myself as a potential podium cyclist, Peter Keen, who would soon become performance director at UK Sport, was emphatic about my prospects. I could hardly believe his words when, on the second last day of the year, my mum pressed an article into my hands. It was from the *Guardian*, on 30 December 2003, in an article headlined:

> **Young, gifted and on track to make headlines in the coming year: Coaches and experts from 12 sports name their top tips to make a breakthrough in 2004.**

The chosen dozen included the cricketers Alastair Cook and Ravi Bopara, the gymnast Beth Tweedle and the footballer Andy Reid. Graham Saville, described as England's youth guru and a member of the Essex County Cricket Club committee, considered the credentials of Cook who, then, was only eighteen: 'Cooky scored a fifty in each of his first three matches for our first team. He's a talented cricketer and I'm told he was a very good singer – a leading chorister at St Paul's cathedral, apparently, until his voice broke.'

Lewis Hamilton was the penultimate name on the list of twelve. He was nominated by Martin Whitmarsh, the Managing Director of McLaren, who wrote of his 'unusual talent'.

I was last on the list. Reading the words, I had tears in my eyes, hardly daring to believe that anyone could show such faith in my future:

Peter Keen, British Olympic coach: 'Victoria Pendleton is the fastest emerging British cyclist in my book, with another sprinter, the Scot Ross Edgar, not far behind. She is 23 and will be pitching for a medal in the women's sprint and 500m time trial. She was fourth and seventh in those events in the World Championships, but her rate of improvement is so fast and the gaps are so tight that if she goes 0.2 seconds faster it starts to look interesting. Vicky is bright, learns quickly and has natural speed and power that have only come through since she's put in the strength training. Superficially she looks fragile, but she's incredibly determined. She's a complete sprinter now, and 2004 could be her year.'

It's hard to tell how I got from there to here. I'm sitting on my bed, in my bare room, down an anonymous corridor at the hotel in Aigle, Switzerland, which doubles as the base for Frédéric Magné's and the International Cycling Union's racing academy. There is a Swiss Army knife on the white pillow. It has a bright red grip and two sharp blades of differing lengths. It also contains, at the flick of a wrist, a corkscrew, a can opener, a wire stripper, a key-ring, tweezers and a small pair of shiny scissors. The longest blade fills my gaze. I have been here before. I know what I need to do to make a new pain which will feel more clean and honest than the knotted mess inside me.

This year, 2004, has not been easy. It has been confusing and distressing. There have been a few uplifting moments. I won my first World Cup, in the individual sprint in Manchester in April. But there was also frustration. My Manchester victory was meant to be the perfect launch for a big breakthrough in the World Championships in Melbourne the following month. I qualified eighth fastest and then beat Yvonne Hijgenaar in the first round, Clara Sanchez, the French rider, next, before, in the quarter-finals, defeating Tsylinskaya, who had won the World title two years before. In the semi-final I faced the defending champion from Russia – Grankovskaya. It was a disaster. Adjudged to have crossed the line, and moved out of my designated racing area into Grankovskaya's lane, I was relegated from the race and consigned to a scrap for the bronze medal.

As my mood dipped, so my desire wavered. I lost both third-place races to Lori-Ann Muenzer – who I knew so well from Fred's academy. Lori-Ann had turned thirty-eight the week before and I felt dispirited that I had lost a World Championship medal to a rider who was fifteen years older than me. Even worse than that, when we shook hands on our bikes soon after crossing the finish line, Lori-Ann held mine and, with a smile, said: 'You will always be a princess – but you will never be queen.'

From the stands people would have only seen her smiling at me as we completed our warm-down lap. In calling me 'a princess', she seemed to be implying that I was spoilt and pampered. I knew that she received no support from her academy in Canada while British Cycling paid for my entire stay in Aigle. But there was something else in her barbed comment. I felt Lori-Ann looked down on my kind of femininity. She had short and spiky blonde hair, with lots of piercings, and she was assertive and relatively intimidating. I had tried initially to befriend her but I found her closed and even cold towards me.

Our relationship had not improved whenever I rode much more quickly than her up the mountains – as the climbing suited my smaller frame. Yet I was still shocked and even distressed by her taunting of me as a princess on the track.

After eighteen months of training under Fred I did not seem to be making the progress I should have done. In my depressed mood I considered fourth place at the Worlds a failure – as it repeated the same finish from the previous year in Stuttgart.

Grankovskaya defeated Anna Meares in a close final, by two races to one, but the younger Australian was a clear star in Melbourne. Her sister, Kerrie, was still out of competition with a back injury but Anna, just three days shy of being exactly three years younger than me, followed silver in the sprint with gold in the 500m time trial. I finished a lowly ninth. I was losing to riders both older and younger than me. It was hard to ignore the beaming joy of Martin Barras and the happy tears of the Meares sisters.

'I'm ecstatic,' Anna told the press corps after she had completed a lap of honour, draped in the Australian flag and acclaimed by tumultuous applause. 'I probably didn't expect a result like this. I thought it would be another year or two away. But Martin changed my training programme in the lead-up. We went back to the basic building blocks then trained me up for this. But I can't tell you what we did. That's a secret.'

I didn't really care about the secret training routine of Anna Meares and Martin Barras. I just wanted to get the hell out of Melbourne and back to Aigle where, I hoped, Fred Magné would lift me out of my fourth-placed rut. I wanted to be like Chris Hoy, who had again won the kilo at the Worlds, or Theo Bos, the men's new world sprint champion. I needed Fred to galvanize me.

Fred was cool and charismatic. He was also friendly towards me but, increasingly, I noticed how different he was around Ross. 'Oh,' Fred always laughed, 'Ross is my favourite.'

I also loved Ross. He was great. But, secretly, I envied the relationship he had with Fred. They were able to kid around, and make each other laugh. Even more significantly, Fred went out of his way to boost Ross and to make him realize how much he had progressed. I wished Fred could believe in me as much as he believed in Ross. I knew I was being petty and so I never said a word to anyone. I just pedalled away, silently, hoping that one day I would be good enough to be called Fred's favourite. I was so insecure and vulnerable, and in such desperate need of being liked, that those confusing thoughts tightened inside me.

Logically, disappointment at remaining in fourth place in successive World Championships was a healthy sign of my raised expectations. But the pride I had felt in Copenhagen and Stuttgart, at my first two World Championships, had soured in Melbourne. I felt stuck – and emotionally blocked.

My problems had started months before Melbourne. I guess they really began when, early in 2004, I resolved to prove to Fred that I was worthy of his highest praise. It seemed to me that, unlike most of my rivals, I lacked core strength. I had studied core stability at university and thought I'd include some additional abdominal exercises in the gym. Determined to pull myself up from the same static level and, having a degree in Sports Science, I considered myself sufficiently qualified to decide whether another set of work on my abs would be of benefit.

However, as I soon learnt, the regimented order of Fred's training programmes meant that any deviation or change was discouraged. Someone told Fred. They dobbed me in – as I might have said if I was still a teenage schoolgirl. Fred called me into his office. 'What's the matter with the programme I give you?' he asked angrily.

'Nothing,' I said. 'I just thought I was being proactive ...'

'No,' Fred said cuttingly. 'You're being disrespectful to the programme – and to me.'

'I'm really sorry,' I said. 'I should have asked for your permission.'

'You should respect me more ...' Fred said coldly.

I was mortified. My respect for Fred ran so deep that I ached for his approval. I could not believe that, instead, I had unleashed his disdain. In a recurring theme of my youth I had always feared letting down figures of authority, my dad most of all, and so I felt diminished by disappointing Fred.

Later that week, at the end of a hard training phase, I was literally blowing after a morning on the track. I felt finished. That sense of deep fatigue disturbed me. I needed to work still harder. So the next morning, I added another ten minutes on the rollers before breakfast. I thought my body needed it; and it was just a way of getting a sweat on before the day's real work began.

Again, someone chose to report me to Fred. I was called once more into his office and, this time, he tore strips off me. I had never been chastised so severely. Dad might have used his silent treatment on me, when I was a girl, but this was different. Fred ripped into me.

'Not only did you do this once,' he said furiously. 'You did it twice. I cannot believe you would do this again!'

'I'm so sorry,' I said in a familiar echo. 'I'm just not thinking straight.'

Fred was unrelenting and I felt terrible. Our relationship deteriorated from that point. He doubted my integrity. How come, he seemed to ask every time I spoke to him, I was the only person at the academy who felt the need to disregard a programme he had planned so methodically? My apologies could not change anything. It felt as if something had broken between us.

I spent many hours in my room, alone, feeling an outcast. Castigating myself for letting down Fred, I questioned my own worth. It got worse. I cried to myself and became still more withdrawn. The hurt inside me was like a raw wound. I needed to take my mind away from such a dark place.

At first I just stuck my fingernails into the skin of my palms. It was not enough. I needed the next step. I felt like hitting myself. I was that low and stupid. I wanted to bruise myself as a kind of penance. I know men sometimes punch walls in frustration. They even crack their skull against the bricks to draw blood. It's violent and it's angry but it offers some kind of release.

I didn't feel violent or angry. I just felt desperately sad and unworthy. I felt the urge to mark myself.

The first time, before Melbourne, I used the knife almost thoughtlessly. I did not sit down and decide, consciously, to cut myself. It was almost as if, instead, I slipped into a trance. I held the Swiss Army knife in my right hand, feeling the solid weight, as if it promised something beyond the empty ache inside me.

A shiny blade traced a faint line on the pale skin of my left arm. It didn't hurt, as I had yet to add any pressure. The slight indentation was at least three inches above my wrist. I had no wish to cause myself lasting damage; and there was no thought of me using the knife to open up the blue veins in my wrists.

I did not want to kill myself. I just wanted to feel something different.

Pressing down harder I had a sudden urge to make myself bleed.

The cut, when it came, did not really hurt. It was a sharp and clean sensation. I only drew a little breath at the sight of a thin line of blood. It was a tracer of my shame. After staring at the cut for perhaps a minute, seeing how it opened just a little wider as the blood trickled from the sliced gash, I cut myself again. I pressed harder and deeper and, this time, I felt it more plainly.

My skin opened up like a peach. The blood looked very red. It flowed more quickly.

I felt calm. It was not a bad cut and the bleeding soon stopped, taking away some of the pain inside. My arm stung a little but, mostly, numbness spread through me.

The next morning, waking early for training, I looked down at the red lines running down my arm. One looked much angrier than the other but, as I pulled on a long-sleeve top to hide the scars, I could not really regret what I had done. It had happened and, for a while, it had helped. I put it out of my mind.

It happened again, and again, and each time the same soothing numbness spread through me.

So here I am, once more, post-Melbourne, reaching for the same Swiss Army knife. I hold it in my hand. It carries the usual comforting weight. I look around me. The walls in my room are white and clinical – and very different to the redness of the cutting. I think of the gorgeous scenery outside. I know how lucky I am. I am living and working in a place of remarkable beauty. Other people are paying for me to ride a bike around in endless circles. I am fortunate. I love the training. The pain of pushing myself hard satisfies me. I relish the gruelling work.

Knowing how lucky I am, that my problems are so trivial compared to the trauma that people all around the world face every day, I feel ashamed. I don't want to be weak. I don't want to be self-indulgent.

I know the truth. I am not starving. I am not in a war zone. I am not being tortured. I am free from persecution and injustice. I am a white, middle-class twenty-three-year-old English girl from the Home Counties. I am in the midst of an opportunity of a lifetime. What right do I have to feel so bereft?

The question goes round my head as if, like me, it's riding a bike in circles on a wooden track.

I think of Fred, and his disappointment in me, his certainty that I no longer respect him. I feel, again, worthless and useless.

In my bad moments I have sometimes managed to ward off the need to cut myself. I turn to a cutting instead, with Peter Keen choosing me as his sporting figure to watch in 2004. I keep it in a slim plastic wallet. Now, trying to be rational, I put the knife down. I hold the plastic wallet in my hands and, through the shiny surface, I re-read some of Peter's words about me:

> Vicky is bright, learns quickly and has natural speed and power that have only come through since she's put in the strength training. Superficially she looks fragile, but she's incredibly determined. She's a complete sprinter now, and 2004 could be her year.

I am determined. I know it. I've been determined since those early Sunday mornings when, chasing Dad up a hill, I pedalled hard until it felt like my heart would burst. I never lost sight of Dad. But I not only look fragile. I *am* fragile. I feel as if I could crack and splinter into hundreds of pieces.

Peter Keen's sentences blur beneath the plastic. I don't feel bright or speedy or powerful or strong. I don't feel like a complete sprinter. I feel like a wreck. I feel like a waste of space.

I put down the plastic wallet. I pick up the knife. I know I am about to cut myself again.

Calmly and coolly, I go to work. I open up my skin. I am careful to avoid any veins. I don't want anyone to know what I do in the sanctuary of my room with a trusty Swiss army knife.

I start to bleed and, with the blood, the pain seeps out of me. I cut myself again, for the last time. I watch the redness trickle out of me and I wait. I want to feel different. I want to feel better.

*　　*　　*

LOST IN THE MOUNTAINS

The following morning, I again wear a long-sleeved top to hide the signs of my inner strife. Fred does not live in the hotel with the rest of us but, still, I instinctively know it's best to keep my personal choice secret from everyone else. I don't want to think about the cutting in the day. It's only some-times, on rare occasions at night, when I bring out the knife.

Today, I turn up for breakfast and reach the train and the track on time. I am about to pull on my helmet when Fred sees me. His gaze lingers on my lower left wrist. I see him staring. The bottom cuts are visible.

'What's happened?' he asks, in surprise.

'Nothing,' I say quickly, as I move towards my bike.

'Aren't you hot?' he asks, pointing to my long sleeves on an early summer day.

'No,' I say, forcing a smile. 'Don't worry …'

I turn away before he can look more closely. It feels the same as when I speak to my mum on the phone – only it's less graphic. On the phone, calling home, it's easier to put on a brave face. Mum can't see me. I speak to her in a deliberately bright voice. I tell her that I'm working hard, that everything's alright.

'Are you sure, Lou?' Mum asks. 'Are you looking after yourself?'

Every time I tell her that I'm fine – just a little bit tired from the training. I don't want Mum to worry.

I also, really, do not want Fred to worry. My issues with the knife belong to me alone.

I'm on my bike and down the banked wooden tier of the track before we can talk more.

Slowly, I circle the track again. My arms are covered. My head is helmeted and lowered. My legs turn. Round and round I go, picking up speed as I pedal.

I'm on my own, going nowhere fast.

* * *

A visitor comes to see me in Aigle. Steve Peters is a grey-haired man. His face is kind and warm. I like him the instant his hand takes mine. Dave Brailsford, the new head of British Cycling, asked Steve to fly to Switzerland. Steve is a psychiatrist. But I can see, immediately, that he is a man before he is a doctor. Compassion and understanding pour out of him even before I begin to talk to him.

I melt into his company. He explains that they were worried about me. Fred had suggested to Dave that I was struggling. Steve wants to help me. His whole life is built upon his desire to help people.

Steve asks me a few routine questions and, within five minutes of meeting him, I am hunched over in tears. It feels as if I cannot stop crying. I cannot answer the simplest questions that Steve has asked. One of the first, delivered in a quiet and gentle voice, invited me to list my qualities. I am mute, but for the crying. I am silent, but for the crying. I am empty, but for the crying.

Then, changing tack with sensitivity, Steve turns his attention away from me. He asks me about my family. We stumble over the imposing figure of my father. I haven't even begun to tell him about the girl on the hill. But it feels as if Steve already knows. Steve can read me like a book he has just opened.

The words and sentences and pages about me are brought to life in his head. Steve Peters reads me. He understands me. Steve starts talking about me as if the truth is written all over my scrunched-up face.

I look at Steve, through the blurring tears, and I say, 'Oh my God, this is so embarrassing ...'

He smiles back at me. It's his way of telling me that we need to move beyond embarrassment.

I'm still shocked. How can a man who has just met me know the secrets I've lodged inside myself for so many years? Am I that transparent? Am I that exposed?

'It doesn't matter,' Steve murmurs. 'I'm not here to judge you.'

He waits and then, after I have nodded my grateful understanding, he says six words of salvation.

'I am here to help you ...'

Later, Steve and I look back at our first meeting in Aigle. He tells me then how proud I make him feel. Steve says that when he meets people who are vulnerable, or damaged, it's important that they should want to change their lives. Some people, Steve suggests, are happy living a life of misery. I am not one of those people. I want to get better. I'm tired of the guilt and the feelings of worthlessness. I want to feel more hopeful about myself. I want to improve – as a cyclist and, more importantly, as a person.

I trust Steve and so, together, we start to unravel the darkness within me. He becomes my friend, rather than a psychiatrist. I talk to Steve and I listen to him.

And so, when we know each other well, Steve tells me the truth about his return to Manchester in May 2004. He flew back from Geneva and, at the velodrome, Dave Brailsford pressed him. The Olympic Games in Athens were just over two months away. Could Steve have me ready to chase down a medal?

Steve looked at Dave and shook his head. 'It's going to take more than a few months,' he said of his aim to make me better. He knew he was right about me. 'This is going to take a very long time to sort out – at least a year. Maybe longer. There's no quick fix. This girl has serious issues.'

4 | RAINBOW COLOURS

Fred Magné was, again, disappointed in me when I flew home early in the summer of 2004. He felt I had made a mistake that would haunt me for years. Fred did not understand the extent of my distress; and he was convinced that training in Aigle remained the only possible route for me.

Eighteen months, however, marked the end for me. I had to break the cycle. Sometimes I felt it so literally I could have taken a hammer to my bike and smashed it to pieces. I sometimes wanted to quit cycling and start a new and happier life. Escaping the isolation and depression of my last months at the academy became essential.

Steve Peters had urged me to not to make any impulsive decisions about my long-term future. He reminded me how hard I had worked to secure my selection for the Athens Olympics that summer. Rather than walking away from cycling forever, I should pause, draw breath and give myself a chance to think more clearly. The prospect of achieving such serenity would be enhanced if I was back with people I liked and respected. It was time to return to my team.

Fred had little faith in the coaching system in Manchester. But world champion riders like Chris Hoy and Bradley Wiggins were improving constantly. I wanted to emulate them and so, for a few days before we left for a pre-Olympic training camp, I took a room in a rented flat with Chris. The routine was very different to Aigle. Rather than being on my own at night in a small box, feeling lost and alone, I kicked back in the living room with Chris Hoy. We watched television and ate lots of cereal in a surreal combination that would not have earned the approval of Fred Magné. But I liked the way that Chris, who always seemed to be hungry, would regularly jump up during a night of slobbing out in front of the telly to grab another bowl.

'More cereal, Vic?' Chris would ask.

'Yeah, go on,' I'd say with a laugh. 'Why not?'

After eighteen regimented months of eating the same sort of food, at the exact same hour, day after day, week after week, it felt deliciously decadent to have another bowl of cereal at 10 o'clock at night.

It did not fit the brief of the UCI training academy; but if it was good enough for Chris Hoy, it was great for me. In training, with his imposing will, no-one worked harder than Chris. I knew he was on course to win his first Olympic gold medal in Athens. I was just going to try my best – a statement I would have found impossible to say a month earlier.

My fragility was obvious amid the stress of an Olympic Games. Everything felt sharp and clinical in the Olympic village in Athens. There were white walls everywhere, and small rooms. It resembled an institution. Surrounded by thousands of athletes, most of whom were edgy and jittery, I felt vulnerable and insignificant. Minor issues caused yet more anxiety. I worried about finding my way around the vast labyrinth of the village; and fretted about catching the right bus to the velodrome. The boys in the team would arrange to meet up for a meal and I would feel excluded and like a little girl on her first day of school – uncertain where I might sit in the dining hall.

It helped that I knew Emma Davies, the pursuit rider, and I hung out with her as often as I could. But, still, there were many days in Athens when I'd wander into the food hall on my own and have a little inner crisis about where, and with whom, I would sit. My first Olympic Games was a fraught experience. Considering the dark place I had occupied just a few months earlier, it could hardly have been different. But I was still shocked by how consuming the Olympics were in comparison to the World Championships.

I had been selected for two events: the 500m time trial and the individual sprint. On the Friday afternoon of 20 August 2004, in an Olympic velodrome as searingly hot as it was intensely pressured, I climbed on my bike just after 3.30. I had spent all my time in Aigle preparing for the sprint and so the time trial would merely be a prelude. Unlike in the sprint, where I had two successive fourth-place finishes in the Worlds, I was not really expected to compete for a medal in the time trial.

The beeps started. I held the bars tighter and took a deep breath. I put my head down and, my mind turning blank, I rose up out of my saddle. And, then, I began to race. I pedalled and pumped my legs as I hurtled around the track. The colours and sounds flattened into one long blur of painful movement.

I flashed across the line in 34.626. I had taken the lead in a new British record; and I began to breathe again as I circled the track more slowly.

My first ride as an Olympic cyclist was over, and applause rolled down the steep banks of seating. Only six riders were left. If four of them were slower than me I would win an Olympic medal. But, even amid the hot glow of competition, I was realistic. The quickest time trialists in the world were about to race.

The second rider after me, Natallia Tsylinkskaya, was a full tenth of a second faster. I would not be a shock Olympic champion after all.

Yvonne Hijgenaar then also went quicker than me. I was clinging onto a medal place – alongside chances marked slim and none.

Simona Krupeckaité of Lithuania killed off slim – moving ahead of me and Hijgenaar and into second place behind Tsylinkskaya.

Only two riders were left – Jiang Yonghua of China and Anna Meares – and they were both faster than everyone else. A back injury had forced her big sister, Kerrie, out of the Games but Anna, still only twenty, followed her World Championship victory in Melbourne with Olympic gold. She won in a new world record time of 33.952. I was 0.674 seconds slower and four other riders separated me and Meares. Jiang and Tsylinkskaya had silver and bronze – in contrast to my modest sixth place.

Just over an hour later, a few minutes before 5pm, Chris Hoy achieved something far more dramatic. He won the first British gold medal of the 2004 Olympics by blitzing the kilometre time trial – the same event Jason Queally had seized so vividly four years before in Sydney. As the very last rider, Chris had seen Jason's Olympic record smashed three times that steaming late afternoon in Athens. Arnaud Tournant of France held the lead as Chris finally followed him onto the track.

He was marginally in front of the pace he needed on each of the four laps and, as he rocketed through the final metres, his face etched in pain, Chris Hoy showed why he was such a supreme competitor. Using every gram of strength in his 66cm thighs he powered over the line in another new Olympic record.

Chris was unusually affected by his gold medal and spoke in a way that moved me profoundly. 'It's so hard to accept and believe it,' he said in his post-race interview. 'It's what I've been training for all this time. I was so emotional I could not get my hands off the bars. I was in tears as I went round the track.'

Later that night, in another unforgettable ride, Bradley Wiggins won the individual pursuit – narrowly beating his Australian rival, Brad McGee.

The two riders I looked up to most on the British team were both Olympic champions.

Two days later, on Monday 23 August, any faint hopes I carried of matching them with a medal were obliterated. I qualified poorly, in tenth place, and was drawn against Tamilla Abassova.

It felt as if I was beaten even before we took to the track. I rode badly and Abassova won easily. She would eventually reach the final – losing to Lori-Ann Muenzer, the new Olympic queen to my ruined princess. Anna Meares won bronze.

I had won nothing; and I just wanted to escape my miserable Olympic experience.

In the media zone, one of the British reporters asked me to analyse my performance.

'I don't know,' I shrugged sadly. 'My mind just wasn't there ...'

Fred Magné wanted to bring me back to my senses. He wanted to drive home the folly of my ways. He wanted to make me understand the extent of my stupidity.

We crossed paths as I was leaving the Olympic pits for the last time. Fred grabbed me by the arm. He steered me towards a deserted area behind the main stand. I could see thousands of spectators above us but no-one looked down. It was just me and Fred on the late Monday afternoon of my failure. There was no time for empty condolences. We both knew that I should have finished higher in the sprint. I had let myself down. I had let Fred down. All that training in Aigle had amounted to nothing.

I knew the reason for my mediocre display. I had been in distress for months and, still not free from the pain, I had arrived in Athens with blunted expectations. In return, I rode bluntly.

Fred seemed to take my disappointing display personally. It was as if I had insulted him by riding with so little spark. Still gripping me by the arm, and holding on as if he would not let go until I understood the truth, Fred made a bitter connection between my departure from Aigle and humiliation in Athens. Hadn't he told me I would be haunted by my idiotic decision to run home? Did I not realize how different the outcome would have been if I'd remained true to his programme? Why had I disrespected everything he had tried to give me – and thrown it back in his face?

Fred was a passionate and determined man. I understood his perspective and so the torrent of questions unleashed a matching flood of apologies from me. But every 'sorry' that fell from my crumpled mouth only seemed to deepen Fred's anger.

His frustration with me, for wasting the potential I had once shown, boiled up inside him. He began to shout at me and I broke down. My tears must have seemed pitiful because Fred kept on at me. I was soon crying hysterically, mumbling the word 'sorry' between gulps of sorrow.

The barrage continued. Fred did not seem able to see how much he had upset me. He kept asking 'Why?' Why had I disrespected him? Why had I given up on his programme? Why had I ruined everything?

I began to hyperventilate, struggling for breath in a way that had never happened to me before. We defined the anguished heart of Olympic competition. The frustrated coach,

Fred, reduced to shouting; and the bereft athlete, me, hunched and sobbing.

For years, that terrible scene would fill my head whenever anyone asked me about the Olympic Games. Of course, I dared not speak the truth. I churned out another platitude about the Olympics being amazing and overwhelming or, more honestly, I said nothing. I remembered the parting of Fred and me beneath the towering shadow of the velodrome, knowing how sorry I felt and how angry I'd made him.

Years later, I regret that Athens only evokes miserable memories in me. I wish I could have absorbed the thrilling nature of representing my country in my first Olympic Games. Yet that piercing experience eventually instilled a determination in me to succeed. In Beijing, four years later, the image of Fred haranguing me unleashed a driving need to prove him wrong.

I was inconsolable after Athens. My depression increased and I rarely went out. I stayed at my parents' house, and allowed the wound to fester. In the days following my return I piled all my Olympic kit and paraphernalia into the bin. I never wanted to see anything of Athens or the 2004 Olympics again. My embarrassment and dejection ran that deep. I just wanted to hide away.

My mum, being sensible and practical, fished a few things out of the bin. She hid them away, saving them for me. While she understood my disappointment, Mum thought that, one day, I might feel proud that I had actually competed at an Olympic Games. I'm ashamed to admit it now but I yelled at her. She knew how devastated I was after Athens, but she didn't understand how worthless every single memory made me feel.

Mum allowed me to scream at her and then, kindly, she said she did not want me to regret throwing away everything in haste. One day, she was certain, I would feel differently.

I slammed my bedroom door shut, as if I was thirteen and acting like the spoilt teenager I'd never been, but my mother's words must have sunk into my cluttered head. She was right. I did keep some of my Olympic kit and it's now tucked away in the loft at home, and in a less disturbed corner of my head.

The first sign that I might finally emerge from my stunned stupor came when, at last, I agreed to go with my granddad Alf, Mum's dad, to his Irish social club. Every lunchtime, Granddad went there for his pint-and-a-half of beer, to keep him strong. He wanted to take me down to the club, to show off his grand-daughter, who had ridden for Great Britain in the Olympic Games. Of course Granddad knew nothing about Fred Magné or my broken-hearted despair. He just knew I had made it all the way to the Olympics.

'You'll win it next time, Victoria,' he promised.

I smiled; and made the short walk with Granddad. I even drank a small glass of beer with him, while he showed me off to his friends. Granddad pushed the beery boat out that afternoon and had an extra pint. He was in a good mood and used some of his favourite words like 'blighter' and 'dolly-birds'.

'I feel a bit tipsy,' he chuckled as I led him back home. But then, halfway down the path, he stopped and gave me his most cherished slice of advice.

'Don't forget one thing,' he said seriously. 'Tell all of 'em to call you "Champ" … because that's what you are.'

'C'mon, Granddad,' I said with a lighter laugh. 'It's time we got you home.'

I found new hope in Mallorca. That November, as a tumultuous year wound towards a quieter end, I left Manchester with the men's sprint squad for a winter camp on the Spanish island. Alongside the male Olympians, I had missed the first World Cup of a new season, in Moscow, but we would all travel in

December to Los Angeles for the next leg – in an annual series of track cycling competitions held in different cities around the globe.

A full-time sprint coach had yet to be appointed at British Cycling, and so I arrived in Mallorca with the usual feeling of being a slightly lost outsider in an otherwise tight-knit group of confident male sprinters. In Manchester, I still trained largely on my own, trying to keep pace with the men, while I rented a room in a house belonging to Jackie Marshall, one of the endurance cyclists. I was on my own – without any clear direction.

Craig MacLean, however, changed my cycling life. Showing generosity and insight, he approached me in Mallorca. Craig must have seen how I was struggling, alone, and he offered his help. Would it be of any use, he asked me one mild winter evening on the deserted holiday island, if he helped me plan a training programme? I could hardly believe that a cyclist I so admired, a world champion sprinter and an Olympic silver medallist in 2000, would give up some time to help me.

I nearly hugged Craig. He gave me belief and structure. As a former piano tuner, appropriately, Craig also brought me harmony and balance. In my two years as a professional I had spent so much time in Switzerland that I had not forged a real relationship with the men's squad. Craig built a bridge for me by explaining how the men organized their training programme. They had become much more sophisticated than in the days when, first operating without a coach, they would try out all kinds of ideas doing the rounds. If someone told them that the Germans might have attempted ten flying 500m training runs then the GB boys would give an outlandish whisper a whirl to see if it worked for them. Craig, Chris and the others now knew how to craft a more appropriate schedule.

We talked through my own ideas, as I explained where I felt I was weakest. Craig added his knowledge and experience to a disciplined programme. I sensed excitement rising inside me because Craig was a bloody good rider and a very smart man. He laid down a path which would lead me out of uncertainty. I suddenly believed I could find a different kind of future for myself.

More immediately, I no longer operated anxiously on the margins of sprint cycling. The kindness of one rider had taken me into the clear heart of a previously mysterious business.

An almost instant improvement was evident. Just weeks later, in December 2004, Craig's new training routine boosted me in stark psychological terms. I went to Los Angeles for the second World Cup of the season. The World Cups are far less significant than the World Championships, partly because there are four or five every year, but the best riders attend most of them. LA was especially busy because everyone had travelled in preparation for the World Championships which would be held three months later in this brand new venue.

In the sprint, I lost in the quarter-finals to the eventual winner Natallia Tsylinskaya. I eventually finished sixth overall. Anna Meares was also out of the medals, in fourth place. But I shocked everyone by winning the keirin – the strange event, invented in Japan, where a man on a small, pedal-powered motorbike leads a group of six or seven riders around the track. At first, the motorbike, or derny, travels at a deliberately slow speed of around 20mph which gradually increases lap by lap. The cyclists are compelled to remain behind the crash-helmeted man and can only begin to race over the last few laps when the motorbike peels off the track with the riders approaching top speed.

The keirin is usually chaotic and even dangerous as we fight for position. In the final, after two earlier rounds, Meares and I both were up against the often imperious Tsylinskaya and three other women. We fought our way to the front and, even though Meares pushed me hard, I just edged ahead of her to clinch my second World Cup victory. It felt like an important milestone after the desolation of Athens.

The new year also began well when, early in January, I reached the sprint final of the next World Cup in Manchester. Having qualified fifth, I beat Kerrie Meares in the last sixteen by riding the fastest time of the round. I then defeated Guo Shuang, from Fred's academy, and another bruising rival in Tamilla Abassova. If felt like a grudge match because I could not forget how Abassova had taken me out of the European Championships two years earlier.

My main aim all season was to build my strength, and so I was mildly stunned to have made the final. I duly lost both races to Germany's Christin Muche – who seemed so surprised to have won that she let out an eerie scream just seconds after crossing the line ahead of me. Victory clearly meant more to her than me but, under the informal guidance of Craig MacLean, I had racked up gold and silver medals in successive competitions. I had also beaten both the Meares sisters. As I got ready to return to Los Angeles for the World Championships, I felt strangely settled and concentrated.

The World Championships began with early British success in the men's team sprint as Jamie Staff, Jason Queally and Chris Hoy qualified fastest. In the final, against the Dutch, a searing last lap from Chris secured another World Championship. It was his sixth major title in three years, counting the Olympics and Commonwealth Games victories alongside his World Championships, and it inspired our squad.

On that same opening Thursday of the Worlds I was content with my performance in the 500m time trial. Having not trained for the event I finished fifth – missing a bronze medal by 0.161 seconds. Tsylinskaya beat Anna Meares to gold by the even narrower margin of 0.02 seconds.

During a quiet morning session on day two, in qualifying for the sprint over a flying 200m, I recorded the eleventh best time. I was safely through to the last sixteen where, in a single match, I faced the highly-touted Dutch rider, Willy Kanis. She was still only twenty but, with power to burn and faster in qualifying, Kanis was expected to beat me.

Yet I won our heat decisively and, in the quarter-finals, I again surprised many of my rivals by speeding past Guo Shuang. It was another little marker from me – as much to Fred Magné as Guo who was as quiet off the track as she could be thunderous on her bike.

For the third successive year at the Worlds, I had reached the semi-finals. I completed the quartet alongside three beefier riders who all liked to bully me. In the first semi-final Abassova would face Kerrie Meares while, in the lower half of the draw, I was matched against Anna.

I left the track for a long rest at our anonymous team hotel just a few miles from the velodrome. The best-of-three races in the semi-final and final would only take place the following evening. In the sultry warmth of a spring night, I felt weary. I needed a break to prepare myself for a battle which loomed as a potentially defining moment in my career. Could I hold myself together and stand up to the three most physically imposing women sprinters in the world? I tried to push the question out of my mind as the yellow street lights flashed past our speeding bus. I closed my eyes and leaned against the window. My head bumped against the glass as we raced through the dark.

Doubts and thoughts of my past tangled around me. I was heading for another wobble; but I just shut my eyes a little tighter and tried to hold on.

Steve Peters, once again, came to my rescue. He listened quietly as I voiced the demons inside me. After the initial spurt of happiness at making the final four, I told Steve that I couldn't really believe I had made it that far. I did not feel I deserved to be there. I had just got lucky. A rider as unforgiving as Anna Meares would demolish me. How could I face her down when I felt so vulnerable?

There was not much time for Steve to work his magic in our hotel. He kept it simple, reminding me that my chimp, rather than the demons, was chattering away. Steve has this theory that we all have a 'chimp', lurking deep inside us, who unleashes feelings of irrational negativity when we are at our lowest and weakest. A real chimp is, obviously, a wild animal which, when threatened, will either flee or fight for survival. In Steve's analogy, the 'chimp' represents our raw emotional being which emerges when we are under pressure or consumed by anxiety or doubt. Our more considered human self thinks logically and takes control of these impulses.

Yet the chimp, if harnessed correctly, can also be a positive and galvanizing force. This is especially true in elite sport, when you need to be adrenalized to release your power and strength. The key point is to recognize the shadow of the chimp and realize when he has taken charge – and then replace his excessively negative emotion with calm thought.

Steve said my chimp, especially with me being a female cyclist in such a masculine environment, was actually a gorilla. That made me laugh. I could not let the gorilla get the better of me. I listened as Steve told me there was no point thinking of the past. All I needed to do was concentrate on the present – by resting and then going out and riding like I had never ridden before.

'You've got to ride this race like it's the last race of your life,' Steve said. 'Do that and you'll beat her.'

I nodded; and then I smiled. The gorilla had settled back down again. On the inside, I felt quiet and calm.

* * *

Shane Sutton was pure Australian; and so he understood the mentality of the traditional Aussie sprinters. They were taught to be aggressive and brutal. Shane, who would hold me up on my bike before my races against Anna Meares, reminded me that our semi-final duel was always going to be physically and psychologically testing. Meares knew how much it mattered to me to make the final after failing to do so the two previous years. My disappointing fourth place in Melbourne had contributed to my downward spiral and departure from Aigle.

I suddenly felt desperate to beat Anna; but I had never defeated her in the sprint. Steve Peters, however, had quelled much inside me the previous night. He checked on me in the morning and, realizing that I had recovered, he gave the nod to Shane to talk to me.

In his stark but inspirational way that Saturday morning, on day three of the Worlds in LA, Shane reminded me how I had beaten Anna in the keirin on this same track three months earlier. Shane spoke in plain old Australian. He motivated me as he told me how much I needed this win, and how certain he was I had the desire and speed to beat Anna. Instructing me to hold firm in the likely event she would try to out-muscle me again, Shane urged me to take to the track and, echoing Steve's mantra, ride the semi-final as if it was the last race of my life. Between them, Steve and Shane had slain my gorilla – at least for a while. I steeled myself for the task ahead.

The day still dragged.

I was relieved when finally, that evening, Anna and I sat alongside each other on the hard-backed chairs in the confined but exposed waiting area near the entrance to the starting line of the track. As her sister and Abassova took to their bikes for their first race, Anna and I gazed straight ahead. I did not yet feel quite ready to stare her down.

An official offered me a choice of cards, dictating who would win the right to ride from the back. Trying not to hesitate I tapped the card closest to me. The '2' was good news for me. Anna would take the less advantageous role of lead-out rider in race one.

Dimly aware that Abassova and Kerrie Meares were already on the track I re-folded my gloved hands on the blue GB towel covering my legs. I resumed my blank gaze. The noise of the crowd flattened into a hum when the first semi-final began.

Shane gave me the nod and I hoisted myself out of the chair. I led the way, and Meares trailed behind us. I wanted to show her that I was ready.

Abassova dealt effectively with Kerrie, still on the come-back trail from injury, and won their first race easily. The two riders pedalled past us on their post-race lap and I tried to breathe calmly.

My black bike was supported by Shane. He held the back of the saddle and the handlebars while I rested my left elbow on his right shoulder. Shane was so close to me that he blocked the number, 77, on my shirt while he said a last few encouraging words to me. We cut an intimate picture but, by then, I was so concentrated I barely heard anything Shane murmured.

Anna was below me, supported on her yellow bike. Level with her, and a foot higher on the lower incline of the start line, I could just see her shape, hunched over the bars. Australia's yellow and green hoops ran around the middle of her white lycra. I was in my red, white and blue GB kit.

Shane slowly rolled me down as, at the start, Meares led us out. She slipped into the ritual position, turning her head so that she could watch me over her left shoulder as she settled into place close to the blue rim of the curving wooden track. Meares, compelled to maintain a speed faster than walking pace for the first half-lap of our three-lap race, pedalled steadily. She mimicked me when I made the first move and climbed the steeply banked incline of the track. My main objective was not to allow her to pin me at the top even as she jerked and shimmied her bike my way. She eventually moved back down the track again and I followed her, still purposely leaving a gap between us.

As we began our second lap I headed upwards again, allowing the space between us to widen a little as Meares decided not to attempt pinning me this time. She began to pedal faster, with more intent, but I responded. Meares now banked up towards me and I weaved one way and then the other as if I just might be out to launch an early attack. She followed my every move and then, as the bell sounded for the last and decisive round, Meares added power to her speed. I joined her and rose out of the saddle to sharpen my acceleration, waiting for the moment when I might glide out of her slipstream and, racing a few kilometres an hour faster from the back, take her by surprise.

I veered hard to the left, trying to slip past her on the inside. She was ready. Meares closed the door on that glimmer of an opening. She held the line between the black and red bands of the track, forcing me to travel further than her by attempting to overtake her on the outside. As we hit the final bend, there was still a wide patch of daylight between our wheels.

Then, as we took the curve and hurtled towards the final straight, I gave it a real spurt. I felt my bike shoot forward in her slipstream, narrowing the gap suddenly. Meares lowered her head in a massive effort to hold me off. My eyes fixed on the line as my front wheel edged closer to her. I kicked again and, almost miraculously, another burst of speed made it feel as if I was flying.

I knew, instinctively, that I had her. I inched ahead of Meares just before we flashed across the line.

The first race was mine. I peeled away from Meares, dancing on the inside, as my bike veered up the curve. I slowed my pedalling, not even looking down at my opponent.

I cruised down the back straight as the result was confirmed by the trackside commentator and the computerized boards.

The number 1 gleamed next to my name. I needed to win just one more heat to reach my first World Championship final.

Beating Anna Meares would be the making of me. Defeat could unhinge me. I had little time to recover before we would sprint again.

For Abassova, at least, there was early confirmation. She sailed past Kerrie Meares to secure her place in the final.

When my turn came to race from the front, with Meares stalking me, I held onto Shane again as I waited for the signal to start. I reminded myself to keep her as close to my hip as possible. The aim of my strategy would be to build my speed gradually so that Meares would not have the chance to out-jump me with a burst of acceleration. I knew that, one down and unable to afford another defeat, she would be gunning hard for me.

I led us out and, like a nervous young horse, my head nodded up and down as I tried to settle into an easy rhythm. Before I had even begun to monitor Meares's movements over my shoulder, she shocked me. Meares overtook me as soon we crossed the halfway point of the first lap. I was taken aback by her dramatic tactical shift. She led me round the track and, in an effort to claw back some of the initiative, I took to the upper tier. Meares held her line for a moment and then she came for me in a gliding motion. Like a big shark launching a mock attack she rode straight at me, her front wheel almost forcing mine into the railing. I could have fallen or crashed as her wheel blocked mine but I turned sharply to the right, avoiding her, and just held on.

Meares had attacked me with such naked aggression that the crowd erupted into a communal gasp. An 'oohhhhh!' echoed around the arena. They knew her less well than I did.

She coolly steered away from me and returned to the lower part of the track. Meares watched me closely to see how I might react. I tried to stay calm and not betray any sign of weakness.

Meares did not allow any respite. She came back up the track again but I held the distance between us. I was not going to give her another chance to get up close to me.

Sticking close to the barrier, I increased my speed. Yet, blocked by Meares, it was hard to see any opening. I sat back down in my seat and waited.

The trackside commentator's voice echoed as he spoke about 'a cat and mouse game' and 'a little intimidation'. Meares and I were heading towards another dramatic culmination.

Peeling away to the left, I raced down the banking. I slid briefly into the lead but, reacting with a shudder of power, which made her wheel twitch like that shark's tail at the sound of the bell, Meares responded and sped ahead again. The full length of a bike opened up between us and Meares hurtled down the back straight. I chased hard, dipping and weaving this way and that as I tried to carve out the space to fly past her. But Meares was as cute as she was tough. Each time she cut my line and I had to try again.

Half a lap was left when, with both of us sprinting hard, I took the only option left to me – to try and overtake her on the outside. I was ready to back my speed against hers. As we arrowed around the final turn there was still a wheel of space between us. Her head, once more, was down as Meares strained with the effort. I kept my gaze locked on the prize and, the track blurring beneath me, felt the space between us tighten and close.

I was catching her. I could feel it and, soon after we sailed over the line, I swept past her.

But the line beat me to it. I overtook Meares after her wheel crossed the finish, fractionally ahead of mine. I had left my spurt too late. Meares had beaten me, tactically and physically. We were back in the old routine. Victory for Meares. It was 1–1 after two races.

We were down to the decider. I tried not to fret as I circled the pits, guiding my bike into a small corner of space. I rode round and round, at the far end of the pits, my mind turning blank with each rotation. Everything would be decided by this last battle.

I was still in a kind of quiet trance when, having warmed down, I slid off my bike and found a seat on which to recover in the GB area. It had been another strong championship for our team. After winning gold in Thursday's men's team sprint, Jason Queally and Chris Hoy had picked up silver and bronze in Friday's keirin. But GB secured the medal that our bosses, Dave Brailsford and Shane Sutton, wanted most when, finally, the men won the team pursuit.

Dave B led the chorus of praise. 'Even before we arrived in LA,' he told the British press, 'I said we had unfinished business to resolve in these championships. If there has ever been a team that deserves to win a World Championship then it's the pursuit guys. They have been so professional, time and time again. It shows that if you knock on the door long enough you get your reward.'

I knew how much unfinished business lay between me and Anna Meares. And it felt, after my turbulent results in the Worlds and the Olympics, as if I had been banging on the door long enough. I was desperate for it to open at last, and I did not dare allow myself to be distracted. Shane must have seen my look because he said just a few simple words of encouragement before steering me back on to the track for the third and final time against Anna Meares.

We waited alongside each other on our bikes, my black frame against her gleaming yellow. This was the moment just before, I hoped, I would show the best of myself.

I was drawn as the lead-out rider again and, from the outset, Meares rode hard on my back wheel. We both had the pattern of the previous race embedded in our brains. I watched her closely. But I decided to let her go when, just before the turn curving towards the home straight, she dipped inside me and unexpectedly took the lead.

On the second lap Meares kept me fixed in her sights, pedalling at a fast lick, while I tracked her from up high. We were both waiting for the moment one of us would strike.

There was little space between our bikes as we approached the final bend of our penultimate lap. And it was then that, with sudden clarity, I saw an opening. I flew down the banks and slipped past her on the inside and re-took the lead just at the sound of the bell. A whoop went up from the crowd and I really got moving down the home straight, opening up the space between us.

Meares closed on me just as we began our sprint on the last lap. She rode above me, in the arcing middle of the track, while I held my line between the two big lanes of colour. We raced hard down the back straight, Meares low-slung in her saddle while I rode a little higher in my stance. I was still leading as we came out of the final turn and headed for home; but Meares had inched closer.

I could feel her bearing down on me, replicating the way I had shrunk the gap between us in our first race, and I poured everything of myself into the finish.

We careered towards the line, with little separating us. I ducked my head as we flashed past the line.

It felt desperately close but I had won. I had done it.

Meares flew up away from me, taking the incline, while I kept pedalling, in dazed rapture, round the inner ring of the track.

I was in the World Championship final. I had won, at the very least, a silver medal. But it mattered more to me that I had the sprinter's scalp of Anna Meares.

*   *   *

There was no time for celebration. Tamilla Abassova led us out in the first heat of the final. She did not try to shadow me when, after half a lap, I took to the upper bank of the track. Abassova remained at the bottom, watching me warily. It was only during the second lap that she climbed high to ride along-side me. But she not did carry the same twitching threat as Meares. I allowed her to speed ahead of me and then, at the bell, I sprinted hard.

I cut sharply down to the left and the crowd erupted as I took the lead, surprising Abassova. I was fractionally ahead as we headed for the last bend. The British team members were whooping 'Go, Vicky, go, go!' as I raced towards the line. I surged away from Abassova and won by a clear bike wheel.

In race two I was the lead-out rider. Abassova fiddled with the strap of her helmet as I pedalled calmly around the track. I picked up the pace, lifting my bum in the air, and headed up the track. Abassova, almost lazily, followed me. There was a significant gap between our bikes.

At the bell I again took the initiative. I spurted down the incline and, along the back straight, I was out of my saddle while Abassova stayed low. Finally she came at me. Chasing me round the final bend she narrowed the gap between us to almost nothing.

'Go, Vicky, go, go, go, go, go!' my friends on the team screamed again.

'It looks like Pendleton on the inside!' the commentator whooped as we blurred past the finish.

I had won. I was the new world champion. The words swept through me down the back straight. Around the turn, I lifted my left hand off the bars and held it high. I clenched my hand into a fist. I pumped it in rapture. My face broke open into a smile of joy as the applause rolled around me.

I looked behind me for Abassova and, seeing her, my left hand dropped back into place. I stretched my right hand towards Abassova, taking hers in consolation – and acknowl-edgement for me.

I didn't know whether to laugh or cry when I climbed off my bike; and so I did a little of both as the team engulfed me. I finally belonged with them. Happiness surged through me.

I was about to pull on the rainbow colours of a world champion. I was no longer a fraud. I could hardly believe it.

'You'd better believe it, Vic,' Shane Sutton hollered. 'You're the champion of the world …'

5 | RIVALS

I evaded my father's pressing questions when I returned home in April 2005. Dad asked whether I had brought my rainbow jersey with me. When I shook my head, and said sorry, he nodded in disappointment. He wondered how I could have forgotten. Didn't I know how much he wanted to see the white jersey, with the rainbow hoops, they had presented to me as world champion in late March? I had worn it on the podium in Los Angeles and I was conscious how blissfully happy I'd looked. It was far more stressful letting down Dad gently.

'Next time, Dad,' I said. 'I promise.'

Mum thought it was a lovely idea. She knew I planned to frame the jersey and give it to Dad as a secret birthday present. But Dad wouldn't turn sixty until 1 May – which meant I was ducking and diving all April.

'I'd really love to see it,' he said again.

'I know, Dad, I know,' I replied. And then, with actorly frustration, I sighed. 'I can't believe I forgot.'

It was even trickier trying to frame the damn thing myself. Instead of getting the job done professionally, I thought I'd keep it personal and do it just for Dad. I might have just become world champion but, clearly, I was not about to win any awards for my framing technique. It took me hours to finally complete it – and it was easier then to write the message I had long planned for the big day. In black ink I wrote:

Thank you Dad
This One's For You
Lots of Love
Victoria x

Finally, with the glass frame covered in beautiful gift-wrap, I went home to Stotfold. There was no need for evasive apologies this time. I could just kiss Dad, wish him happy birthday and hand over his present.

At first, as he unwrapped the paper, he looked quizzical. He was obviously not expecting to see my rainbow jersey encased inside the glass frame.

I had never seen my dad cry because he's not a man who easily shows vulnerability. Over the years I had learnt to read his dark moods. I could tell when he was angry or dejected, frustrated or incredulous. But Dad preferred to hide his more tangled feelings. I think he saw it as a weakness to reveal them.

It was impossible, however, to conceal the feelings coursing through him as he looked down at my gift. Dad couldn't speak and he couldn't look up. Instead, my father just stared at the frame, his hands trembling, as he held it. Finally, when he did lift his eyes to me, I could see how hard he worked to stop his tears from falling. He did not give in and start crying but he came so close that I could not help myself. My own eyes welled up and I moved towards him. I held my dad close.

As I hugged Dad I thought of all those Sunday mornings on his unforgiving hills. I pictured myself, with a pale and wet face, fixing my gaze on the distant figure of Dad as he never looked back. It had been so hard to keep up with him, to try and please him, but he had turned me into a world champion.

If it had not been for Dad I would never have begun cycling. I would never have learnt the tenacity and resilience that allowed me to defeat Anna Meares when it mattered most. I might once have thought he was breaking me but, really, Dad had made me.

My father shook his head quietly when we parted. He thanked me, in a voice still thick with feeling, but he also said he didn't feel he deserved my rainbow jersey. Dad reminded me how hard I had worked for it. The jersey was a beautiful symbol of my becoming world champion. He could not take it away from me.

'You've earned this, Vic,' Dad said. 'It's yours …'

I felt even more certain than he did. I wanted Dad to have the rainbow jersey.

'I'll never wear it, Dad,' I said, truthfully. Every time I rode as world champion over the next year I would be supplied with the official UCI-designed rainbow skinsuit. But the first jersey, the one awarded to me less than an hour after I beat Tamilla Abassova, would never be worn in actual competition. If I kept it, the rainbow hoops would remain hidden in a box at the back of a darkened cupboard. It would be much better to keep it at our family home – so Dad might see it every day and think of all we had achieved together.

When I'm in the mood I can argue just as convincingly as Dad; and so he surrendered. He gazed again at the framed jersey, and then me, and his tears were pushed down inside him. In their place, a proud smile lit up Dad's face.

'Thanks, Vic,' he said. 'I love it …'

Richard Caborn, the Minister of Sport, underlined the success of the GB team in heading the medals table at the World Championships. 'We have to give credit for this to the governing body,' Caborn said. 'There's no doubt that there has been a major modernization in recent years, a renaissance in the sport.'

At UK Sport, Peter Keen, who had started the lottery-funded cycling system, responded to our achievements as a team in Los Angeles by saying, 'Whichever way you look at it, Britain is currently the top nation in world track cycling ... we're on the verge of something even more special.'

I was proud to be part of our dizzying rise. Winning also moved me closer to the heart of the GB squad, and ended my feelings of isolation. No longer the newest member of the team, and older then medal-winning debutants like Ed Clancy and Mark Cavendish, I was relieved that I finally belonged at the Manchester Velodrome. I had become only the third British woman to win a World Championship track cycling gold medal after the great Beryl Burton won her fifth and last title in 1966 and Yvonne McGregor in 2000. Their victories had come in the pursuit; I was the first British woman sprinter who could call herself a world champion. Yet not even that slice of history, and a rainbow jersey, could banish all my doubts.

Steve Peters was unsurprised. In the year at British cycling I had shared with Steve – a sports psychiatrist with his most complicated student – I came to value his support and understanding above anything else. Steve described himself as 'a mechanic of the mind' and we both knew that I was in regular need of repair. He had met me at my very lowest, amid the cutting and the crying in Aigle, and in twelve months he had rebuilt my shattered psychology. But it needed tweaking and strengthening every week.

Steve had a very ordered mind, which was partly a product of the maths degree and logic theory he had studied before he turned to medicine. His structured intelligence worked well in tandem with the emotional empathy he brought to his work. Steve spoke simply when he said that, essentially, all he wanted to do was to help people become happier.

He had dealt with more cluttered minds than mine, for Steve had worked in forensic psychiatry and with patients suffering from personality disorders at Rampton Secure Hospital in Nottinghamshire. But I presented him with a difficult challenge. My psychological make-up was unsuited to the brutal world of elite sport. And yet my talent and determination belied those apparent frailties. Steve's task was to help me control the worst in myself, and uncover the best, while assisting my development as a person and as a professional cyclist.

Steve was very different to my dad, about whom he had begun to learn a great deal as we probed my past, because he described his methods as being 'all carrot and no stick'. Dad would never have analysed himself in such terms but I always thought he was a stick-and-no-carrot man. I loved Dad, and it meant so much to have won a rainbow jersey for him, but I far preferred Steve's talk of carrots and chimps. I liked the carrots; and with time I would learn to control the chimp, or gorilla, as Steve still described the dark forces of my negative self, and turn it into a jolting source of inspiration.

His methods of working were clear and exact. Steve separated our programme into three distinct stages. In the first he guided me deep inside my own head so that I could begin to understand how I interacted with the world both now and in the past. We were about to move into the second stage, as Steve helped me fathom how other people thought and acted, before I would finally be ready for his third tier of learning – where I would improve my communication skills.

Steve had already taught me to try and stop worrying so much about pleasing everyone. We knew that this was one of my most draining flaws and he again used three groups to clarify my thinking. There would always be some people, Steve said, who would care about me and love me. In contrast there would also be a select group of people who would never warm to me – no matter what I did. And in the middle came the overwhelming mass who were largely indifferent to any of my failures or triumphs. I needed to understand that most people didn't really care what I did or said. All my anguish about how they might perceive me was redundant. Steve helped me realize that I spent too much time trying to please those oblivious people in the middle or, more problematically, the small group who would never change their critical opinion of me. I should concentrate on the people who really did show concern for me.

He also focused on my unduly negative claim that I was lucky to have become world champion. I did not believe I really was the best female sprint cyclist on earth and so, typically, I undermined my own achievements. I told Steve that my World Championship win needed to be considered in the context of a post-Olympic year. It was an unequivocal fact that the best riders considered the first year after an Olympic Games as the least important in their four-year cycle of preparation.

Steve calmly asked if I had believed Anna Meares, as an Olympic champion, had dismissed the significance of the Worlds the night before our epic semi-final? I had been full of talk then that she was far too formidable and that I felt unsure we even belonged on the same track. What had happened since then to change my view? I had beaten her and become world champion.

'I got lucky,' I said.

'And Meares and Abassova just rolled over and allowed you to win – that sort of luck?' Steve asked.

Steve was such a gentle and compassionate man it was hard to argue with him. I knew Meares and Abassova hadn't just let me win. But I couldn't quite shake the feeling that I must have been fortunate to have won the rainbow jersey.

'You don't become world champion by luck,' Steve said. 'You're too smart to believe that …'

I smiled and shrugged.

'Well,' Steve murmured, 'you'll have to go out and win it again – and prove to yourself that you're more than just lucky.'

I liked the sound of the hard work, and fierce training, such a task entailed on the track at the velodrome and in the gym with Mark Simpson – my strength and conditioning coach at British Cycling. In Steve and Mark I had discovered two men who had begun to transform me mentally and physically. As different as they were, for Mark was a much younger mixed-race man, they shared an emotional intelligence that made them stand out amongst the hardcore men in elite cycling. Just like Steve had always been able to read me, so Mark could gauge my state of mind as soon as I walked into the gym. He knew precisely how to treat me every new day – which meant he and Steve both had the same rare gift.

Mark's role in the development of British Cycling was plain to me. He spent more time with the sprinters than any track coach and, rather than Shane Sutton and Dave Brailsford, it was Mark who was attuned to our daily regime and all our fears and hopes. I was sorry he had not been in LA to see me win my first World Championship because I felt that, in part, it belonged to him after all the hours he had spent helping me. But British Cycling did not allow low-key staff members to share in the glory – and it bothered me.

'Don't worry about it,' Mark said with his usual smile. 'We're Team Pendleton anyway.'

Steve, Mark and I were the founder members of our invisible Team Pendleton. I knew that they both were intent on looking after me. Neither of them, unlike other coaches or mentors in my past, ever spoke down to me. And so I felt able to be myself with both of them; to be a goofy chatterbox one day and a vulnerable doubter the next. They each encouraged me to take even firmer charge of my own training programme so that I could feel responsible and in control. Stable, consistent and emotionally sensitive, Steve Peters and Mark Simpson gave me hope that I could make it, on my terms, in a harshly thrusting and male-dominated environment. I was not, after all, alone.

The drugs testers were also determined to offer me their company; and I was soon on excellent peeing terms with various anti-doping officials. It seemed as if they were always popping in and out of the velodrome. At least once a month I'd have to do my thing with a small specimen jar while they waited patiently for me. There was even a day, when I won two titles at the 2005 National Championships, that I was tested twice in the space of six hours. Each victory, in the 500m time trial and the sprint, was followed by a request from the drug detectives to supply them with a little sample. I was happy to keep winning, and peeing, as I moved towards the next big block of competition.

In cycling there's always another race and, after the Nationals, I turned to the World Cup events to prepare myself for the following year's Commonwealth Games and World Championships. In early November 2005, at the first World Cup of the season in Moscow, I reached the sprint final – and lost to Natallia Tsylinskaya.

Building towards something more substantial, I was set on winning the next World Cup sprint in Manchester the following month. My ambition was obvious from the start as I rode the fastest time in qualifying. Tsylinskaya was second quickest while Anna Meares was considerably slower – and tenth in qualifying. We were drawn together in the last eight after I won my first round.

Meares and I again split the first two races. She won heat one; and I took the second. The third race was the quickest and, determined not to lose to Meares on my home track, I just held on to a narrow win to endorse my world champion tag. In the semi-finals both Tsylinskaya and I won clear-cut 2–0 victories over, respectively, Guo Shuang and Simona

Krupeckaitė. My times were notably faster and I went into the final against Tsylinskaya with real confidence. After winning the first heat, I rode the slickest race of the day, in a time of 11.886, to secure the gold medal. Tsylinskaya also endured a relegation for moving across her line and effectively cutting a corner. It made her defeat seem absolute. It also meant I completed my first year as a world champion with another World Cup victory.

I returned to battle with the Meares sisters in their backyard at the Commonwealth Games in Melbourne in March 2006. We knew that, three weeks later, we would be at it again on my side of the globe – during the World Championships in Bordeaux. Even if competition at the Commonwealths was not as steep, because the European riders were missing, I faced a testing week against the tough Aussie mining girls.

Attention focused on the Meares sisters because their parents, Marilyn and Tony, would watch them ride for the first time in an international competition. There was already enough of an edge between us to mean that I liked the idea of beating them both in the sprint at home and in front of their mum and dad.

We began with the 500m time trial, Anna's domain as world champion, and the two of us were given the final two rides. Kerrie had already set the quickest time of 35.210 when my turn came to climb on my bike. I felt concentrated but relaxed as, unlike in the sprint, there was little expectation I might come close to defeating Anna in her specialist discipline.

My legs churned with real pace and rhythm, and I knew I was quick. But I was startled to see how far I had dipped under 35 seconds. My time of 34.662, two-tenths of a second faster than my previous personal best, glittered on the scoreboard. I had set a new Commonwealth Games record.

Anna Meares lowered her head and, as she admitted later, 'I can't really repeat what I thought. "Oh gosh!" might be a nice way of putting it! I saw 34.6 come up on the board and I was straight back looking down at the ground thinking, "You do your own race, don't worry about the time."'

She was a champion, of course, and proved it again just a few minutes after me. Meares powered round two laps of the track, from a standing start, in a time of 34.326.

Anna and Kerrie, having won gold and bronze, climbed into the crowd to embrace their parents. 'They were crying after the finish,' Anna said afterwards. 'Having them here was so important. It's the second fastest time I've ever done, so I'm pretty pleased with it. I felt strong all the way.'

I smiled more demurely when called in front of the press. Acknowledging that I had ridden well, I added some needed context: 'I got beaten by Anna, and I couldn't have gone any faster. She's the world record holder and Olympic champion – of course she's fast. It's the closest I've ever been to her in competition, and I'm not really a 500 metre specialist.'

The implication was obvious. I was determined to show the sisters why I was world champion in the event that mattered most to us. I stood on the podium after the time trial, a silver medal draped around my neck, and smiled again as they waved to their cheering supporters.

Two nights later, on 19 March 2006, I avoided a semi-final against either Meares girl. Kerrie set the fastest early time in qualifying for the sprint, at 11.725, which was soon lowered by Anna to a perfectly rounded 11.700. As world champion I was last out and in the mood to send a message to them. They would not find it easy to match me for speed. I hurtled round the velodrome. My white English jersey, with a big red cross running down the middle and around the back and sides, must have looked like a gleaming blur against the more colourful backdrop of a packed Sunday night crowd. My time, of

11.275, sent a little gasping ripple around the venue. It showed everyone how much quicker I had ridden.

As the fastest qualifier I faced a relatively straightforward semi-final against New Zealand's Elizabeth Williams. The Meares sisters, in contrast, would race against each other in the lower half of the draw. I was pretty sure Anna would win but I could only imagine the conflicted feelings she would need to overcome in beating her older sister. It seemed a very long time since I had sped past my twin brother on the grass track of Heckington; and I was relieved that my own big sister, Nicola, had opted out of cycling years before I started to ride competitively.

Williams took an early crack at me in race one. She pinned her hopes on surprising me with an instant burst of acceleration at the very start. The gap between us after three-quarters of a lap was significant but I had so much time to reel her in that my win was never in doubt. I cruised past her on the final straight and sealed my entry into the final with another straightforward victory in the second race.

The sisterly semi-final was more tense and competitive. Kerrie Meares, in her blunt way, said, 'After the second round with Anna I nearly heaved ...' It was confirmation that she had poured so much of herself in an attempt to beat her younger sister – but Anna was still too quick and powerful and narrowly won both heats. We would confront each other again.

Anna Meares led us out in the final and, gradually, I took to the slopes. She tracked me to the top and for over a lap and a half we raced close to each other. Meares did not try to pin me but the threat was obvious. I held my line, unflinchingly, and she eventually peeled away. I followed her at a distance, feinting and weaving, to let her know an attack was imminent. Strong and confident in my riding, I dipped down in search of space but Meares blocked me again. I backed off and steered away to the right, knowing that I still had time.

Riding high above her I increased my pace as we neared the final turn before the bell. Meares quickened with me but, even though she was looking up at me over her right shoulder, I still stunned her. I suddenly turned on the burners and flashed down the bank, blasting through the narrow gap she had left. I was gone before she could react and, rollicking ahead of her, I opened up four bike-lengths of velodrome pine between us. Hoisting my rear high out of my saddle, as my legs pumped beneath me, I maintained that gap down the back straight.

Meares came back at me, as always, on the last bend. But I kept my bike ahead of hers, despite her straining rush to the line, and the first race was mine in a time of 11.822 at a speed of 60.903 km/h. Tactically and physically, I had been the superior rider. And, psychologically, I was sure she could sense the difference in me. The days of being bullied and cowed were surely over.

In the second heat she tracked me impassively. Her face looked like chalky stone as she rode in my slipstream. I tried to unsettle her by climbing out of the saddle and cranking up the rhythm. But Meares, hidden behind her dark goggles, didn't react. It was only deep into the second lap that she tried something different. Meares swept upwards. I glided towards her and then, fiercely, she pedalled hard and overtook me on the outside. Knowing that I had not been quite cute enough to head off her charge, I let her go.

As we came out of the high curve of banking, I picked up momentum. We had one lap left. Riding hard, I raced on the outside, close to her shoulder. Meares crouched low over the bars, her nose just inches from the metal, while I was much higher in my gait. My teeth bit down on my lower lip as I plunged forward, rim to rim with her at last.

'Shoulder to shoulder,' the commentator screamed as, briefly, we careered against each other.

'Oh, they collided there!' the commentator yelped. 'But Pendleton rode it well.'

I wobbled on my bike and Meares gained a few centimetres on me. Still, I came back hard at her.

'Now the finishing straight,' the commentator roared, 'and the lunge for the line.'

Our front wheels seemed locked together but the commentator made his instinctive cry. '*It looks like Meares ...*'

It still needed an agonizing photo-finish to separate us. Meares edged it, by millimetres. 1–1.

I was angry with myself. I had let her outmuscle me on the last straight and lost a race which should have been mine.

In the break before the decider I took to the rollers. Shane Sutton spoke urgently to me as I pedalled on the rollers. We had been here before, at the Worlds in Melbourne, locked together at a race apiece. I had beaten Meares then; I could beat her again. I'd just have to find a way to ride more strongly than her. Shane reminded me that I was his pick.

'You've got her,' he said.

On the line, in the crunch match, Meares adopted a curious pose. Held up on her yellow bike, just like I was supported on my black frame, she turned to her right and stared straight at me. Her gaze burned into me. She rolled down at the whistle and, slowly, I followed her. We made a striking pair – a reigning Olympic champion, in the 500m time trial, against the current world champion in the sprint. A real rivalry, and personal history, had begun to build between us.

I rode close to her back wheel before, finally, I took to the piney hills. Meares watched me climb to the upper slopes, her searing stare never leaving me. I made a couple of small mock attacks but Meares did not waver. She either held her line at the bottom of the track or made a detour up top, as if to tell me that she had me taped. One-and-a-half laps from the end I darted down the banked track, looking for a break on the inside, but she held me at bay.

The bell rang, tolling its warning that the gold medal would be decided over the remaining 250 metres. Meares still looked back at me, over her right shoulder, but we were sprinting now. We were riding hard and true. Meares led the way out of the last bend but I could feel the burn of my sprint. I had further to travel on the outside but I ate up the track, my black bike hurtling towards Meares. She hunched low again, trying to find the force to withstand my speed.

We flew down the flat track together, the commentator whooping in his box: 'Into the finishing straight, this is the decider. Ooooooo, on the line,' he yelped. 'Looked like …'

He hesitated, checking the veracity of his gut.

'… Pendleton got it!' he exclaimed.

I took the upward curve, my mouth opening in relief and hands falling loosely at my sides. I sat up in my saddle, absorbing the sweet certainty of my victory.

'Pendleton!' the commentator roared. 'For my money she's got that. The Commonwealth champion and gold medal winner. It was very, very close … but the celebrations are already starting.'

I raised my arms in the air and then, extending them straight, I also stretched my fingers up to the roof of the velodrome. Feeling jubilant, I pumped my arms before wrapping them round the handlebars. I blew air from my cheeks while my ponytail flew up in delight from beneath my blue helmet.

'Victoria Pendleton getting the better of Anna Meares,' the commentator cackled as I lifted my left arm again and held one finger aloft. 'And she's signalling that fact …'

Then, as if I could no longer help myself, I again raised both arms as I pedalled serenely around the packed velodrome. The applause rolled towards me. I loved the feeling of being a champion.

We soon met the press in the mixed zone. 'After that second heat I was pretty annoyed,' I said. 'I had a few hard words to myself. I was confident going into the final, but you have to focus on the race. We're so close – me and Anna. There have been times where she's beaten me twice in a row. It goes back and forth. We're both very similar, and it's swings and roundabouts really.'

Meares talked in a similar vein. 'When I come up against Victoria I know that I'm going to have to give it everything,' she said. 'I always want to beat Victoria.' Meares paused and, then, as if to reinforce her words, she said again, 'She's someone I always want to beat; she's a great competitor. We bring out the best in each other. I gave it my absolute all against her tonight – I really wanted to win that gold medal again, but Vic is the reigning world champ and I hope I get another chance against her in three weeks' time in Bordeaux.'

I slipped on my spectacles and looked very innocent and English as I stood on the podium with two Australian sisters alongside me. I split them right down the middle, leaving Kerrie on my right, holding her bronze medal, and Anna on my left, flashing silver, as I felt the comforting weight of gold around my neck. In the ensuing photographs we looked deceptively friendly.

Two days before we arrived in Bordeaux, on Tuesday 11 April 2006, UK Sport announced a significant increase in the funding of the track cycling as a means of preparing us for an unprecedented assault on the Beijing Olympics in 2008. Dave Brailsford, the performance director of the national squad, responded with a stark message. 'UK Sport and the government have delivered and there can be no excuses now,' he said. 'There are not many nations in the world that have the same backing. It's scary because all the obstacles have been removed and there is nothing for us to hide behind.'

We weren't hiding but it was hard to escape the fact that so little time separated the staging of the Commonwealth Games in Melbourne and the World Championships in Bordeaux. 'It's rubbish timing,' I told the press, 'complete rubbish. Three weeks is bad enough but throw in the thousands of miles of travelling, and all the jetlag, and it's going to be a real killer. The only consolation is that it's going to be just as hard for the Aussies as it is for us.'

Dave B and Shane Sutton had always prioritized the Commonwealths ahead of the Worlds. They were held only once every four years and it seemed important to set down a marker on the home track of our bitterest rival: Australia. Brailsford tried to lower expectations of us in Bordeaux, by pointing out that all the European nations had been training and resting at home while the Aussies and the British, and all the other leading Commonwealth cycling nations, had been taking chunks out of each other in Melbourne. 'You can't go on peaking as we did, travel halfway round the world and expect to be as fresh as nations targeting this one event. It's a slightly different World Championship for us this year, because of those reasons, but I'd still like to think we can be competitive.'

Attention was already turning towards Beijing. Closing on the two-year mark before the start of the 2008 Olympics, you could sense the shifting of priorities. Chris Hoy made the most obvious statement when he confirmed that, in Bordeaux, he would ride the kilometre time trial – the cherished kilo – for the final time. The kilo had been dropped, controversially, from the Olympic programme. It had long been considered one of the traditional blue-riband events on the track, the ultimate test for a male sprinter, and there was much bitterness that it had been dropped in favour of the BMX.

I felt sympathy for the traditionalists, and especially for Chris, as the kilo was his best race, and yet I was pleased that young riders like Shanaze Reade, a teenage world champion from Crewe, would have a chance to compete on her BMX in Beijing. Shanaze had more raw talent and power than any other young woman rider I'd ever seen and it seemed appropriate that she'd compete at the Olympics. The rest of the Olympic programme, however, was skewed badly against women.

Chris could grumble about the axing of the kilo but he still had three events to target in Beijing: the individual sprint, the team sprint and the keirin. But every woman sprinter had been condemned to a single race in the Olympics: the individual sprint. We were scandalized that the 500m time trial, which Meares won in Athens, had been ditched alongside the men's kilo.

The disparity kept recurring in my head. I would race hard for one gold medal in Beijing. Chris Hoy had his sights fixed on three. It was a decision, in the twenty-first century, devoid of equality and justice.

It was hard, therefore, to approach the 500m time trial in Bordeaux with quite the same seriousness and application I brought to the sprint. The time trial was still the first race of the World Championships on the fast Vélodrome du Lac and so I put my head down and went for it. I recorded a personal best – 34.614 seconds – and I was just 0.005 seconds away from the bronze medal which went to Lizandra Guerra of Cuba. Anna took silver and, at the age of thirty, Natallia Tsylinskaya won an impressive seventh rainbow jersey.

Tsylinskaya was just as imposing in qualifying the following morning in the 200m sprint – setting the fastest time of 11.052 seconds at a rollicking speed of 65.146km/h. I was content in fifth place, while Meares, who described herself in broadest Australian as 'stuffed' from her previous night's exertions, finished twelfth. Her big sister was even further down the list, a lowly eighteenth place. It seemed as if the Commonwealth girls were not quite as fresh as our European equivalents.

Kerrie was knocked out in the first round of the match sprint while Anna and I both reached the last sixteen. Her poor qualifying time meant that she was drawn against Tsylinskaya who, again, was too quick for Meares. I beat the Italian Elisa Frisoni, who had defeated Kerrie, and then squeezed home in the quarters against Simona Krupeckaitė – whom I just beat by millimetres in the third and deciding heat.

The following evening, on day three, I raced both the semifinal and the final of the sprint. In the first I beat Guo Shuang – but it was hard not to notice that Tsylinskaya was quicker in dispatching the local French heroine, Clara Sanchez. She was nearing the end of her career but Tsylinskaya was also in the form of her life. I still believed I had the beating of her, even on a track that I loathed. I didn't feel comfortable racing in Bordeaux and when Shane Sutton asked me about the track I responded sharply, 'I don't like it. I just don't get it.'

It should not have stopped me from retaining the rainbow jersey but, in both races of the final, lacking real concentration, I made the same fatal error. I allowed myself to end up in a hopeless position on the track, by climbing the bank, and I was outjumped twice by Tsylinskaya. I could hardly believe I had given up my world title without any real fight.

Less than twenty minutes after such disappointment I had to try and sound measured to the press. 'Natallia is phenomenal,' I said, paying tribute to her eighth world title. 'When she's on form there's no-one who really comes that close. I think I did well to end up in the final after qualifying nearly half a second off her. That shows what great form she's in right now.'

I could not resist making a more telling point because I still believed that I was a better sprinter than Tsylinskaya. Trying not to look too miserable I said, 'I didn't think it was going to be that hard – I thought it would be quite easy to maintain the form and the focus, but really that first week back after the Commonwealths was a real downer. You come out of competition and the athletes' village and in Manchester it's cold, and it's raining. I kept telling myself, "Come on, pick it up, we can do this ..." But, in the end, I couldn't quite do it. It's been quite hard for everyone to try and turn it around in such a short space of time. Give it another week and I'm sure it would have been a different story; three weeks is one week to recover, one week on and one week to taper – it doesn't give you much time. I should be smiling. I've got a silver at the Worlds, but it doesn't feel that great.'

I felt less than great. I felt furious. Even as I stood on the podium, with a sickly excuse of a smile just about reaching my face, my thoughts had already turned to the keirin. As the Belarus anthem played, I hunkered down in my head, talking silently to Tsylinskaya and the Meares sisters. 'I haven't won the sprint, you bitches,' I said, sounding unusually bitter for me, even in my most amusingly vengeful moments. 'But I'm gonna win that one tomorrow. Just you wait ...'

Day four in Bordeaux. I was certain that I would end the last day of the 2006 World Championships with a new rainbow jersey on my back. It hardly mattered that I only finished third in my opening heat of the keirin. Yvonne Hijgenaar and Kerrie Meares were fourth and fifth behind me – while Anna Meares was also third in her first race. It meant that a formidable line-up had been forced together in the first repechage – heats which give losing riders another chance to qualify for the final stages.

Only two riders out of these six would make the cut: Anna Meares, Kerrie Meares, Simona Krupeckaitė, Tamilla Abassova, Lizandra Guerra and me.

'Hello! This is me . . .' and this is my first-ever bike shot in our back garden in Stotfold. I seem to be getting in the mood for future years as I wave to an imaginary crowd and wear a medal-like dummy around my neck.

Mum and Nicola are in charge of me and Alex – as we sit in our embarrassing yellow carriage that Dad made and then attached to the back of his bike.

Alex and me on a family holiday in France. 'C'mon, Al, give me a kiss!'

Nicola, Alex and me at home in
Stotfold in 1984. The staff at Great
Ormond Street worked wonders for
Alex and our family that year.

Dad encourages me as, huffing and
puffing, I get an early taste of life on
the rollers. This comes from 1989
and I'm nine years old.

Alex and I take a break on another family cycling holiday – this time,
in 1990, at the age of 10, we're riding around Snowdonia in Wales.

Dad and Alex in 1989.

I'm racing Alex again and, at last, I'm starting to beat him. Dad and other people are beginning to notice my speed on the bike.

People often ask me when I first became aware of my potential as a cyclist and I always say that it was the day I became a world champion for the first time – in Los Angeles on 26 March 2005. I looked so happy that day because I finally felt as if I belonged to the GB cycling team. It was almost as if becoming a world champion was the minimum entry requirement to that gang of brilliant boys.

In April 2007, in Palma de Mallorca, I won three gold medals at the world championships. Here I am, in the keirin, completing the hat-trick as I race away happily from my rivals.

In March 2008 I stripped off for the cover of the *Observer Sport Monthly* – which ran the cover line of VICTORIA PENDLETON: One Cyclist with Nothing to Hide. It's a photograph of which I am still very proud as it shows how far I had moved from the insecure girl who used to hide behind a towel on the beach.

'Me and my hero . . .' Here I am, in May 2008, enjoying a chat with Chris Hoy on a training day at the Manchester Velodrome. We were just a few months away from each of us winning gold at the Beijing Olympics.

Scott and I went to Wimbledon in June 2008. We had just told Shane Sutton of British Cycling that we had fallen in love. Shane suggested that Scott take his place as my guest at the tennis – even if we were advised to keep our relationship a secret from the rest of the team until after the Beijing Olympics. This was my moment in the Wimbledon limelight, with Scott, to my left, looking very dashing. But the rest of the day was low-key and lovely – and I enjoyed meeting Olympic athletes like Steve Redgrave, Kelly Holmes and Jonathan Edwards.

Between the Lines . . . and I'm on my way to defeating Anna Meares in the final of the individual sprint at the 2008 Olympic Games.

I've just won gold at the Olympic Games on 19 August 2008 in Beijing and, standing on the podium, I feel strangely numb and drained of feeling. It's almost as if I'm not even there, with Anna Meares to my right and Guo Shuang to my left, as we listen to the national anthem. It was one of the most surreal days of my life – and, even if I did not know it then, I would be heartbroken just a day later when Scott and I were accused of a terrible betrayal for falling in love.

I finally get to meet one of my heroes – Dave Grohl [far left] from Foo Fighters and Nirvana – at the *GQ* Men of the Year Awards in 2008. John Paul Jones and Jimmy Page of Led Zeppelin are to my left while Pippa Wilson, the Olympic sailor, is to my right. Meeting Dave was probably more exciting than winning an Olympic gold medal.

Here I am doing my best Audrey Hepburn
impersonation for a Hovis commercial.

In 2009 I went to the Chelsea
Flower Show, where a rose
had been created especially for
me. It was even named after
me. The bloom was yellow
– which was the closest the
horticulturalists at Harkness
in Letchworth, near my family
home in Stotfold, could come
to producing a golden rose.

Reflections of a world champion . . . riding in the rainbow jersey.

I'd drawn the last place in the procession which would slowly follow the man on the motorbike. Anna was one place ahead of me while Kerrie was tucked in just behind the bike. I felt confident and strong as we pedalled slowly around the track. My mind was clear and I knew that I would attack early, riding hard on the outside so that I could seize control of the race.

The sisters, however, had hatched a brutal plan. They had decided to work as a team and ensure that at least one of them sailed through to the final. Kerrie was freshest and so, one place ahead of me, Anna would take me out. Their plan was that crude and dangerous.

As I mounted my first attack, driving hard from the back and moving to the outside, Anna just turned her wheel smack into mine, sending me hurtling towards the bars of my bike. I skidded sideways, the rear of my bike tilting to the left. My head was down and the advertising boards flashed beneath me. I almost somersaulted into them. It was the kind of calculated assault that could have smashed my collarbone or broken my arm but, somehow, in mid-air, I clung onto my bike and stayed upright. It was a tactic of such naked aggression and foul play that, instantly, she had ruined my race.

I was riding on Dugas tyres. They were very light, fast and delicate and a large section of the tread had been ripped off. I had no grip left and I was riding on the remnants of silk from which they were made. They could have exploded and I was either pretty skillful, or very lucky, to have held on at that point.

My front wheel had burnt a mark up the back of Meares's Achilles. The collision had been entirely pre-meditated on her part and she was immediately relegated. It did not help me because, unlike in the sprint, regulations do not allow a restart of the keirin. Krupeckaitė won, Kerrie was second and Anna and I were history.

The French crowd booed, whistled and cat-called Anna but I don't think she cared. She had helped her sister by removing me from the competition.

Ernie Feargrieve, our lovely bald mechanic whom I always call Ernbeam, was one of the first of our team to reach me. He checked that I was alright and then, gently, told me how well I had done in keeping upright on my bike. 'I don't know how you stayed on,' Ernbeam said. 'You showed incredible skill.' I thanked Ernie but I was still shaking with the shock of being attacked on the track.

Anna Meares soon came to find me. 'I'm sorry,' she said. 'I didn't mean it ...'

I looked at her with cold fury. 'You didn't mean to turn right on me?' I asked incredulously.

'I did ...' she hesitated. 'But I didn't mean it to turn out like that ...'

I knew what she had meant to do to me. The two of us had been riding up close together for so long that there were no secrets between us any longer.

I prided myself on riding fairly. I would never want to win by bending the rules or deliberately running someone off the track. Anna and Kerrie had been brought up differently. They had been coached to ride in an aggressive way. They were ready to do anything on the track to beat me. It did not seem to matter to them that they could have put me in hospital or ruined my career with such a dangerous plan.

'Don't talk to me,' I said as I walked away from her. In the silence, as I moved as far from her as possible, I could feel something stirring deep in my gut. It felt like a burning sensation – a kind of angry fire inside me. I didn't think I would ever forgive her for what she had done; but I would make her pay on the track. I would burn her by beating her fairly, again and again.

6 | HAPPINESS

A time of bliss had begun. I went to the Manchester Velodrome every day feeling happy and hungry for work. That unusual combination of serenity and desire made me believe, for once, that I was almost unbeatable. Life seemed sweet. And I seemed strong.

My mood was underpinned by the team that had emerged around me. Apart from Steve Peters and Mark Simpson, my enduring mechanics of the mind and body, I also relished working with the more practical mechanics on my bike – Ernie Feargrieve and Mark Ingham. They were warm, generous and gifted in their trade. Luc de Wilde, a former sprinter from Belgium, was my *soigneur* – the man responsible for looking after me and all my needs, from food to clothing, during the long days of competition. But Luc did most by offering me uncluttered and staunch emotional support. His work was rarely noticed by others but, to me, Luc was indispensable.

Three specialists in track sprinting had been added to the staff at British Cycling. Iain Dyer, Jan van Eijden and Scott Gardner were a diverse trio – an Englishman, a German and an Australian – whose backgrounds and skill-sets complemented each other almost ideally.

Iain brought a coherent structure to the GB sprint programme. He provided a logistical overview and plan that bound us tightly together. Meanwhile, as a former double world champion, in the individual and team sprints in 2000, Jan instilled a contemporary racing perspective and tactical awareness into my training. He raced for the last time in 2006, at the World Cup in Sydney, where he finished third in the keirin, and at the age of thirty he joined us soon after that event as a full-time sprint coach and tactician.

I liked Jan from the outset. He was warm and supportive and I obviously respected his achievements as a rider. Jan was also the first true sprinter we'd had on our coaching staff and he helped me enormously in training and by enhancing my strategic knowledge.

There was also a touching human side to Jan and, soon after his arrival, Shane Sutton tested him at a World Cup event. Just before I was due to race, Jan received an instruction from Shane that he would be holding up my bike. Shane would give up his usual role with me and, instead, he would simply watch us from high up in the stands. Despite his vast experience as a competitor, Jan had never before supported a sprinter on the track in that time of great intimacy between a rider and her coach. He did not want to let me down and, as he told me wryly later, he'd had to use all his considerable strength to control himself and stop shaking as I leaned against him on the start line. Jan, of course, was just fine; but it gave me an insight into a more vulnerable side of him.

As new boys together, Jan and Scott shared a flat in Manchester and they became close friends. Scott, at least to me, was the enigma of the group. A sports scientist, with a PhD in sprint cycling that considered power output and muscle mechanics in a way that bridged the gap between bio-mechanics and physiology, Scott was an intriguing addition to our backroom staff. He was the antithesis of the traditional brash and strutting man I had grown used to seeing at tracks all around the world. Scott was highly intelligent, quietly spoken and accomplished in his scientific field. He brought a theoretical insight, and hard statistical evidence, to every sprint cyclist that worked with him.

Australia had dominated world cycling during the period, from 2001 to 2005, when Scott was their physiologist and an assistant performance analyst. While researching his doctorate he had worked closely with Martin Barras. It represented a real coup for the GB team to have enticed him to Manchester after Matt Parker, the endurance cyclists' head coach, had first noticed Scott's impact. They had been at a conference together and, hearing Scott present a paper, Matt realized how much he had contributed to Australia's success. It helped that they struck up an immediate rapport. Soon after his return to Manchester, Matt told Shane Sutton about Scott's work in considerable detail.

I guess I might have picked him out in a line, if you'd pressed me, and identified Scott as 'the Aussie boffin', but I had no idea that Shane had grand plans to poach him from our closest rivals. In Bordeaux, at the World Championships where Anna Meares and I had our violent dispute in the keirin, Shane ambled over and plonked himself down in an empty seat next to Scott. It was very informal but, as one Aussie talking to another, Shane told Scott about his own move to Manchester and stressed how British Cycling was intent on an even deeper period of supremacy. There were quips and laughs but Shane, in his blunt way, made it plain that Scott was wanted in Manchester.

'We could do something special together, mate,' Shane promised Scott before they parted in Bordeaux.

The following month, in May 2006, Scott was in Utah at an American College of Sports Medicine conference when he took a call from Shane.

'C'mon, mate,' Shane said across the miles, 'are we gonna get serious now?'

'Maybe,' Scott said with a light laugh.

'OK,' Shane grunted as if he knew Scott was on his way. 'Get over here ...'

Three months later, in August, Scott arrived in Manchester to begin working for British Cycling. Jan followed and, with Iain already in place as a manager, I felt transformed by my coaching triumvirate. It was almost as if, working together, they removed all the persistent doubts from my mind. They produced a training programme in which I was utterly confident.

Iain ensured the smooth running of our work together while, on the track, Jan often raced alongside me on his bike. It allowed him to show me how best I could harness my speed and tactical acumen. Jan was not shy of riding against me at the velodrome in a physical way that replicated the technique of Anna Meares. Most of all, he instilled in me a belief that I was the best woman sprinter in the world.

Of course I had my low moments – it would not have been me if I had become utterly convinced in myself – and it was then that Jan produced the reams of statistical data and scientific analysis that Scott shared with him. Scott's tables and charts provided unequivocal proof that I was on an upward curve in training. There was no point arguing with the clear logic of my progression – and I liked the way in which Scott's work endorsed my training.

I was just a little confused that Scott chose to liaise with Jan rather than talk directly to me. He adopted a different path with Chris Hoy. I used to notice how Scott and Chris would sit down and assess the training data together. This was partly due to the fact that Chris was so confident within himself – but I still wondered why Scott chose to avoid me so studiously.

Dr Gardner, in my most secret moments, seemed pretty damn mysterious. I would have loved to have had the chance to talk to him personally but whenever I tried to instigate conversation he seemed to be looking away. He did it so cleverly that it never really felt rude but, rather, that he didn't even register my presence. I didn't like it much – being so invisible to such a smart man – but I decided he obviously didn't rate British women. He must have been hung up on Aussie girls. Or perhaps it was just that I seemed a little silly to him. Maybe, worst of all, he found me repulsive?

I had no idea whether Scott was married. If he was, I felt sure it would be some no-nonsense, button-sharp woman from Melbourne or Sydney. I pretended not to care. As long as Scott's computerized numbers kept telling me and Jan that I was getting better and better on my bike I could live with him ignoring me.

It helped that I already had a boyfriend and so I could survive the cool nonchalance of a maddeningly intriguing Australian scientist. I couldn't quite work him out but eventually, for the sake of my sanity, I decided the Aussie idiot didn't know what he was missing. And so, instead, I concentrated on blitzing his countrywomen and all the other leading sprint cyclists in the world. I was on a mission to crush them all.

In 2007 I hit the form of my life. At a World Cup event on my home track in Manchester, in late February, my legs felt so fresh and springy I was almost scarily assured. There were moments when I did a little double-take at my unusually deep self-belief as I set about winning three gold medals in preparation for a similar yet far more significant hat-trick of attempts at the following month's World Championships in Palma. It did not take me long to remember the reasons for my new confidence.

Apart from the input of my new coaches, I had worked hard for over two years with Steve Peters. His official title at British Cycling was relatively grand, as Dr Peters was designated as the Olympic Podium Programme's sports psychiatrist. But, to me, he was just Steve – a lovely man who cared about me. Steve gave me many profound insights into myself, and life, during our weekly sessions in his office at the velodrome. He calmed and soothed me. I think he also achieved something miraculous in turning the lost and vulnerable girl who used a Swiss army knife on herself into a world champion sprinter.

Steve taught me how to like myself more, and to be less harshly critical of my failings, and we continued to work on my constant need to win the approval of other people. It was a long old battle but we both felt we'd end up winning the war. In terms of pure performance, the benefits of Steve's measured approach were increasingly evident.

I used to feel close to a complete meltdown amid elite competition. All my psychological frailties were subject to brutal exposure both just before and during racing. I felt tested enough in ordinary life, when I would worry if I had let someone down or if they really disliked me, or even if I might catch some horrible bug from merely touching a door handle, let alone avoiding my personal bête noire of a public loo. Fortunately, those moments of mild paranoia or flat-out craziness were mostly private. The difference at a World Cup or a World Championship was severe. My fiercest rivals and a packed velodrome placed me under such scrutiny it seemed as if every little mistake I made, or doubt I harboured, was magnified. And defeat was unforgiving in the way it highlighted my failures.

In our lighter moments, of which there were many, Steve and I were amused by the irony that I, of all people, a woman consumed by uncertainty and worry, should end up in a world where assertiveness and conviction were everything. Chris Hoy had both. As soon as Chris walked into the velodrome you could feel the force of his self-belief and sense of self-worth. He epitomized the strength you need to portray in track cycling.

At the same time I liked Chris because, away from competition, he could reduce me to uncontrollable laughter with his mimicry and wise-cracking. Chris seemed to have struck just the right balance – in being loose and witty in private but disciplined and implacable in public. Steve always reminded me that Chris and I were distinct characters and that there was no point trying to compare myself to him.

I also sensed that some riders, unlike me, were just very good at hiding their own demons. Yet, at the start of 2007, I had entered a new phase. It was not quite in the Hoy-esque class of indestructible certainty – but I had begun to value my own abilities rather than fretting about my competitors. Instead of wondering how Natallia Tsylinskaya would plan her rides I finally realized that I'd be better off concentrating on my chosen tactical strategy with Jan.

Steve reduced the emotional stress of racing. He taught me not to be swayed by the fact that the success of a track cyclist's year is determined by just a few days of competition. I could train beautifully all year but a loss of perspective could ruin everything during a World Cup or World Championship. In high-stress situations it's easy to succumb to nerves and to forget the basic processes which had allowed me to reach this point in elite sport. Steve showed me how to step back and look more logically at the demands of competition. All I needed to do, in the end, was to race against the same girls I had beaten often enough in the past. If I focused on each race as an isolated entity, rather than imagining it as the trigger for a wildly contrasting chain of consequences, my talent and speed would flourish.

I was heartened by my new perspective on race days. During the opening morning of the World Cup in Manchester I recorded the fastest time in sprint qualifying. Meares and Guo were close behind in a list of twenty-two competitors, but I felt so sure of myself that it hardly mattered who I drew in the match sprints. I had the beating of everyone.

Cruising through to the semi-finals without difficulty I was reminded of another change in my working life. I was no longer the only woman sprinter on the British team. Anna Blyth, eight years my junior at eighteen, had begun to show real potential at the Nationals and in various World Cups. She joined me in the last four after surprise victories over the Netherlands' Willy Kanis in their first two heats. I might once have allowed the pressure of racing against a fast-improving younger British rival to unsettle me. It was clear that I had everything to lose, and little to gain, in racing Anna; but I remembered Steve Peters's advice to focus on my own performance.

I beat Blyth 2–0 and awaited the winner of the latest Meares–Guo showdown. It went to a decider which Guo won after Meares made a tactical mistake and left it too late to launch an effective attack.

In the final, both my races against Guo were initially cagey encounters, But, at their crux, I had so much more speed and power that winning each of them seemed remarkably straightforward. Sprinting had begun to feel easy.

The same feeling framed the next two days in Manchester. I won the 500m time trial in a time of 34.070 – over half a second quicker than my previous best. It was a time that would have made me world champion over the distance in 2006, and it was just outside the world record, even though I had done no real training for the race. Everything was geared towards the sprint, and so I could just smile at the effortless speed with which I covered those two laps of the track. Anna Blyth maintained her rise by taking the bronze medal behind Yvonne Hijgenaar.

On Sunday 26 February 2007, I completed a World Cup clean sweep in the keirin. *Cycling News*, reporting live from the velodrome, seemed impressed. 'Victoria Pendleton signed off a perfect weekend with an emphatic and dominant display of keirin sprinting which surely marks her as the woman to beat in all the power events in the World Championships next month. The final saw plenty of switching for position behind the derny and, as it peeled off, World Cup leader Guo Shuang of China took to the front and looked to have made the right move. At the bell, however, a rampant Pendleton charged around the outside of Guo in an awesome display of power.'

I shrugged aside such gushing praise. It was important to downplay the extent of my surprising new confidence, but I also enjoyed making a point to Meares and Guo. 'I've just been plugging away at my times very slowly and consistently,' I told the press shortly before stepping onto the podium again. 'Jan has made a difference to my training but he's also made me feel more confident. The sprint is all about asserting yourself. You have to intimidate your rivals as much as possible and I can see the other competitors are worried about me.'

A month later we travelled to Palma de Mallorca, where Craig MacLean had rescued me in late 2004 after my disastrous performance at the Athens Olympics. The tormented and lonely girl from two and a half years ago had increasing confidence and a rock-solid coaching team behind her now. Life was simple. There were no issues or problems. Training was fantastic and even racing seemed enticing. I was happy.

Scott Gardner, of course, continued to ignore me, but everyone else on the GB team seemed suitably enthused by the more chilled-out and supposedly imperious me. I was smart enough to know it would not last and so I just allowed myself to enjoy this fleeting sensation of impregnability.

The newly-built velodrome in Palma featured such pristine wood that the track had yet to fully settle when we began our first training runs. As we circled the boards, which were sure to be fast in the sultry temperatures, strange crackling and crunching noises could be heard beneath our wheels. Splinters kept snapping off the virgin pine track and, high up on the sloping curves, the wood felt slightly uneven. It seemed as if our bikes could slide on the splintering boards – which meant it was not the kind of untested track that would suit another clash between hurtling bikes.

In Palma, rather than riding in the 500m time trial as I had done in Manchester and at past World Championships, I would partner Shanaze Reade, the BMX world champion, in the team sprint. Controversy over the disparity between Olympic opportunities for men and women sprinters in Beijing, with their three events to our one, had intensified – and there was speculation that a women's team sprint might be included at the London Olympics in 2012.

My mind was fixed on Beijing; but the prospect of riding in a home Olympics already seemed beguiling. I would be almost thirty-two in August 2012, and it seemed a lifetime away, but Shanaze offered so much exhilarating power I was easily persuaded to pair up with her in Palma while glancing ahead to London. It would be an early test to see if we gelled in an event that shifted the focus away from the individual.

Shanaze was an absolute ace on a BMX bike and, even more than Hoy, she looked a certainty to win gold in Beijing. It didn't matter that she was only eighteen because Shanaze was then in the midst of a three-year reign as world champion. Her incredible potential on the track was just as obvious. Six weeks before the World Championships Shanaze had not even ridden a single lap of a velodrome. It was initially a cross-training exercise, to add something new to her work in BMX, but she was so fast in the velodrome that they drafted her immediately into the track squad. Shanaze was as inexperienced as I had been when, as a naïve schoolgirl, I could hardly sleep after my first taste of track riding because it felt as if I'd been up and down a rollercoaster. Shanaze carried that same look – except she replaced my wonder with belief. Everyone was stunned by the times she reeled out during her earliest sessions.

Shanaze and Anna Blyth raced together in the team sprint in the Manchester World Cup. The girl from Crewe produced an astonishing start to ensure that they qualified fastest – ahead of the Dutch pair of Hijgenaar and Kanis. Kristine Bayley and Anna Meares were third quickest for Australia. I did enjoy wondering, a little wryly, how Meares felt about having her ample behind kicked by a complete novice. GB might even have won the final, against the Dutch, had Shanaze not completed a whole lap at full tilt after she missed the echo of a gun confirming a false start. She and Anna only just lost the re-run against the fresher Dutch girls.

I was happy to accept the offer, made by Shane Sutton and Dave Brailsford, to take Anna's place at the Worlds. The combination of Shanaze's power and my speed, allied to her confidence and my experience, looked an irresistible mix on paper. We were even better on the track. And I loved the way that, before qualifying, it was Shanaze who boosted me after I let slip that I felt suddenly nervous.

'Nervous, Vic?' she laughed before asking a seemingly incredulous question: '*Why?*'

Shanaze brought a simple purity to our new partnership. 'It's just pedalling,' she said.

She burst out of the start gate and pedalled – at a ferocious rate. I took over on the second lap and, following her advice, I turned my mind blank and pedalled. We were half a second quicker than Bayley and Meares, and 0.441 of a second faster than the favourites, Hijgenaar and Kanis.

In the final, the Netherlands pair came back at us hard. It was close, with just 0.0034 seconds between us, but Shanaze and I had become world champions – after just six weeks of training and in only the second track competition Shanaze had ever ridden.

It was hard to know how much faster we could ride if Shanaze and I started training seriously, but I was certain we could shatter all records and produce something extraordinary together. My only regret was that, while the men prepared for the Olympic team sprint, Shanaze and I could not continue our winning partnership in Beijing.

The men qualified fastest on that first evening in Palma – with Ross Edgar, Chris Hoy and Craig MacLean breaking the world record ahead of their perennial rivals France and Germany. But, in the final, the French nicked gold from GB by an incredible two-thousandths of a second. Gregory Bauge, Mickaël Bourgain and Arnaud Tournant were all renowned sprinters, and it was clear that they and the Germans were not about to let the British team take charge as we threatened to do in most other events on the track.

In the end, the men won four out of the ten gold medals on offer to them in Palma. Hoy won both the kilo and the keirin while Brad Wiggins was at his crushing best in the individual pursuit. The team pursuit quartet – Ed Clancy, Geraint Thomas, Paul Manning and Wiggins – was also unstoppable.

I chose to miss the 500m time trial so that Anna Blyth could take my place. She finished eighth with Meares winning gold and setting a new world record. I was more impressed by Shanaze's fifth place.

There were seven events for the women; and I was tipped to win three of them. After the team sprint, I spent the morning of day two qualifying third fastest for the individual event. Guo and Krupeckaitė went quicker but I was content to have finished ahead of the defending champion, Natallia Tsylinskaya.

That afternoon I returned to familiar territory – and endured another dangerous brush against an Australian bike that might have injured me and removed me from the competition.

In the first match sprint, as *Cycling News* reported from Palma, 'Pendleton had a scare when her opponent Kristine Bayley swung up the track on the final lap and bumped her hard. She was still able to win the heat, and the Australian received a warning for her move.'

Bayley seemed intent on doing Meares a favour but I held on. It was not as if she caught me by surprise. I had steeled myself to expect anything from the Australians because Martin Barras obviously still believed I could be bullied and outmuscled on the track. But I felt far tougher than I looked.

I came back fast to outsprint Blyth in the last sixteen and, that evening, I faced Tsylinskaya. It was difficult to be up against the defending world champion in a preliminary round. I'd also had my share of demons with Tsylinskaya, who had beaten me often enough, to ensure that I was more on edge than I might have normally been in an early heat. But I was so much quicker and stronger that I won both our races with plenty to spare. It offered some compensation for losing my rainbow jersey to Tsylinskaya in Bordeaux but, most of all, it was just another marker of my progress in pursuit of three golds. I went to bed that night feeling relatively relaxed and still fresh.

My semi-final, against Cuba's Lisandra Guerra, was equally clear-cut and I again won the first two races. Guo and Meares, as usual, were so close that they were forced into another decider which went to the girl in red and yellow – Guo.

In the final, Guo took the role of lead-out rider and I tracked her calmly, almost serenely. It hardly mattered that she opened up a big gap as we began the final lap. I just turned on the burners and by the time we came out of the first corner of the back straight I was in a perfect position, on her shoulder. It felt almost ridiculously easy again as I swept past Guo. I won by eight bike-lengths, without really extending myself. 1–0 up; and in need of just one more victory to reclaim the rainbow jersey.

Taking the lead in heat two, I watched Guo over my right shoulder as we completed a lazy-looking circle of the track. It was a measure of my conviction that, with over a lap and a half left, I decided to leave her behind. I put aside the tactical niceties and just hurtled forward, my black bike speeding beneath me. Guo tried hard but she was never going to beat me. I flashed past the line, comfortably ahead.

I was world champion, again, in the race that meant most to me. Briefly, I pumped both my arms above my head before I let them fall to my sides, dangling free while I kept pedalling. As the applause deepened I held them aloft again, using both hands to wave to the crowd. It was as if each hand represented a gold medal. I had another still to win and so I nodded once more – as if in reminder to myself.

The keirin was much bumpier; even if it started comfortably on day four when I won my heat ahead of the defending champion, Christin Muche, Tsylinskaya and Bayley. I also raced home first in the semi-final, with Guo and Jennie Read joining me as qualifiers. The prospect of winning a third gold medal suddenly seemed real enough to touch. I was tired, and just a little emotional, but I also felt determined.

There was plenty of trouble in the final. Muche muscled me down onto the bottom blue band of the track, called the 'côte d'azur'. The race was stopped and I was uncertain if I would also be penalized. After a few anxious minutes, as the judges consulted, it was decided that five of us could restart the race. Muche had been relegated for dangerous riding.

We went at it again but, this time, we had problems with the derny. The small, pedal-powered motorbike slowed to a near halt and I could not stop myself from overtaking it on the opening lap. It could have meant disqualification for me but, as the bike seized up just as I had to veer around it, the race had to be stopped. We had to climb off our bikes and wait for a new machine to arrive. It was the kind of delay which once could have unhinged me. But I stayed cool as I also waited for clearance that I would still be allowed to race. That confirmation duly came.

Eventually, as the race began for a third time, I was in fourth place, behind Reed, Blyth and Guo. Meares was on my wheel and, entering the last lap, we jostled for position. I was in danger of being boxed behind the squat shapes of my old Australian and Chinese rivals, but down the back straight I unleashed everything left inside me. I powered ahead of Meares and Guo and, at the last turn, took the lead. Guo had one final crack at me but I was still too quick for her and for Meares. I was the keirin world champion, collecting my third rainbow jersey of the week.

Great Britain had won eleven medals in total, with seven golds, which represented more than 40% of the titles on offer at the 2007 World Championships. Martin Barras, who had once predicted that I would 'annoy' him with my distinct lack of suitability to elite sprinting, was interviewed while he watched me circle Palma's new wooden boards one last time. 'There're no two ways about it,' Australia's sprint coach said, presumably through clenched teeth as his former colleagues in GB cycling jumped up and down in delight, 'we've just had a righteous kick in the arse.'

At last, as I left the track, the tears came. 'I just can't believe it,' I said, crying with helpless happiness. 'I might as well retire. How can I top that?'

7 | NAKED

Catching Scott Gardner's eye was one possible way of surpassing my World Championship treble. Even if we had begun to acknowledge each other beyond polite 'hellos' and 'hiyas' – and the ritual 'How're you doing?' – it still felt as if Scott was being dragooned into some kind of strained interaction with me. As soon as he could, he would slip away down the nearest corridor.

'What do you think of Scott?' I would casually ask people at British Cycling.

The answers always echoed the same theme. Scott, especially to other women, was 'lovely' and 'cool' and 'great'. I didn't see it myself.

'Really?' I would say, innocently. 'You don't think he's just a little bit aloof?'

'You're kidding, right?' someone once said before they regaled me with anecdotes confirming Scott's charm and friendliness.

He wasn't charming or friendly to me. I decided I must be the only person at the velodrome who hadn't been welcomed into his cheerful world. I knew what all the men on the team thought of him. As hard as I tried to coax an admission out of Chris Hoy and the others that Scott was pretty weird, they were resolute.

Scott was 'the business' and 'fucking brilliant.' I still didn't see it.

Well, actually, I did. I liked him, a lot, and I thought he was the most interesting person in British Cycling. I was crazy about the idea of getting to know him, even just a little bit, but it seemed impossible. He was obviously not interested in me. And so I would simply shrug as if I couldn't understand why everyone else raved about him.

I only heard later that Scott and I first met at the Commonwealth Games in Melbourne in 2006. I must have blanked it from my mind – trying to ignore an Aussie – because I really can't remember how he briefly chatted to me and Emma Davies in the stands. I hardly spoke to him but he apparently liked my big and ridiculous Oakley boots. I was in a bit of a Tank Girl phase then; partly as a way of diverting myself from the hideous England kit I had to wear. Everyone else was convinced Scott had his eye on Yvonne Hijgenaar, the rather attractive Dutch cyclist I'd often trained alongside in Aigle.

Scott denies this now, with much amusement, and claims to have noticed me at the previous Commonwealths – in 2002. He had also thought about me in professional terms, as a sprint cyclist, in considerable detail. Even before I won my first World Championship in 2005, Scott had been present at repeated meetings with the Australian team, when he was still working for his home country, as Martin Barras plotted how best to beat me.

Until late 2004, Anna and Kerrie Meares believed they had my number. They thought I was far too skinny to cope with their power. But their mood changed once I beat Anna in 2005. They began to assess me with real seriousness because there was no-one better on the wheel than me. Anna, especially, understood that she did not dare leave a gap when I was approaching her at speed. Flying out of her slipstream I would beat her every time. So they needed to pin me and overpower me. They needed to dictate the pace of a race and dominate me physically.

Their main hope, beyond intimidation, was a belief that I still sometimes raced naïvely and was reluctant to dictate. Martin Barras would remind the sisters that, especially if I was riding at the front, I would rarely commit myself. So once they got to the bell lap, they knew that the first to jump and accelerate would invariably win. They would watch me waiting and then, bang, they would attack. It was the only way they were going to beat me – unless I got bullied first or taken out in a rogue accident.

Scott had since decided that, even though I didn't fit the sprinter's archetype in body shape, I had a physical gift. I was slight and even tiny compared to most of my cycling contemporaries. But Scott told Jan how impressed he was by the power I produced in the gym and on the track. He also knew I had blistering speed and real grit. It turned out that he didn't think I was entirely flaky or weak.

Of course Scott didn't say this to my face. I heard it from Jan, but it was enough to make me feel a little braver. I tried harder and sometimes followed him after we'd said hello, being careful not to look like a stalker, and chatted a bit more. Eventually, Scott didn't race away. He lingered and chatted amiably enough. Our conversations became longer and, wonder of wonders, friendlier. We both loved music – and especially bands like Nirvana, Foo Fighters and The Smashing Pumpkins. It was a start.

I also imagined that, as we were finally talking, there was a real spark between us. But my new-found confidence on the track was not matched whenever I found myself up close to Scott. I couldn't be sure if he felt the same as me. It must have been written all over my face because I was smitten by him. I tried to hide it but I was sure he knew. He was harder to read, being an ultra-smart scientist and a relatively cool Aussie dude, but at least he no longer blanked me. Scott talked to me and smiled at me. He made me laugh and blush and, sometimes, I also got him to laugh.

As I was single again I managed to confirm, through some devilish detective work, that he was not in a relationship either. 'Listen, Scott,' I wanted to say, but did not dare to do so, 'let's go out sometime and see what happens.'

I did not mind stripping. It felt good to remove every shred of clothing. I was naked; apart from wearing a nude-coloured thong. But I did not feel vulnerable. I felt strong. For years I had given up everything. I had simply worked on my body; as well as my mind. Only Steve Peters could see right inside the hidden depths of my mind; but everyone could see my naked body. I didn't feel ashamed. This is who I am, I said silently, this is the product of everything I've done and everything I've denied myself so long. At last, I was ready to show myself.

It was one way to overcome the terrible self-consciousness I'd felt as a teenage girl. I used to be so embarrassed by my body that, on the beach, I would always cover my swimming costume with a T-shirt and shorts. Then, I believed I was the wrong shape – flat as a board and so unwomanly. I felt different at the age of twenty-seven.

Walking to a bike, in the nude but for the flesh-coloured thong, was a strange experience. Beneath the glaring white lights of the studio it was even more surreal. I climbed onto the fixed bike and, after a few moments, I returned to the old ritual. I began to pedal. But I was not a teenage girl chasing her distant father up a hill. I was not a world champion sprinter hurtling around the track. Instead, I was a woman, riding a bike naked, my black hair flowing behind me. I was just me, stripped and strangely at ease.

'Victoria Pendleton is a terrific athlete and an impressive woman,' Richard Williams wrote in the *Guardian* on 26 February 2008, 'but a world champion track cyclist, even a drop-dead gorgeous one, should have no need to broaden her appeal by stripping off for next Sunday's *Observer Sports Monthly*. She was right to be frustrated by her omission from the shortlist for last year's BBC Sports Personality of the Year award but playing the glamour card might not look quite so astute if, in this Olympic year, she suddenly runs into a streak of poor form. Although Pendleton would say, with justification, that Britain's top cyclists need all the publicity they can get, some kinds of exposure have a way of turning sour. Let's hope this is an exception.'

The following Sunday, on 2 March, I was seen on the cover of *OSM*, a serious and widely-admired sports supplement, in all my naked glory. You couldn't see anything shocking or sensational – unless you were titillated by the sight of a taut bum cheek – and the overall intention of the photograph was intended to convey power and strength. It replicated Annie Leibovitz's famous photograph of Lance Armstrong when she captured him naked on his bike. I was also at work, hunched low over the bars and gaze fixed ahead. The hardened shape of my body was exposed by my nudity. It didn't look very sexy to me; but I liked the stark and honest way in which I was depicted. Here I am, I seemed to say on the cover, this is me – bare.

Of course it caused a stir. That was one of the prime aims of the shoot. You don't photograph a woman naked, especially a world champion, and decide to put it on the cover of your magazine, without planning to get noticed. For years I had toiled in anonymity, feeling lonely and vulnerable, stalked by demons, both real and imagined, and it was time for something different. My father had always predicted that fame would follow glory, telling me I had the sort of face that would offer me opportunities that transcended sport. I had never believed him. But it seemed as if my old dad had not been completely crazy.

I was in the shape of my life, having worked so excruciatingly hard to reach this point, and part of me wanted to capture the feeling forever. When I become a little old lady I might want to look back at all I had done when I was so much younger. I figured that, when I was in my sixties or seventies, I might be ready to open the box containing my gold medals. I might want to hold them then, feeling the weight in my bony and wrinkled hands, while absorbing the gilt-edged gleam of their meaning. And, as I would no longer look the same at sixty-seven, I might want to glance down through time and see how I'd appeared to the world at twenty-seven. I thought I would be proud.

Emma John, who interviewed me for the accompanying feature, was generous and perceptive. She began by writing about the body shape expected of a sprint cyclist: 'In a sport that requires moments of acceleration, the men and women have always been physically imposing: short limbs, huge muscles and necks like fire hydrants. Lined up against her opponents, Pendleton – lithe, petite and unashamedly feminine – looks entirely out of place. Yet she is the world champion and – if we dare say it out loud – Britain's surest thing at the Beijing Olympics.'

She praised me still further, pointing out that I had been 'named Sportswoman of the Year at two separate awards last December' and suggesting that, for cycling, I had 'become its charismatic icon'.

It was a pretty relaxed interview, as much as the unbalanced scenario of an interview can ever be relaxing. 'We eat a Wagamama takeaway while we chat,' John wrote. 'Pendleton has ordered a yaki soba without even looking at the menu, a sure sign, I suggest, of a regular patron. She grins. "Food is the one indulgence I can afford myself," she says. Ah, the life of the professional sportswoman – no alcohol, no late nights and, I imagine, a sex ban from the coach. "Oh no, we're allowed to do that," Pendleton says. "Just not with each other."'

No-one knew that I was thinking only of Scott Gardner.

The *OSM* article and cover shoot coincided with the fact that the 2008 World Championships were being held at the end of that month, in Manchester. In the last test before the Olympics, on my home track, I was under pressure to make a statement before Beijing and to shake off accusations that I had become unnecessarily diverted by whipping off my kit for a magazine. 'Pendleton has rocketed from obscurity to cover-girl status since she took three golds in Mallorca last year,' *The Times* suggested. 'But in Manchester this week she has to show she can still deliver on the track as well as strike sultry poses.'

I would be in for a fully-clothed roasting if I failed; and it was a relief that we started with the team sprint. Riding with Shanaze Reade was as reassuring as it was thrilling. In qualifying we simply smashed it – setting a new world record of 33.186 seconds for our two-lap race. The velodrome, which was full to bursting, nearly had its roof blown off by the noise. That same response, from an ecstatic home crowd, echoed throughout an incredible competition for the GB squad.

In the team sprint final, against a young Chinese duo, we did not have to ride as quickly. We still won easily, in 33.661 seconds, over half a second faster than Gong Jinjie and Zheng Lulu. The absence of the event at the Beijing Olympics felt, once more, cruel and unjust.

My concentration, however, soon homed in on the individual sprint as my lone Olympic event. Anna Meares had been badly injured, and had cracked vertebrae in her upper back, during a crash two months earlier. It could have been a career-ending accident but I was genuinely relieved to hear she was recovering and seemed determined to make her comeback at the Olympics. I wanted Anna to be fit and well; and I also knew victory over her would make an Olympic win still sweeter.

All the other leading sprinters were in Manchester, led by Guo, Krupeckaitė and Tsylinskaya. In qualifying they finished, respectively, second, third and seventh. But I was way out in front, fastest in 10.904 seconds. In the match sprint and, on my way to the final, I beat Anastasiya Chulkova, Clara Sanchez, Yvonne Hijgenaar and Jennie Reed without losing a race. Krupeckaitė edged out Guo in the other semi-final.

The first heat in the final was tight. Krupeckaitė held me until the last banking before I rocketed past her to win by half a bike-length. I was more convincing in the second race and, riding from the rear, surged beyond Krupeckaitė to seal the win I had expected. I had already planned to peel away on the track at the spot where my dad was watching. It felt right to find him and give him a hug.

My legs felt amazing all through the Worlds but, on the Sunday, day four, they finally protested. I won my two heats in the keirin and I led as we came round the last turn. Reed was soon on my shoulder and, at the line, she had just a touch more gas than me, and left me with silver.

It slightly ruined my record but, still, in the space of a year, I had won five out of six World Championship events. 'I've had the form of my life,' I breathlessly told the press afterwards. 'I've never felt this strong and confident in a championship of this level. I'm really pleased I won the sprint. It's the Olympic event so it's the most important, way above the rest. This was my last race today, and the first time I've felt my legs saying, "Hang on a minute, you're asking too much of us." But, otherwise, I felt great.'

The mood in the team was also exultant. At the Worlds we had won half of the gold medals on offer – nine out of eighteen – and Dave Brailsford said, 'We've crushed everybody. The opposition will go away and wonder what they have to do with just over four months left to Beijing.'

I had done particularly well – especially for a naked girl on a bike – but the time for talking had ended. I smiled, wiped my face with a towel and retreated into the shadowy bowels of the velodrome where there were no windows, let alone cameras, as I walked slowly down the narrow corridor to the showers.

I was set for Beijing. I knew I was ready for the Olympic Games.

Shane Sutton had often joked with me. 'Vic,' he would say as a small smile curled around his mouth, 'if I was twenty years younger ...'

The implication, at least for Shane, was plain. If he had been in his thirties, rather than his early fifties, he was convinced he would have swept me off my feet – although he more usually told me that I was 'just like a *daw-ter* [daughter]' to him. It was everyday banter on the track; but I knew Shane and lots of other people expected that Chris Hoy and I were more likely to cook up some steamy sexual chemistry.

I always laughed at that suggestion. Chris was my sprint hero, and more like an older and slightly condescending big brother, rather than someone I fancied. He was the world's best sprinter and I would have backed him to win any debate he entered. I certainly knew that, whenever we had a good-natured exchange of views, I came off second best to the more erudite and competitive Chris Hoy. He would demolish my argument while smiling through his words.

My awed respect for Chris's cycling achievements had increased during the World Championships. He matched me with two golds and a silver, the latter coming in the team sprint, but his victories in the individual sprint and the keirin showed the depth of his resolve. He had been world champion in all four sprint disciplines – and the way in which he compensated for the loss of his favourite event, the kilo, was a measure of his unbreakable ambition and discipline. But Chris and I were never going to be romantically involved.

It was different with Scott. We kept on chatting innocently and looking at each other. Even though nothing else happened, each time Scott and I spoke it seemed just a touch more thrilling and intense. Yet we both knew that any kind of relationship between an athlete and a coach was not only fraught with complications – it was regarded as unethical and unacceptable.

They were compelling reasons for such strict boundaries between a male coach and a much younger female athlete. The scope for abuse was obvious if a teenage gymnast or swimmer or tennis player was being courted by her adult coach. I thoroughly supported all limitations which curbed the chances of a grown man taking advantage of a vulnerable girl.

But I had turned twenty-seven in September 2007. Scott was thirty-two. We'd both had our fair share of relationships before and, now, we were single. We were two consenting adults who just happened to work in the same field, in elite track cycling, for the national squad. I couldn't really see any problem; but I could tell that Scott was more wary of the complexities. I began to appreciate why he had been so diffident and distant for so long. Scott knew there would be trouble ahead.

I didn't care. I just wanted to see more of him. I wanted to meet him away from the velodrome, because when we were together we didn't talk track cycling. We wanted to talk about our shared interests and ask questions about each other's pasts. It began to feel more natural and easy – especially when we spoke on the phone or swapped the odd text. He really did seem to like me then. But still, me being me, I needed to know for certain. I decided one night that I would leap off an imagined cliff in my heart. I would take the plunge and tell Scott Gardner some of the thoughts locked inside my swarming head and tangled heart.

It was embarrassing but, the next day, I stumbled on with my rambling introduction of a tempestuous subject. 'I'm going to have to say this,' I began, before stopping and then starting again. 'I don't know if I'm being stupid and barking up the wrong tree but, you know ...'

Scott looked at me, with a quizzical but wry eye, and waited patiently for me to reach my tortuous point. 'I think we should talk about this,' I tried again, before blurting it out, 'because I really like you.'

I must have glanced away from him then, staring at the floor or some invisible spot on a wall, as I thought, 'Oh, please, don't let me be totally wrong about this ... because, if I am, it will be the most embarrassing thing I've ever done.'

The silence between us seemed excruciating. I dragged my gaze back to his face. I saw that Scott was half smiling. It was a complicated smile, crammed with feeling, and then he spoke: 'Well,' Scott said, 'I really like you too. And that's the problem we've got here ...'

Deep inside of me I let slip an exultant 'phew' of relief. He liked me. Scott Gardner actually liked me. He liked to quip in later years that I had chased him down and then thrown myself at him. It was actually far riskier, and more poignant. I had taken a giant risk and, emotionally, I had laid myself bare in front of him. And my happiness, in Scott responding as he did, made me positively giddy. We arranged to meet away from the track and talk more about our feelings.

Scott is not a scientist by coincidence. He has a logical and analytical brain and it did not take long for him to detail the massive difficulties we faced. We would break the protocol that is meant to keep an athlete's private life separate from her coach. In the view of others around us at British Cycling we would have crossed a dangerous line. I thought he made us sound like star-crossed lovers. He said it was more serious than that. Scott knew the consequences of becoming involved with me. He pinpointed the career-denting problems that could ensue if we, as a member of the coaching staff and an elite athlete, became embroiled in a relationship.

We had both committed our whole lives to sport, and to the pursuit of excellence, and we had tasted real success. Australia, with Scott on their staff, had swept the board at the Athens Olympics in 2004. Four years later our GB squad, with Scott a vital member of the backroom team, was expected to be even more dominant. And now he was on the brink of becoming involved in a supposedly 'illicit' relationship with me – a complicated sprint cyclist who currently held two World Championship titles. We were doing all right, me and Scotty; and then we went and fell for each other.

'It's happened,' Scott said with a happy shrug. 'We can't fight it forever.'

I felt delirious. But I was not stupid. I knew it was serious. We would have to move slowly, and think very carefully.

I looked at Scott, my eyes opening wider still at the wonder and trouble of it all, and I told him straight. I understood we could not be flippant or carefree and so I was not about to reveal my feelings to anyone else. His work was too important to ruin it with a silly fling. We would find a way and decide, together, what we might do next.

'OK, Vic,' he said, his hand lightly squeezing mine. 'Sounds good.'

From late May 2008, ten weeks before the start of the Beijing Olympics, we began to have some amazingly intimate and earnest conversations. There was no idle chit-chat or drunken flirting between me and Scott. We could not be seen together in public and so we had to confine ourselves to long and involving phone calls to each other, usually at night, as we discussed the tricky questions and the hard decisions we knew we would have to face even before we approached the first delicious stage of actually going out together.

'How are we going to work this out?' Scott would ask.

'I don't know,' I'd admit, 'because we're not in a relationship yet. We won't know until we give it a try.'

And then I'd backtrack, a touch awkwardly, and wonder out loud if it was best we didn't try it out – simply because of the damage it could do to Scott's career.

'But then we'll never know,' Scott reasoned. 'We'll always be wondering "what if ..."'

Round and round we went, in circles, like two love-struck hamsters on a wheel, or a cyclist and her coach looping round the same old piney track, again and again, one long lap after another.

It was far too risky to meet for a drink or go out for dinner, or to the movies, because if anyone spotted us it would be obvious why we were together. People would just need to glance at my face to know that I was not meeting Scott to quiz him about my progress on the track or the gym. I was not that interested in statistical data about my flying 200s or work with weights. I knew I looked like a girl who was falling crazily in love – and I had to hide those feelings. Scott, in turn, could not dare show how he really felt about me to people with whom we worked.

So, inevitably, we spoke for hours and hours about the implications of giving in to each other. It was a very strange way to start a relationship but, if nothing else, it made us talk soberly about the future in a manner that ordinary couples do not even consider until they start discussing living together or getting married. It had to be that deep and heavy because, if we were going to take the risk, we knew we had to be sure it was going to be worth it. My hopes for the Olympics, and

Scott's hard-won career, could easily be derailed if we just followed a whim and had some fun. We had to know, for sure, that we were meant for each other. That process often felt curious because it's difficult to ask such questions of a person that you're only just starting to understand – while they, in turn, are only just beginning to get close to you.

Yet, out of such unusual circumstances, we forged an emotional intimacy that, again, normally only emerges over a long period of time. We might have had to curb our desire in an effort to think straight, but we were free in the way we admitted the growing depth of our feelings for each other. In private, on the phone, we were going somewhere. It felt good. It felt right. But, still, we had to move delicately.

Even though I saw Scott at work every day we had to emulate the same pattern of polite distance that had always defined us. Occasionally, as we passed each other in a passage or at the track, we'd acknowledge each other with a brief smile.

It was difficult to plan a meeting away from prying eyes. We had my training to consider and, with the Olympics hurtling towards us, we needed to remember that I could not go off to a gig or a pub where I might stand on my feet for a couple of hours and stay up late. I was meant to be resting at home, with my feet up, and at that stage I was still in the midst of buying my first house in Wilmslow. Until that day came, and I lived on my own, without any house-mates, we would have to wait. In the same way, with Scott and Jan sharing a flat, I could not exactly pop over to his place for a coffee after training.

Cycling had always dominated my life. Ever since those teenage years at home, when Dad would make me feel guilty if I said I wanted to go out to the movies with my friends the night before our big Sunday morning bike ride, I had given in to cycling. All my boyfriends, grudgingly or not, accepted they had to fall in line behind my bike. It wasn't much fun for them, or for me, but that's the way it had always been. I had sacrificed so much, for so long, that I was shocked by the impact of this new test. I had initially given up so much for the bike because I knew how much it pleased my dad. And then, as I got better and better and started chasing world titles, I did it for my coaches, my team and, just maybe, myself.

Now, the bike did not seem to matter much when set against my longing to be with Scott. Yet, confusingly, we had been brought together by cycling and our futures were so immersed in our continuing work at the velodrome. It was enough to make my head spin.

We had not even kissed each other, Scott and I, despite having talked with such graphic feeling. Our relationship remained physically innocent. But, at its heart, it seemed furtive. Scott, in particular, felt uncomfortable with the apparently illicit nature of our discussions. He's not a liar and the necessary deceit of our old-fashioned courtship unsettled him. We agreed that he should talk to Shane Sutton, and tell him the truth. Shane had been a crucial and supportive figure in both of our careers and it felt right to explain to him that we were falling in love.

Shane had, on occasions, picked up on the frisson between me and Scott. He sometimes made cryptic and light-hearted quips that we would be wrong to imagine that he was 'stupid'. Nothing more was said then. Essentially, Shane had no idea about the depth of our emotional involvement.

During a few days away from the velodrome for the track cycling coaches, at Celtic Manor in Wales, and about eight weeks before the Olympics, Scott walked to Shane's hotel room and knocked on the door. He was ready to break the news about us.

Scott started slowly, with a familiar joke: 'Shane, you remember what you said about you and Vicky, and if you were twenty years younger ...'

'Yeah, Scotty,' Shane said in a deliberately neutral voice, 'I remember.'

'Well,' Scott paused before he told the truth. 'It's happening between me and Vic.'

'What?' Shane said in genuine surprise. 'You mean …?'

His voice trailed away and Scott nodded. 'Yeah …' he said, as if that one word was enough.

'Well,' Shane said with a bemused smile, 'I guess you gotta go for it. Vic's a good sort.'

Scott explained how our relationship had evolved. He underlined the point that we had discussed the implications with real care, but that we were serious about each other. We had not started a fling. We were committed to each other – even at the very outset of our becoming a couple.

Shane seemed remarkably understanding. He did not spell it out to Scott but it seemed obvious that he'd pass on the news to Dave Brailsford who would then inform Steve Peters. But it would need to stay within the boundaries of senior management and Shane thought we should take our relationship no further at this stage. That last hope seemed like an impossible request; and no demands were issued. Shane seemed to accept we would remain discreet and that my focus would be locked on winning gold in Beijing.

A little later, during a track session at the velodrome, Shane pulled Scott aside for a quiet word. He had, rightly, informed Dave of the situation. It soon emerged that Dave and Steve were equally calm and agreed that it happened all over the world, in all forms of business, as a romantic bond was forged between work colleagues. So we were not dealing with anything alien or distressing. No-one else was involved and so they respected and understood that something natural and good had unfolded between me and Scott. The only unfortunate aspect, Dave implied, was the timing. His instinct, like that of Shane, was for us to maintain our low profile. There didn't seem much point in diverting anyone else on the team as we approached the most important weeks of our careers.

So, for the next few months, we wouldn't tell Jan and Iain – or say a word to any of the other cyclists.

It was difficult but, finally, one weekend, Scott and I had a chance to be together. Jan went home to Germany for a couple of days and so Scott and I, like guilty lovers, plotted a date. I went to his flat with the idea that we'd move on to the Gaucho Grill for dinner. It felt special. It felt good. It actually felt better than an ordinary 'date' because we then decided to stay in. Scott cooked me dinner – and I was far too happy to tell him that neither chicken wrapped in prosciutto nor chargrilled roasted peppers were amongst my favourite dishes. I like my peppers raw and crunchy but, that night, I could easily tell him that everything was simply delicious.

We also told each other sweetly ordinary anecdotes about our contrasting pasts in Bedfordshire and Tasmania, about our parents and siblings, the involving mess of family life. We spoke about songs we both loved and later, much later, we went back to the deep and meaningful themes and again said what we meant to each other. We couldn't say we loved each other, not yet, but we came to the conclusion that we both felt the same way. We might have a real shot at having something special together, something that could last a lifetime. It was weird saying such words out loud but it was what we believed; and we were honest with each other that night.

'I really think we should give it a go,' Scott said.

'Me too,' I murmured, my face almost breaking with all the smiling. 'Me too …'

Scott and I were ridiculously happy – except for our shadowy secret. It seemed abnormal to hide the reason for my constant smiling. People must have thought I was revelling in my world champion status rather than imagining that I was day-dreaming about Scott. At least I was able to tell my mother all about

Scott because, otherwise, I would have surely burst from the prohibited need to blurt out my news – '*I'm in lurve ...*' – to everyone else. My mum even met Scott when they both helped me move into my new home, a little house I had bought for myself in Wilmslow. She liked him, of course, and gave me the instant thumbs-up.

Our relationship was still mostly based on telephone calls. I needed to be in bed, asleep, by nine o'clock every night, to help my body rest as much as possible before Beijing, and so there was no wild cavorting for me and Scott. Instead, he would call me each evening on his way home from the gym and we'd chat on the phone for an hour or so before I said good night and shut down my phone.

As the weeks passed, we found the courage to share the odd day together. Scott even took me into the countryside, when we went to the stables to see the horse he owned. It was also striking that, after I had invited Shane to come to Wimbledon with me, as the Lawn Tennis Association had sent me two Centre Court tickets, he suggested that I ask Scott instead. And so my secret love and I went to the grass courts of Wimbledon on a beautifully sunny day.

There was just a small tremor in me when I was invited to stand up in the Royal Box and wave to the crowd. Scott, wearing dark glasses and looking very dashing, applauded politely next to me. We were relieved that the television cameras were consumed by a different match elsewhere. No-one seemed to notice our joint appearance on Centre Court.

Soon, back home in Manchester, we prepared to pack our bags, and my bikes, for Beijing. There would be time enough, in the wake of a triumphant Olympics, to tell the world what we meant to each other.

8 | BEIJING

I worked hard in the sultry heat and humidity of Beijing. It was a long wait, over two weeks, before I'd ride the Olympic Velodrome during qualifying for the women's individual sprint on Sunday 17 August 2008. Two knockout rounds would follow but they were spread out over the Sunday and Monday evenings. The semi-final and the final were scheduled for Tuesday 19 August. On the GB squad, only Shanaze Reade would be made to wait longer for her Olympic competition to begin. Every other cyclist would have gone into battle before us.

The burden of being the overwhelming favourite for gold could not be ignored. There were moments, and even chunks of days, when it dragged me down. It helped, then, that I could talk to Steve Peters. In Beijing he reminded me that there was no point trying to imagine the moment when I might win the Olympic final. At the same time it was just as illogical to fret about the wait or the threat of any late hitches. All I needed to do was concentrate on the present and maintain the training rituals that had enabled me to make it so far.

Steve even got me to admit again, in a confession I'd first made to him after winning three World Championship gold medals in Mallorca, that I was far more than a 'lucky' rider. That hat-trick in 2007, and two more World titles in

Manchester in the final event before Beijing, told me that I was better than anyone else in women's sprint cycling. I just needed to hold my nerve.

The numbers, churning out of Scott's laptop, told us that I was flying in training in Beijing, with the only concern being that I'd peak too early. A similar measurement of progress and hope applied in the gym as I lifted heavier weights than I had ever done before. I felt incredibly strong.

My mind, however, was more skittish. Away from Scott, and only able to see him occasionally in Beijing, and always with other people around us, I relied on his calls every evening to keep me upbeat. It was still hard. I shared an apartment in the Olympic village with Shanaze and the two pursuit riders, Rebecca Romero and Wendy Houvenaghel. We each had our own room but everything else was communal.

Rebecca had won an Olympic silver medal as a rower at the 2004 Olympics in Athens. She had since switched sports and, astonishingly, had become a world champion cyclist in Manchester. Rebecca and Wendy would now slug it out for the Olympic individual pursuit title – but, just like Shanaze and me, they were denied the chance of riding together in a team event. Wendy, who was nearly six years older than me and Rebecca, had also travelled an impressive and circuitous route into elite cycling. Squadron Leader Houvenaghel was a qualified RAF dentist from Northern Ireland who had only started riding six years earlier. I'd been on my bike for twenty years, and so, unlike Rebecca and Wendy, it felt like I had been building towards this moment for much of my life.

Remembering my miserable experience in Athens, it felt important that I should come away from Beijing with some uplifting memories. But each day, once the cycling started, it became more difficult.

Nicole Cooke won the first GB medal in any sport in Beijing when, on Sunday 10 August, a full week before I rode the velodrome, she was victorious in the Olympic road race. Her unexpected triumph galvanized the entire British effort. Emma Pooley followed with silver in the road time trial, but it was in track cycling, more than any other sport, where the British effort gathered dizzying momentum.

The men's team sprinters were the first to claim gold in the Olympic velodrome. I felt sympathy for my friends, Ross Edgar and Craig MacLean, who missed selection, but Jamie Staff, Chris Hoy and Jason Kenny were chosen. On each of the three occasions they raced together in Beijing, they set the fastest-ever time for the event. The French, who had been world champions for the last three consecutive years, edging out GB every time, were beaten comprehensively in the final. We were on our way.

I sat inside the apartment back in the village, on my own, watching the medals roll in as the small television screen filled with the triumphant faces of people I knew so well. On the second evening of track competition, there were bronze medals for Chris Newton, in the points race, and for Steven Burke in the individual pursuit. I felt strangely emotional as Brad Wiggins, who had just won a more widely anticipated gold in the same race, ruffled Steven's hair as they rode around the track in a post-race lap of triumph. It was a touching moment of almost brotherly affection.

Rebecca and Wendy, meanwhile, were the two fastest women in the pursuit and ensured that they would meet in the final – and guarantee our squad gold and silver in another display of dominance. I knew that the atmosphere in the apartment would be a little tense as they prepared to race each other the following evening. But their monumental achievement, so far, was shared.

I had already begun to hug my pillow, while staring at the screen alone, feeling the pressure growing inside me, thinking, 'Shit, shit, shit ... I have to win to be part of this story. I need to win.' Anything less than gold, for me, would define failure. I knew that Steve Peters would instruct me to avoid letting my thoughts drift into such dangerous territory. It was obvious that I should just relax and only consider the logical next steps of my task – rather than getting carried away by emotion.

But I cried when, in the men's keirin, Chris and Ross seized gold and silver that same evening. I knew Chris would win but I was moved that Ross, a close and constant friend, had also surpassed expectations. I thought of the eighteen months we had shared in Aigle, when Ross had been such a favourite of Frédéric Magné, and of all the pain I had been through high up in the Swiss mountains. So much had changed since then, not least the glorious sight of Ross with an Olympic medal around his neck. But I couldn't bear it if I missed out this time, just like I had done in Athens when Fred had torn into me afterwards.

I clutched the pillow tighter as I watched the medal ceremony. Chris beamed happily as he held up his second gold of the Games. He still had one more to win. Ross just grinned, flashing silver and knowing that his work in Beijing was done. He had fulfilled his dream. The camera cut away to the rest of the GB squad, applauding and whooping.

My happiness for Chris and Ross turned to personal dread. 'Shit, shit, shit …' I whispered softly to myself, 'if I don't win I'm not going to be part of this team.'

It did not help that I was in the midst of my period. It had started two days earlier, and so I bled again. My irregular menstrual cycle meant that, no matter what stage we reached in a specific month, my period always kicked in just as I was about to begin another major competition. The stress brought it on – just when I least needed it. I knew that, in Beijing, my low and edgy mood was probably due as much to PMT as the Olympic jitters. I also consoled myself, while laughing about

Sod's Law with Scott, when I told him that I had won more World Championships and World Cups on my period than free from it. I sometimes wished that the men who complained about my variable moods could experience riding a World Championship or Olympic race in the midst of bleeding and aching and feeling a little blue.

Scott knew me well enough by now to guess that it would be a good time to give me a call. The evening session had just ended and he phoned from the back of the velodrome. As the stands emptied Scott could see the mechanics packing away everything for the night. He knew I was only twelve hours from arriving at the arena, at last, and he was immediately aware that I was in the middle of a minor meltdown.

'It sounds like you're having a bit of a moment,' he said softly down the phone.

'I am,' I admitted with a teary sniff. 'I'm happy for Ross and Chris and everyone but ...'

'I know,' Scott said simply. He did not need to add any more words to underline the extent of his understanding. He had already cheered me up considerably earlier that day when, on my return to the apartment from lunch, and confined to my room for rest again, I discovered that he had delivered a letter to me. It was a handwritten letter, printed out neatly on blue-squared paper, and it was filled with words of love and inspiration. There were also some photographs of me, winning the races which had turned me into a multiple world champion, and the whole package made me smile.

'I got your letter,' I told Scott.

'Did it make sense?' he asked.

'Absolutely,' I said, grinning down the phone, and repeating aloud the gist of the words which had struck me the most.

I lingered over Scott's suggestion, in his letter of love and good luck, that I put myself through my Olympic trauma for three reasons. I endured the pain and angst and strife because

I was doing it for the people who had loved and supported me so long. I deserved to win gold for the people who loved me – but, yes, for myself too.

The third and more shadowy group, Scott told me in his beautifully written letter, could also be useful at such a crucial time. In the Olympic Velodrome I needed to push myself to the edge of my ability so that I would shock all those people who hadn't believed in me during the long and lonely years.

'I got that bit totally,' I said, with a light laugh.

'Good,' Scott said. 'I knew you would.'

'I feel better now,' I told my secret love. 'I'm OK …'

I woke early the next morning. On Sunday 17 August 2008, after two hot and clear weeks, it was rainy and foggy when I pulled up the blinds in the apartment. It was also cold. My heart plummeted with the temperatures. The heat had produced fast conditions at the Laoshan Velodrome, which suited me, as the tight bends of the track were best taken at speed by a smaller rider like me. I'd struggle to replicate my blistering times in training while the cold air would help the heavier frames of my rivals.

A grey, nasty morning seemed a sinister omen. The rest of the apartment was quiet. Rebecca and Wendy were awake, in their separate beds, waiting for the race of their lives. As I walked across the room I felt better. My legs were springy and full of power. All the weeks of tapering and resting meant they were bursting with energy. They were ready to fire me around the gleaming Olympic track.

As world champion, I would ride last in qualifying. There were only twelve women in the Olympic individual sprint, which was far less than a World Championship entry. Yet every one of them, apart from the Japanese entrant, Sakie Tsukuda, was an established presence who had won medals at major events around the world. Qualification was just a means of seeding us – with the fastest rider drawn against the slowest, and the second quickest facing the eleventh-ranked racer until the pairs for all six match sprints were established. Apart from wanting to avoid a dangerous first-round opponent, there was a chance to lay down a psychological marker by out-qualifying everyone else.

I calmed myself by remembering my last training run. I had left the track feeling certain I hadn't done well. My legs were so devoid of any burning pain it was almost as if they had become numb. I was surprised when, smiling broadly when they looked up from a laptop, Scott and Jan told me I'd been on course to break the world record.

'Oh …?' I said dumbly. 'Really?'

Scott showed me the stats for my last flying 100. It had taken me 5.33 seconds. If they doubled that, and I sustained such pace over a full 200m, which I often did in producing almost even time-splits, the world record would have been blown to smithereens.

I nodded before telling them that I barely registered any sensation in my legs. They pressed down on the pedals, and turned at a whirring rate, but they did not once twinge in complaint.

'That's because you're ready,' Jan said simply. 'You're in perfect shape.'

I savoured those words as, at the velodrome, one rider after another followed each other out onto the track. Time began to accelerate.

I was already on my bike, circling the pits, as the qualifiers reeled past me. It was nearly my turn, after so long, to do what I did best.

Anna Meares went out early, when the lead was held by Svetlana Grankovskaya of Russia in an average time of 11.544. I knew Anna would be quicker but, having just returned from her horrendous injury, it was hard to know quite how fast she might qualify. There had been concerns that, after her cracked vertebrae, she would be in a wheelchair rather than on an Olympic bike. But I knew she was brave and determined.

The noise in the arena, still only half-full during morning competition, began to gather as, during her warm-up, Meares picked up speed just before racing against the clock. I could hear various Australian voices shouting above the banging boards and stamping feet.

'Come on, Anna!' they echoed each other. 'C'mon!'

She looked utterly healed to me as, in her typical low-slung gait, Meares hunched close to the handlebars, her helmet a white blur as she hurtled around the track.

'Go, go, go, go, Anna, go!' the Australians whooped, for they could tell she was riding fast. Meares came round the last turn and, visibly, she cranked out yet more effort down the home straight. As she crossed the line, she ducked her head with an exaggerated nod. It was as if she were telling me she was back. The Aussie contingent hollered and then made an even louder racket when her time registered on the board.

The number 1 next to her name confirmed that she was the fastest rider so far but her time, 11.140, led to the biggest eruption of noise. The words 'Olympic Record' said all I needed to know.

Anna Meares had smashed the record which Michelle Ferris, her Australian predecessor, had set twelve years before – at the 1996 Olympic Games in Atlanta.

Meares was back. My mouth felt dry and there was a small tightening in my gut. OK, I told myself, as I slowly orbited the pits, you'll just have to set another Olympic record.

Jan walked towards me. He did not need to say anything. I stared at his deep blue GB top and tracksuit bottoms, unable to look elsewhere. My own skinsuit was white, with Great Britain written across the middle with a flash of blue down my arms. The shorts were blue, too, but the visor hiding the top half of my face was black. My helmet was covered in the famous old red, white and blue colouring. I pedalled slowly behind Jan, waiting for the moment when he led me onto the Olympic track.

The number 88 was pinned to the back of my GB skinsuit. Eight was meant to be a lucky number in China. I felt in need of some good Chinese luck.

Simona Krupeckaitė went fast, her time of 11.222 for 200m being a mere hundredth of a second slower than Ferris's previous best. Willy Kanis ratcheted up the intensity. Third last out, following Krupeckaitė, she also rode quicker than Ferris's old mark and slipped into second place in 11.167 seconds. Two riders, so far, had broken the old Olympic record.

We were on the track at last. Jan held me up, his right hand steadying my saddle and his left gripping the handlebars. I leaned against him, my gloved hand curled around Jan's upper arm for support. I fiddled with the black strap of my helmet as we waited silently. Guo, the last rider before me to roll down the banking, increased her speed as she approached the start of her timed run. The Chinese crowd chanted her name and clapped their hands rhythmically, their belief in her adding boldness to the roar.

In that excruciating moment I waited for Guo to reach the mark of her final flying 100m – which would be the signal for Jan to let me go.

At the bell, as Guo crossed the start line at speed, her rear raised in the air and her head held low as she pedalled with violent power, I could feel the noise in the pit of my stomach.

I drew in a sharp breath as Jan, with a delicately measured push, set me on my way with an encouraging murmur of '*Go!*'

Guo thundered down the back straight. I didn't dare look at her but the bedlam told me was she was on course for something very quick.

Pedalling smoothly round the track, still trying to breathe calmly, I could not avoid the cacophony around me as she ended her run. I couldn't see Guo's time – 11.106 – but it was enough to tell me that she had taken the lead. Meares's new Olympic record had lasted less than ten minutes.

I looked down, my gaze clear beneath the dark visor, and went to work. Riding high on the boards, the whistles and cries of 'C'mon Vicky!' resounding around a suddenly hushed arena, I pumped my legs faster. They responded effortlessly and my bike began to whir beneath me.

Approaching the bell, I hoisted myself from the saddle and turned on the burners. I sat back down again, angling myself low as the bike veered around the first tight curve of my lap. The pine flashed beneath me as I went faster and faster. A bellow of surprise, at my speed, rose from the crowd as I flew towards the back straight. I must have looked frighteningly quick as I put my head down, the long and pointy end of my helmet aiming at the rafters as I raced towards the line.

A louder roar let rip as my time flashed up on the screen and the commentator boomed his confirmation. Guo's new Olympic record had gone. It had lasted less than a minute.

I had qualified fastest; and dipped under 11 seconds. The number 1 shone next to my name on the black screen and my time stood out in beautiful yellow digits: *10.963*.

The rest of the day disappeared in a haze. In heat one of the knockout rounds I faced the weakest qualifier, Tsukuda, who had ridden more than a second slower than me in qualifying. I was never under any threat and, seamlessly overtaking her on the last lap, I cruised away from Tsukuda and won by a huge margin in a leisurely time of 11.736. Guo, Meares and Sanchez were all quicker than me in winning their heats, but they needed to be, and we were joined by Kanis and Reed. Krupeckaitė and Tsylinskaya finally made it through to the quarter-finals after winning their rides in the repechage.

I scanned the list of heats set for the following evening: Pendleton vs Krupeckaitė; Guo vs Tsylinskaya; Meares vs Sanchez; Kanis vs Read.

Our apartment's internal battle had also been resolved. Rebecca Romero defeated Wendy Houvenaghel in the individual pursuit final – in a stressful situation for my flatmates. William Fotheringham, in the *Guardian*, had detected the tension: 'Romero arrived at the British pits early, Houvenaghel much later; Houvenaghel clearly attempting to remain composed while Romero exchanged a brief word with the sprinter Victoria Pendleton but otherwise remained locked in her own bubble, dark glasses over her eyes. There was nothing to counter Houvenaghel's assertion that they were "colleagues" rather than friends.'

The first day was done. I stepped out into the clammy darkness of Beijing, and headed for a different kind of atmosphere in our apartment. After offering my congratulations and commiserations, I knew it would be best for me to hunker down alone in my room. I would re-read Scott's letter while I waited for his nightly call. I felt weary, but calm.

A rush of gold medals had lifted the entire British Olympic squad. Apart from our success on the track, that weekend also sealed triumph for Rebecca Adlington in the pool, for the men's coxed four in the rowing and for Ben Ainslie and the self-styled 'three blondes in a boat' in sailing. Britain would end the weekend on twelve gold medals, six of them for cycling, as Brad Wiggins, Ed Clancy, Paul Manning and Geraint Thomas clinched a crushing team pursuit victory over Denmark. Great Britain had climbed up to third place in the overall medals table for the Games – behind China and the USA.

I had a more modest plan in mind – to beat Krupeckaitė in the quarters – and return to the village to rest up and prepare for the biggest day of my sporting life. The best way to do that was to sweep aside Krupeckaitė in successive races, avoiding a decider, and then pass another night without obsessing about Olympic medals of maddeningly different colours.

For once, everything went to plan. Krupeckaitė was a talented rider but I was too quick for her both times. I was into the semi-finals – alongside Kanis, Meares and Guo – who each sailed through the quarters without losing a race. We were down to the final four.

The draw presented me with the match my fastest qualifying time ride had warranted. Meares and Guo would race each other in the first bruising semi-final. I'd face Kanis in a slightly less daunting encounter.

A long evening session began at three-thirty in the afternoon as, an hour before the semis, I prepared myself in a packed velodrome. In the men's sprint, Chris Hoy and Jason Kenny would ride against, respectively, Mickaël Bourgain and Germany's Maximilian Levy. Tony Blair was one of many British luminaries to appear in the posh seats. I knew they were mostly there to see if history could be made – with Hoy winning a third gold medal. For me, however, everything boiled down to this lone event.

At 16.30, exactly, Guo and Meares spooled across the start line. The Chinese favourite led them out while, in the pits, Kanis and I circled each other in the ritual warm-up. I kept one eye on the track as the home supporters kicked up a cacophony of noise by beating giant clappers against each other. After half a lap, Guo led Meares towards the upper banking. Down below, pedalling in a parallel warm-up with them, Kanis and I kept pace in the inner ring of the velodrome.

It was brutal, above us, as Guo and Meares tested each other psychologically. Guo was the first to bring her bike to a complete halt, standing tall in her clamps with her wheel angled hard to the right. Coolly, Meares passed her, almost brushing against Guo, before she brought her own bike to a stop half a wheel ahead of her opponent. They must have been able to hear each other breathing as they waited for someone to crack. The clappers made even more noise as my two rivals continued their strange dance which remained static but for the slight twitching of their bikes. A burly Chinese man suddenly appeared behind them, ostentatiously looking down at his watch in reminder that there was a time limit on their stationary pause. It was permissible for a rider to remain motionless for only thirty seconds.

After twenty-five seconds Guo eased ahead but, a couple of metres later, she stopped again. Meares had to pass her; before bringing her own bike to another halt. Chants of 'Aussie … Aussie, Aussie, Aussie …' rose above the home support.

Guo made the next move, and retook the lead. She controlled the rest of the race and jumped early on turn three before the bell. Guo carved out a sizeable lead and was three bike-lengths clear of Meares as they began the last lap. Meares chased hard but Guo had made the vital break. 1–0 to Guo.

Jan, wearing white after two days of blue and red shirts, pushed me down the track, as Kanis led us out. She watched me over her right shoulder. I held back, without any need to play the bruising mind-games of Guo and Meares. It was only deep into lap two that I made my first significant move. I headed up the bank, and Kanis stuck close to me, watching and wondering what I might do next.

At the bell I was on Kanis's right shoulder, feeling utterly in command as we sped down the back straight. To give myself the spurt I needed I shifted out of my saddle and churned my legs harder. I zoomed past Kanis and the win was over in a flash. I was just one race away from the Olympic final.

Meares kept the second heat to a crawl, feinting with threats to stop her bike, and she and Guo swapped the reluctant lead three times. As they finally began to race near the bell, Meares was positioned perfectly to take advantage of the slipstream. She closed the gap and outsprinted Guo on the back straight. 1–1.

It was now my turn to lead Kanis in our second race. Happy to rely on my natural speed, I was less tactically cagey than Meares and Gou. I set a steady pace until, on the turn before the bell, I let Kanis slip past. As we began our racing lap I set about tracking her as if she were now my prey. For the last half-lap we raced shoulder to shoulder, our elbows brushing together as we matched each other pedal for pedal. And then, with the line in sight, I kicked hard and edged ahead. I was over the line first, narrowly ahead but still with a clear enough gap to mean there was no question. I had made the Olympic final.

The identity of my opponent took much longer to establish. Guo fell in the first attempt at a decider and they had to restart the race. It was another close and physical struggle. Meares jumped early on turn three and, trying to pin her back, Guo bumped the Australian down onto the blue band. It looked an illegal move but they kept racing and Guo just snatched the win. She celebrated for a few minutes while Meares waited. Eventually, to the disappointment of the Chinese crowd, it was announced that Guo had been relegated. The race had been awarded to Meares. She was in the final.

Meares vs Pendleton. Again.

Despite my sympathy for her neck injury, I was not about to melt away at the memory of our history together. We could go to war if we had to but, instead, I planned on blitzing Meares in the final.

I could be alone with my thoughts as the rest of the GB squad around me, in the pits, excitedly absorbed the fact that Hoy and Kenny had made it an all-British men's final. I was set for a more personal battle.

Laoshan Velodrome, Beijing,
Tuesday 19 August 2008

At 18.30, according to the velodrome clock, I led out Anna Meares in race one of the Olympic sprint final. All was quiet for the first lap. Meares kept her distance and we pedalled round the track as if enjoying a serene Tuesday evening ride on our bikes in Beijing. The pattern continued for all of lap two and the tension could be heard in the sudden cheering of the crowd as we both rose out of our saddles and headed for the bell. Meares went high, far on my outside, as I held the centre of the track. The bell echoed shrilly amid the chaotic noise.

I held a comfortable lead down the back straight even though Meares tried desperately to take a chunk out it. She had no chance. I held her off in one of the most straightforward races we'd ever had. 1–0 to me, and just twenty-eight minutes left before we went at it again.

I'm going nowhere fast. On a set of whirling rollers, with my head down, I'm flying without moving. The bike below me shudders a little from side to side but it never moves forward. It just spins on the gleaming drums, the wheels of an otherwise stationary machine whirring endlessly.

I'm just one race away from becoming an Olympic champion.

'*It's yours to lose,*' I tell myself. '*Take it … take this chance.*'

To me, feeling so strong, it seems as if a giant hand has extended down from the sky·above. The hand has opened in front of me and, in the centre of its massive palm, I can see my gold medal. I just need to stretch out and take it – and win one more race against Meares.

I want to win so badly. And I know I am going to do it. I feel the certainty pumping through me.

It's taken my whole life to reach this point. The little girl trying desperately to stay in sight of her dad, pedalling up a hill until it seemed her heart might burst, would not believe we'd end up here. There were no Olympic dreams then. That small girl, me in a different world, just wanted Dad to slow down or look back to see that I was alright. Churning the pedals on the rollers I can now imagine Dad driving me on, never glancing over his shoulder while I struggled to keep up with him. I just wanted Dad to love me, and be proud of me, and so this is where I've ended up.

I'm riding this one for you, Dad, despite everything, because you, more than anyone, made me who I am – this racer going somewhere, chasing something that would make you very proud.

And this one is also for you, Mum, because you never wanted me to be anything but myself. You'll love me just the same – whether I come home with a gold medal or, instead, I just give up and slip off this bike forever. I'll be the same Lou to you.

I slide the mask across my face, the mask that will tell Meares I'm going to blitz her like she's never been blitzed before. I allow myself to think once more of Scott. On the rollers I remember his letter tracing all the people who should motivate me now. Beyond my parents I'm doing it for everyone who either loves me or has supported me so long – for my family and my friends, my coaches and for Steve Peters and Mark Simpson, my mechanics of the mind and the body. I'm also doing it for Ernie Feargrieve and Mark Ingham, my actual bike mechanics, and for Luc de Wilde, my trusted *soigneur* in the GB team.

Of course, more than anyone now, I'm doing this for Scott. And, yes, I'm also doing it for me.

There is one last shadowy group in my life. I think of all the people who doubted me. They dismissed me. They hurt me. It's time I show them how wrong they were about me. It's time I make them change their minds about me forever.

Suddenly, I see Frédéric Magné, the coach who had made me cry so hard in Athens. Fred is walking around the pits. He's training the Chinese girls now and, specifically, Guo, who has just won the bronze medal race against Kanis. Fred keeps drifting in and out of my eyeline but, now, I hold him in my gaze.

I look right through him as if he's not even there.

I can feel the resentment surging inside me on the rollers. Staring through Fred, it's as if I'm looking beyond him to that moment when he tore into me in Athens, believing that I had slighted him and let him down. His words cut me far deeper than my own knife.

My legs keep turning, moving faster and faster, and my face is utterly blank. I am not the same frightened and confused girl I was in Switzerland.

I see Martin Barras next, still Australia's sprint coach, and seared in my brain as the man who decided I was far too girly and puny to ever make it.

Well, Martin, here I am, seven years later. I'm one-up on Meares. I'm one-up on you. I'm one-up on Fred.

I feel like I am about to start growling on the rollers as my gaze switches from Fred to Martin, from one doubter to another. My uncomplaining legs pump harder as the darkness descends.

I'm going to show all of you, I swear to myself.

I'm not just going to beat Anna Meares. I want to annihilate her, by not only winning the Olympic final but by opening a gap of an entire straight. I want to be, undisputedly, the fastest sprinter in the world.

I've never felt like this before. Adrenalin courses through me. There is so much tension and expectation in these last minutes. It seems like I've been touched by fate.

'*It's yours to lose,*' I tell myself again. '*Take it ... take this chance.*'

I feel, at last, like I'm going somewhere fast.

I look straight into Meares's face. Her eyes avoid mine and, already, in that moment, I know it's all over. I've put the hex on her. She simply does not believe she can stop me. My speed will burn her off the track.

I lower the black visor over my face. Only my mouth is now visible, and my lips, usually soft and feminine, are hardened in determination.

The wait, for once, does not feel painful. I use the time to compose myself, to make sure my aggression is controlled and channelled into the ride of my life.

Meares still looks down, away from me. She rises slowly when the call finally comes a minute before 7pm.

She leads us out and, as if riding on instinct, her bike twitches boldly towards mine as I coolly ride up the banking. Meares then drifts away down to the bottom of the track. I follow her and keep a perfect bike-and-a-half-length distance between us. Her head is cocked awkwardly behind her right shoulder but I appear completely impassive – pedalling steadily and implacably without stirring in my saddle.

The pattern continues until midway through lap two when I meander up to the slopes again, dragging her with me. She knows it will not be long before I come at her. Still, I allow the gap between us to widen and Meares retreats down to the bottom again. The noise escalates as we approach the last turn before the bell. We both rise, me almost lazily, from our perches.

Seconds before the bell, I begin to sprint. I'm past Meares even before the next turn and my lead extends down the back straight as she strains to cling on to me. But, fluidly and powerfully, I fly around the track, the gap between my bike and hers seeming to widen with each new rotation of my legs. As I enter the final straight Jan has already turned away from me at trackside. With his back to me, he's almost running to the finish, his arms raised in jubilant disbelief at my demolition of Meares.

I am not finished yet. I race on, faster and faster until, unknown to me, Meares surrenders just around the last turn. Meares, the formidable fighter, simply gives up. She raises herself from her hunched sprint and sits up, accepting mutely that she has been destroyed in the Olympic final. I am so crushingly far in front of her, at twelve bike-lengths, that I register my biggest-ever margin of victory in a time of 11.118.

As the velodrome rocks, with the British contingent roaring and whooping, I finally ease off. Half a lap later I lift myself out of my racing zone and take both hands off the bars in front of me. I pedal around the velodrome, my hands raised high in the salute of a new Olympic champion.

'It's over,' I say softly to myself. 'You've done it ...'

9 | THE FALL-OUT

I had three minutes before the focus shifted. Three minutes to accept a Union flag and hold it above my head in a ritual gesture of victory while I looked briefly tearful at the release of winning. Three minutes to stand in front of the snappers, arms above my head, fingers clutching the flag, as I stared dazedly at the clicking and popping cameras. Three minutes to smile and try to look euphoric as a whirl of feeling tore through me. Three minutes to compose myself and savour the pure relief of winning.

And then they were gone. The eyes and the lenses turned elsewhere. They moved away from me to the giant shadow of Chris Hoy. At the start of his second race in the men's sprint final against Jason Kenny, everyone edged closer to the track, willing him to make history. I sat down on a chair in my designated corner of the pits in the centre of the velodrome. There was no doubt in my mind. I knew Chris Hoy would win again. He would secure his hat-trick of gold medals five minutes after I won my only Olympic final.

I might have won three myself but for the ruling that women should have only a third of the opportunities available to men in Olympic sprinting. Without the team sprint and the keirin my ordeal had been one of waiting; Chris's task had been more physically gruelling. On his fifth straight day of competition he needed just one more big ride to become the first British sportsman, since the swimmer Henry Taylor 100 years earlier, to win three golds at the same Olympic Games.

Another few minutes later and Chris Hoy had done it. His mental fortitude and indestructible power were too much for Kenny, twelve years his junior at the age of twenty, and the final was settled by a two-race sweep for Hoy. It seemed as if everyone around me, from British Cycling to the media crews running after him, moved helplessly towards the king of the track. I was the queen, apparently, but I felt strangely lost and solitary. The switch away from me was painless; I only felt stricken when I thought how much I needed to see Scott. I wanted to get away from the track and be with him. I wanted to be normal again.

There is nothing ordinary about waiting to step on to the winner's podium after you have won a gold medal at the Olympic Games. It is, rather, such an abnormal experience that I felt myself turn numb at the prospect. My mind reeled before the surreal mystery of it all. I had seen the convention played out on television hundreds of times before. A delirious and tearful Olympic winner waves blissfully to an exultant or appreciative crowd before bowing low so that the heavy disc of gold can be draped around his or her neck. They then stand straight, gazing into a faraway place, heads swarming with thoughts of triumph and vindication, as the national anthem echoes around a respectful arena.

I had always wondered what it would feel like to be in such a place – and yet I seemed no closer to understanding the emotion that is meant to consume you in that rare moment. Instead, the blankness spread deeper inside me as I took my winner's place. On the outside, I smiled and blinked, waved and looked up to the heavens. It was different inside me. A dense and heavy fog clouded my mind; and my body felt drained. I hardly felt anything. Questions like 'Is this it?' and 'What now?' did not even dent the deadened incomprehension. There was too much to absorb, especially when I was so aware of the contrasting and searing emotions I was supposed to feel and the way in which I was expected to act.

In the end, it was all an act. I just about got away with it. My glazed emptiness could be excused as disbelief or ecstasy. I just knew it was not meant to feel this way.

My mood changed with Scott. We felt bold enough, now that I had won and GB had taken seven of the ten gold medals on offer at the Olympic velodrome, to sit together and watch Shanaze Reade in the BMX heats the following afternoon. She fell; but still struggled up to make it into the semi-finals. Shanaze would eventually crash again and fail to win a medal, when gold had once seemed destined to belong to her. We did not know it then but Scott and I were heading for an even more dramatic and painful fall.

Exactly twenty-four hours after I had beaten Anna Meares, just past 7pm in Beijing on Wednesday 20 August 2008, our lives changed forever. It started with a small beep on Scott's phone. The text was from Shane Sutton – who had been taken aback by seeing us alongside each other in support of Shanaze. We were, apparently, still meant to be maintaining our guilty secret and staying apart in public. Shane's text suggested it was time we met to 'discuss the future'.

I wanted to stay in the present. For two years I had been forced to project myself into the imagined future of an Olympic final. Almost everything I had done had been geared towards the pursuit of this moment of anticipated triumph. And now it was over I did not yet want to look towards the next 'goal' or 'target' or even the months and years ahead. After just one night and day as an Olympic champion I had begun to relax into the role. I had started to enjoy myself. All the grief and stress had gone; and even the numbness of the podium had melted away into a happier glow.

It helped, of course, that I was with Scott. We had gone together, with my agent Chris Evans-Pollard, to a champagne reception which a sponsor had laid on for the British medal-winners. The three of us were chatting cheerfully to the rowing boys, whom we had just met. We were also in the midst of enjoying the delicious champagne and Chinese canapés as I indulged in the giddy realm of an Olympic champion.

Then, with its curt beep, Shane's text brought us tumbling down. We considered the implications with Chris, a friend close enough to be allowed into our secret, and I was bewildered. Surely we could be allowed to enjoy ourselves for a few days? Surely a showdown could wait until we got back to Manchester?

Emotions were raw for everyone. The agony of the long build-up, the intensity of competition and the comedown following the medal ceremonies and obligatory media inter-views had left us all frazzled. No-one, clearly, was thinking straight and so we decided we might as well front up to Shane and Dave Brailsford. There was no point hiding away, even if their timing in calling for a meeting seemed inappropriate. It did not appear unreasonable to expect that Shane and Dave should allow me the pleasure of this moment. They also deserved a break to revel in our shared achievement – as cyclists and coaches.

'I don't think this can wait,' Scott said sagely. 'We'd better go see them.'

We swapped a champagne reception for two meetings of bile and bitterness. A sweet day turned dark with acrimony. Scott's working future depended on his encounter with Shane and Dave and, when the four of us faced each other, it was apparent I also had other people to confront. Jan van Eijden needed to see me. As a coach, Jan had won all four of the sprint cycling medals available at the 2008 Olympics – and he could even claim a small portion of the silver medal awarded to Jason Kenny after his loss to Chris Hoy.

Jan and Iain Dyer had tried to remain scrupulously fair in their coaching of the two British finalists. They each took a turn to hold up Chris's bike, and Jason's too, and agreed not to pass on any tactical advice to either rider. I also knew how Jan had taken such pleasure from the demolition of my rivals. Yet it was made obvious that all his pride and joy had soured in the moment he was told that Scott and I had been together for weeks before the Olympics.

Arrangements were made for Jan to see me in the village apartment that evening. I had no idea how deeply he felt; and so his anger was like a whirlwind. It seemed strong enough to knock me down. I was stunned. And then I was reeling as he set about me with a volley of words loaded with heavy meaning.

Jan spoke for a long time, and with a hard edge, as he spoke of being 'disappointed' and 'hurt', 'let down' and 'betrayed'. I felt terrible at first. I liked Jan, and I respected him. But he made it seem as if Scott and I had been unbearably cruel in 'carrying on' behind his back. In my default mode, I slipped back into repeated apologies as I tried to explain our relationship and the need for secrecy.

Word, of course, has a habit of slipping out. Rumours and gossip had been flying around and Jan said that Rebecca Romero had told Dan Hunt, coach of the women's pursuit team, about us. It soon turned out that everyone in the GB squad, except for Jan and Iain, knew about me and Scott.

'We should've been the first to know,' Jan said bitterly.

I apologized again. It seemed right that Shane and Dave, as the head coach and performance director, should be informed first. But they had advised us to tell no-one else; and we couldn't stop others reaching their own conclusions.

'You were wrong not to tell us,' Jan said stonily. I was sympathetic because I knew how much time Jan had spent with both Scott and me over the last six months. He was also Scott's flatmate.

'We wanted to tell you,' I said simply. 'We wanted to be open with everyone.'

'So why did you betray me?' Jan asked.

Talk of betrayal and treachery unsettled me. It seemed to bear no relation to our situation. I stopped myself from saying it but I wanted to point out to Jan that, actually, I owed him nothing in my private life. I was happy to acknowledge and praise all the work he had put into my Olympic success. In fact, I wished Jan and I could sit on the floor of my village apartment and share a drink and a few laughs together as we pored over the way we had, together, achieved Olympic gold. Our tactics, and preparation, had been exemplary. So why couldn't we just celebrate our professional triumph rather than tear each other apart over my personal life?

In that life, as a private person, I did not have to answer to Jan. He was not my father. He was not a priest. He was not even Steve Peters. There was a clear line between Jan, as my sprint coach, and me as a twenty-seven-year-old woman entitled to a personal life away from cycling. I was not sure why I needed to take such vitriol from Jan; but I nodded and listened and tried to understand.

All I really knew, however, was that the night which was meant to be one of the happiest in my life had turned out to be so miserable. I sat in a corner of my small room in Beijing and listened to all the repeated accusations of betrayal and treachery.

Jan and I eventually parted but the wounds were so deep that I felt bereft. We would not recover easily.

Scott had also seen any remaining illusions about his working future stripped bare. We both knew that working with me would be seen as a blurred 'conflict of interest'. But all our other expectations and hopes had gone. Scott was made to understand that his future boiled down to a stark choice: his career at British Cycling or me. Protocol, apparently, demanded it.

I was devastated. In my opinion, Scott was the world's best performance analyst in sprint cycling. He had worked hard for a decade to establish his prowess and reputation. And now that work seemed to count for nothing – unless he ditched me. If he dumped me then he could stay at British Cycling. But he could not possibly continue his work if we remained in a relationship.

That ultimatum was delivered to him in much smoother terms, with more diplomacy, but the outcome was the same. Work or love? He had to make his choice and live with the consequences.

'There's no choice to make,' Scott told me softly as I began to cry. 'The choice was made weeks ago.'

I looked at him, and I knew what he meant. For months we had agonized over our involvement, considering every possible twist and turn we would face as a couple. And, after we had thought so long and so hard, and spoken so intimately about our feelings for each other, Scott and I had resolved that we should be together. He was not about to back away now.

Relief, and love for Scott, mingled with anger and guilt. I was suddenly enraged that we should have been treated so cruelly by the coaches who were also meant to be our friends. The same old questions echoed again. Could they not have waited until we returned home so we might have tried to find a happier way out of this tangle? Did they have to shatter us the night after I won the Olympic final?

If anyone else had been involved, and Scott or I had been romantically attached to someone different, their response might have been justified. I could also have understood their reasoning and timing if anyone was in danger of being hurt or left in a vulnerable position. But we had both been single. I was just over a month away from turning twenty-eight. Scott was almost thirty-three. I was an Olympic champion. He was a doctor of sports science. We were, hopefully, two successful and intelligent adults capable of making consensual and rational decisions about our private lives. It seemed to me as if we deserved to be treated reasonably – rather than being issued ultimatums and accused of terrible betrayal.

I was inconsolable. It seemed as if everyone felt they could get stuck into us, and take a chunk out me and Scott, while we ourselves remained voiceless. No-one wanted to hear our story. Instead it seemed that, because they were in pain, they wanted only to hurt me and Scott.

I cried a little harder, and Scott held me close. We would get through this, he promised me, and we would rise above the egos and jealousies and find a way to be happy.

'What about your work?' I asked. 'What about your career?'

Scott looked steadily at me, his eyes glinting behind his glasses, and then he smiled. 'We'll put you first,' he said simply. 'You can't quit now. You're Olympic champion. You've got to go on and give yourself another four years. I can wait. My turn will come again.'

I buried my face in his chest, my tears leaving streaks on his shirt, and I held on to Scott. I knew how much he would have to give up for me. If I had been a footballer I could have just slapped in a transfer request and moved to a different club. But I could not swap one country for another. If I had been a tennis player or golfer I could have quit all team competitions and simply concentrated on representing myself in the far more important grand slams and majors. But I could not ride a World Cup event or the World Championships, and certainly not another Olympic Games, as an individual. I had to be selected by Great Britain – by the track cycling squad that had just ruined my Olympic success in Beijing and, more importantly, terminated the work of the man I loved.

'Why?' I asked between crying. 'Why've they done this to us?'

I could not believe that Shane had completed a full 180 degree turnaround. Shane had changed from being an understanding and supportive mentor to an angry man who just wanted to expose us. It seemed as if the emotional reaction of Jan and Iain had shocked him; but I was frustrated and disappointed in Shane's new attitude towards Scott and myself. At least Steve Peters was in Beijing to calm down Dave Brailsford and offer him a considered perspective on our relationship. But Shane was not in any mood to listen to Steve. We were heading for a long period of conflict.

Scott just held me tighter. We would need to be strong in the dark and testing days ahead.

There were moments of respite and glitter when we returned home. Occasionally, I could remember I was an Olympic gold medallist rather than a treacherous wench in a star-crossed tryst. On 2 September 2008, at the Royal Opera House in London, I was one of the invited Olympians at the GQ Men of the Year awards. Usually, I lived in a world of gears and sprockets, of sweat-streaked pain and smelly lycra, of shouty sprint coaches and exhausted legs. This was very different – and much more to my taste.

It began with the suggestion that I make my way down to the Burberry warehouse and choose any dress I fancied wearing for the night. Orlando Bloom, I was told, would be clad from top to toe in Burberry Prorsum as he presented the Designer of the Year prize to Christopher Bailey. Lots of models and actresses and singers would also appear on stage in sumptuous designer dresses.

'Really?' I said with attempted nonchalance, as if I'd just heard that Shane Sutton and Jan van Eijden would be wearing shorts and T-shirts again at the Manchester Velodrome.

I was told to choose a dress that made me feel special. As a woman for whom fashion and make-up are actually more interesting and liberating than flying laps and the psychology of track cycling, I had been transported to a giant and heavenly wardrobe. I was allowed to touch the dresses, to hold them against me and, wonder of wonders, to even wear them. I felt a bit embarrassed; but excited when I was told that I could also choose any pair of shoes I liked.

There were racks and racks of clothes and even though a lot didn't fit me, as I'm bigger than a sample size, I loved trying on some dresses. Eventually, in the cramped and tiny changing room, I picked out a black shift dress which I really liked. It looked good even though it was a little tight around the chest and shoulder area. As I tried to peel it off, the dress got stuck at the level of my armpits. It was caught halfway over my head and, suddenly, I could not move. Standing there, in my underpants, trapped inside this pretty dress, I wondered if I should call out for help. But the embarrassment made me decide to keep on trying to wrestle myself free. I began to sweat a little. It was a very expensive dress and the idea of tearing it was also terrifying. The struggle continued.

At last, I escaped. I looked red and flustered as I left the changing room – having decided that I would settle on a slightly looser shift dress. It had a touch more room and a few more zips to help me get in and out of its slinky confines. The dress was simple but elegant; and I chose some shoes with the highest heels I had ever worn. They didn't feel attached to my feet, and I could barely walk in them, but they did look very cool – with studded straps that wrapped all the way around my ankles. My legs appeared very long and very slim and, provided I didn't fall over and totally humiliate myself, I thought it would be worth the aching feet I'd suffer from later.

On the night, while driven through central London in the back of a purring car, I turned and looked, wide-eyed, at Christine Ohuruogu next to me. Christine had won gold on the track, in the 400m, and she laughed with similar disbelief as we glided to a stop outside the red-carpeted entrance to the Opera House.

'It's alright, Christine,' I said as we queued up. 'No-one will know who we are. We can sneak in and watch the celebs do their thing.'

Yet Christine and I were in for a shock. As soon as we made it to the red carpet, with me tottering on my studded heels, which made me look six inches taller than I was in real life, people started screaming. The photographers had the loudest voices and, incredibly, they seemed to know our names.

'*Victoria!*' they yelled. '*Christine!*'

Christine and I gave each other a '*Who? Us!*' look which seemed to send the snappers mad. '*Over here! Victoria! Christine! This way!*'

We turned our heads their way and it was as if we had suddenly looked into the sun. Exploding lights flashed in our faces, almost blinding us, as we blinked helplessly back at them.

My legs were trembling and I thought I was about to keel over. I must have looked like a very small deer in the headlights. I'm not sure how anyone managed to get a picture of me because I was shaking so much I must have been perpetually out of focus.

'Smile, girls,' someone encouraged us. '*Smile!*'

We smiled in confusion. Even when we were encouraged to move down the red carpet the swarm of photographers raced ahead of us so that they could keep flashing their cameras at us.

'*Victoria!*' they shouted again. '*Christine! One more!*'

I had never experienced anything so bizarre – but I liked it. The change from being photographed in the depths of competition, with my face screwed up in concentration or pain, seemed glamorous. I felt in need of some glitz. It made up for being shunned and shamed by a few angry cycling coaches.

We were led over to a group of journalists waiting behind a roped area. Christine and I were told to show them the gold medals we had been instructed to bring with us. As we went through the usual question-and-answer routine – and I lied and told them how 'amazing' it had been to stand on the podium and how 'happy and proud' I was to be part of a triumphant British cycling team – my gaze was snared by an incredible sight. I could not quite believe it. I had to look even harder as we moved away from the press.

'Oh my God,' I whispered to Christine. 'It's Dave Grohl!'

Christine nodded and said, a touch airily, 'Oh … yeah …'

He might not have meant much to her but, to me, Dave Grohl was a god-like presence. If you had asked me that morning if there was one person I would love to meet in music or film I would have said his name, without a moment's doubt.

'I cannot believe I'm going to the same event as Dave Grohl,' I drooled.

Inside the Royal Opera House my surprise did not lessen. Wherever I looked I saw another famous face that usually stared out at me from inside a glossy magazine. Elle Macpherson was dressed in Hervé Léger and sparkly Louboutins. Thandie Newton wore Erdem and killer Giuseppe Zanotti gladiator heels. Lily Allen drifted past in an off-the-shoulders dress by Dolce & Gabbana. I remembered that she and Elton John were hosting the ceremony.

Liz Hurley, Jerry Hall, David Bailey, Tony Bennett, Gordon Ramsay, Daisy Lowe and Jaime Winstone milled around – but I was drawn to the musicians. Primal Scream were there, looking suitably spacey, as they spoke to Jimmy Page of Led

Zeppelin. I had met him at the closing ceremony in Beijing but I didn't expect Jimmy Page to remember me. Instead, I turned away and tried to walk gracefully to our Olympians table.

I sat between Pete Reed, the rower, and Pippa Wilson, the sailor. They had also won gold in Beijing – Pete in the coxless fours and Pippa as one of the 'three blondes in a boat' who had been victorious in the strangely spelt yngling class. I latched onto Pippa and said, in a kind of mantra, 'Oh my God, I can't believe Dave Grohl is here!'

'Really?' she said in a voice that told me she had no idea who I was talking about.

'Dave Grohl!' I exclaimed. 'The drummer in Nirvana! He's now the lead singer in Foo Fighters! He's got loads of other projects as well – like Queens of the Stone Age.'

'Wow,' Pippa said uncertainly. 'I quite like the, er, Queens of the Stone Age.'

'Oh my God, Pippa!' knowing that she was just being polite and had never heard of them either. 'I can't believe you don't know Dave Grohl!'

Chris Evans-Pollard, my kindly agent, came to Pippa's rescue. 'Don't worry,' he reassured her. 'I've never heard of Dave Grohl either. It's just a Victoria thing …'

I spent most of the evening scanning the room, and it was a gigantic room, in the hope of seeing Dave Grohl again. I could barely eat with all the excitement of thinking I might actually spot him. I wasn't about to start stalking him – I just wanted to see him one more time.

It was only when we were called onto the stage, as British gold-medal winners, that I briefly stopped thinking about Foo Fighters and Nirvana. A muted horror took hold of me as I imagined falling flat on my face in front of the massed glitterati – and, damn, Dave Grohl as well.

'Don't trip over,' I instructed myself as I followed Christine, Pete and Pippa to the stage. 'Don't trip over …'

Suddenly, out of nowhere, Ruth Jones jumped up out of her seat and grabbed hold of me. She gave me an almighty squeeze and shouted, in her Welsh accent, 'Brilliant, Vicky ... bloody brilliant!'

We'd never met before but I knew Ruth from watching *Gavin & Stacey* and, especially, *Nighty Night*, the BBC black comedy which, as it also featured Julia Davis and Rebecca Front, was one of my favourite television programmes. I almost keeled over. First Dave Grohl – and now Ruth Jones hugging me. I was amazed she even knew my name.

Somehow, I made it. I clambered up on stage in my skyscraper heels. Another kind of wonder emerged. Elton John kissed me and, then, Lily Allen presented me with a bouquet of flowers while the whole room rose to its collective feet and applauded the four of us as if we had done something extraordinary. I blushed and grinned but I almost wanted to stop and remind them that we were just four athletes – they were the ones with the cool jobs in music & fashion and film & television. I also gave the room another quick scan in search of Dave Grohl. He seemed to have vanished.

The rest of the evening disappeared in a blur and, after the meal was over, awards were presented to The Killers' Brandon Flowers, the most stylish man of the year, and Mark Ronson, for the inspirational but not-so-stylishly titled 'Alfred Dunhill Maverick of the Year'. And, yes, I finally saw Dave Grohl again as, on stage, he handed Jimmy Page and Led Zeppelin a lifetime achievement award. I thought they should have given an award to Dave Grohl himself – just for being the coolest dude in the room.

Afterwards, going down to the bar area for a drink, I caught my breath on the escalator. I was about a third of the way between floors and, at the bottom of the escalator, Dave Grohl was standing there, very casually. 'Oh my gosh,' I told myself silently. 'It's Dave bloody Grohl!'

What could I do? I couldn't turn around and run up the escalator in my four-inch high heels. Anyway, this was my one chance to meet him. I would never forgive myself if I didn't try to at least shake his hand. I had less than ten seconds to compose myself.

As I reached the bottom of the escalator, and the Foo Fighter himself looked up at me, I launched into a long and embarrassing spiel. 'I love you Dave!' I drivelled. 'I mean … I love Foo Fighters and your music. It's great and I can't believe you're here!'

He smiled at me; but the sound of my own voice was enough to make me shudder. 'I'm really sorry,' I said, trying to calm myself.

'Hey,' Dave Grohl said, 'is that a gold medal? Can I look at it?'

'Dave, seriously,' I said, 'take it.'

He looked at it and said how much he liked it, and he asked me what I had done at the Olympics, and I felt better. We actually started to have an ordinary conversation after I told him I'd been to a couple of Foo Fighter gigs and that I loved listening to his music. In fact, I explained, most of the team trained to the Foo Fighters because their music creates the right sort of atmosphere in the gym.

Dave looked surprised. He told me how taken aback he was that, outside of his little bubble of a recording studio, his music could travel so far and reach so many different people – without him even knowing. I was nodding and thinking, 'Wow – amazing! Me and Dave Grohl having this deep conversation.'

We spoke for almost twenty minutes and he compared our worlds, the contrasts and similarities, and it was all so interesting – beyond the fact that he'd played the drums for Nirvana and was in Foo Fighters. Even if he had walked away from me after twenty seconds I would've been delirious and called Scott in a flash to tell him I'd just met one of our heroes. But he turned out to be such easy and sweet company that I almost forgot he was Dave Grohl.

Then, to complete the evening, Jimmy Page wandered over. 'Hello, Victoria,' he said. 'How're you doing?'

I couldn't believe he'd remembered my name. 'Hi, Jimmy,' I said. 'I'm having a great time – talking to Dave Grohl!'

Jimmy and Dave laughed – as they did when I beseeched one of the photographers to take a shot of me with the musical gods. We were joined by Pippa and John Paul Jones of Led Zeppelin.

So there we stood – with me between Jimmy Page and Dave Grohl. I smiled helplessly, not believing my luck.

Glamour soon gave way to the familiar grind. There were no famous musicians or designer dresses at the Manchester Velodrome. Instead, there was just a hard track and the same old sapping routine. I was no longer a fabulously excited girl in a pretty shift dress and dizzying high heels. I looked more like an exhausted hamster – trapped on a wheel and going round and round in meaningless circles.

Rather than stopping and climbing off the endlessly rotating treadmill of training and racing I kept working. I did not know what else to do; and so I had resumed training just five days after my return from Beijing. Scott's future was clouded by uncertainty and I felt too guilty to take a break and revel in my success. Everyone else on the track team stepped back. I was the sole Olympian to compete at the National Championships in Manchester in September. It was ludicrous; but I felt I should keep busy.

My times at the Nationals were surprisingly fast, despite my lack of enthusiasm, and I defended all my titles without coming close to losing a race. It still felt a dispiriting chore – racing in front of a half-empty velodrome and feeling less like an

Olympic champion than a dogged old packhorse. I then turned back into the proverbial hamster and continued training as another competition loomed. The first World Cup event of a new season was set for early November, again in Manchester, and once more I felt compelled to compete.

A week before the World Cup, on 28 October 2008, I was interviewed in the *Guardian*. I wore my glasses and didn't hold back. 'Believe me,' I said softly, 'it's a constant struggle. People say, "Wow, you've achieved it all this year, two World Championship wins and an Olympic gold medal." And I think: "Yeah, but how come I feel so unsatisfied and under pressure all over again?"

'I am an insecure person. I am emotional. I am a self-critical perfectionist … I'm terrible. I beat myself up the whole time because I'm striving for something I'll basically never achieve. I portray this image of confidence, of arrogance, and it's not really me. I'm never satisfied and I'm never content. It means I'm a bit of a mess some of the time.'

The real cause of my distress, of course, could not be exposed in a national newspaper. I could hardly reveal what had happened to Scott and to me. I skirted the topic. 'In some respects I crave a life where I don't feel guilty about staying out late or having a glass of champagne. I would quite like to have a normal life and just enjoy riding my bike – rather than doing everything with such purpose. It's the same with relationships. I struggle with them because in the past I haven't been committed enough to people. Gold medals have always been way above boyfriends – sorry! And that causes problems because it tells a guy he's not my priority.'

I must have let slip that my priorities had changed because it was suggested in the piece that 'her latest relationship is, at least, working out more smoothly.' I didn't name Scott but I said, 'I haven't been going out with him for long – but he's been really understanding so far.'

It almost broke my heart to say those words, knowing that Scott was at home in Wilmslow on an ordinary Wednesday afternoon, having given up his career for me. I wanted to explain the depth and commitment of his understanding. Instead, in the interview, I spoke about children.

'At the moment kids are simply not an option until 2012. But I must admit that as I get older the idea of having kids does become less repulsive than it was a few years ago. Maybe it's a hormonal thing but when I see kids now I sometimes think, "Yeah, it would be nice to have some of my own." As much as I love my life, and the fact I don't sit behind a desk and I experience wonderful things in amazing places, I still crave normality.'

I was more polemical when tackling Olympic chauvinism. 'I don't know how they get away with it,' I exclaimed. 'Three events compared to seven for the men? That's not even half so it's particularly sexist. If this was swimming or athletics it wouldn't be allowed. There've been rumours that they might deign to add another women's event in 2012 but whether it's a sprint or an endurance who knows? It pisses me off.'

To lighten the mood near the end I also offered an impersonation of the Queen – as I'd met her a few weeks previously at Buckingham Palace. 'Simon Clegg [the British Olympic chief] said, "These are our gold medal winners," pointing to us standing there with our medals around our necks. And the Queen said [in my best imitation of the Royal voice], "Yes, I can see that." She peered at me and asked, "What do you do?" I said, "I'm a track cyclist – like Chris Hoy." I chucked in Chris's name – just in case.'

Three days later, on Friday 31 October 2008, I went in pursuit of the hat-trick of gold medals that had been denied to me in Beijing. Chris Hoy was still on the publicity treadmill, as the nation continued to exult in his trilogy of Olympic wins, and he was spared having to ride in the World Cup in Manchester. I was in much less public demand and the pressure was back on me to deliver a series of victories. As the World and Olympic champion I did not want to explain to the media afterwards how I had messed up any of my three events. Defeat would be distressing.

Anna Meares and Guo Shuang, my perennial rivals, had followed Chris's lead in abstaining from this particular World Cup. The long flight to Manchester was a deterrent but they were still both reeling from the Olympics. I was bolstered by the news from Australia. A shocked Meares had asked Martin Barras what she had done wrong when riding against me.

I was told that Barras had given her a blunt answer. 'Nothing,' he apparently said.

'But what could I have done differently?' Meares supposedly asked again.

'Nothing,' Barras repeated. 'You've just never raced against someone that fast. No-one has …'

Anna Meares, I was told, had resolved to go away, recover and then come back and work harder than ever in an attempt to close the gap between me and her. Our shared story was a long way from done.

In Manchester, however, I was way out on my own. In the sprint qualifying on the opening day I recorded the fastest time of 11.162 seconds. I was slower than I had been in Beijing but the track wasn't as fast, conditions were colder and I was weary and less motivated. The two Chinese girls, Lulu Zheng and Jinjie Gong, competing in place of Guo, were the next quickest while Anna Blyth finished in a creditable fourth place ahead of some more renowned riders.

During a long day, in the match sprints, I defeated Helena Casas Roige of Spain and Germany's Miriam Welte before beating Blyth in two straight rides in the semi-final. The final was equally straightforward and I outsprinted Zheng in both heats. The sellout crowd, which packed into the velodrome in a burst of post-Olympic celebration, enjoyed it more than me.

On Saturday I won the 500m time trial ahead of Gong and Welte and followed it on the Sunday with victory in the keirin. It was routine both for me and the team – and the GB women produced a performance of perfect symmetry by winning all eight events over three days. Richard Moore, the respected cycling writer, warned that, 'The British domination, though cheered to the Velodrome rafters by the capacity crowd throughout the weekend, did not meet with universal approval. Some feel that it has gone too far, that track cycling, if it carries on like this, will wither as rival nations, unable to meet the challenge, simply give up.'

I knew such ascendency would not last. Great cycling countries like Australia, Germany and France were not about to abandon their track programmes. In my own event Meares and Guo would return with serious intent. They were both younger than me and had another whole Olympic cycle to hunt me down. From my own recent personal experience, it also felt to me as if not all areas of our sport were as tightly knit as they appeared.

Countless articles were written about the apparently meticulous attention to detail paid every day at the velodrome. Dave Brailsford and Shane Sutton were praised as the most inspired and thoughtful coaches in British sport. The entire backroom staff at GB cycling was held up as an ideal model of excellence. British cyclists, we were told, were the most skilfully and sensitively managed group of sportsmen and sportswomen in the country. There was talk that Dave B should be parachuted into higher-profile struggling sports, like rugby, in order that he could sort them out and replicate the smooth-running and harmonious machine of British Cycling.

'If only they knew,' I said to Scott every night after I got home from the velodrome. If only they knew how different my experiences at work were in reality. Jan van Eijden and Iain Dyer were barely talking to me. Shane was prickly and Dave seemed invisible to us and caught up in more serious business elsewhere. Most of the men in the elite squad were pissed off with me for taking Scott's expertise away from them. Shane was far less sympathetic towards Scott – issuing barbed warnings that I should watch my back. Scott might not be quite the man I imagined. Shane, after all, as he promised me, still treated me like his '*daw-ter*' – but he was quick to slander the man I loved.

I felt increasingly isolated amid such cynicism and dissent. I continued to train with the rest of the group, at the velodrome, but I did my work apart from them. It was clear that Jan and Iain were still hurting and angry with me. Training became a solitary trial. I cycled alone. I sat alone. I ate alone.

The rest of the group, meanwhile, seemed to be cracking along happily without me. It was painful to see how the coaches seemed to go out of their way to laugh and joke with all the other riders, and to praise their achievements, while ignoring me. I am sure they felt that I had cut myself off from them; but, at least to me, it was as if their body language and behaviour underlined the fact that they did not want to bridge the chasm with me. Instead, they appeared to take special pleasure in the improved performances of young sprinters like Jess Varnish and Becky James. It was almost as if, in boosting them and ignoring me, I would eventually disappear and life would become much easier for everyone else at the velodrome.

The contrast between this miserable experience and the sheer pleasure and unity I felt when I won my hat-trick of world champion titles in Mallorca in 2007 could not have been starker.

Yet, on the surface, British Cycling had never been stronger or more cohesive. The plaudits and honours continued to roll in. Chris Hoy was knighted – not too long after he'd won the 2008 BBC Sports Personality of the Year ahead of Lewis Hamilton and Rebecca Adlington. Lots of people wrote in support of me, arguing that if I had been allowed to compete in three Olympic sprint events, I would have rivalled Chris for the award and been made a dame. I didn't make the shortlist for the BBC award that year but I was happy to receive an MBE – and I knew how proud it made my mum and my dad.

The awards and the titles, however, mattered less than the loss of everything Scott and I endured. I was worried and sometimes even bereft over the fact that, because he had fallen in love with me, Scott had been forced to move from British Cycling. At the same time I had lost the respect and affection that had once bound me and my track coaches together. I had lost all sense of peace and harmony in my training. As we moved into a new year, 2009, it seemed as if I had lost more than I'd won. I did not feel much like a World and Olympic champion.

10 | THE BREAK-UP

I wrote my letter in a jagged rush to the man who had made me. He had helped conceive me and he had shaped me more than anyone else. I loved him. Max Pendleton, after all, was my father. He will always be my dad. But, as the words poured out of me, I told Dad that it felt as if something had broken between us. I was not sure how we'd ever repair the damage after he split our family apart.

Max was not the man I had once idolized. He was not the unbreakably honest man of my imagination. Max was flawed and just a little cruel. I know we're all flawed, and capable of equally thoughtless cruelty too, but a girl does not expect to find such weakness in her father. A girl, especially a girl like me who used to be in such awe of her dad, is simply stricken when a more tangled truth is revealed.

I used to see Dad as a man of unyielding principle. He could be domineering and inflexible, but I always respected him. Max was tough but he was also solid. He had great passion and a real sense of fun when he was happy. I thought Dad lived his life much like he rode his bike – full of grit, determination and truth. As an amateur cyclist, and to me, he had always been a winner.

I wanted to be honest and strong and uncompromising – just like Dad. He deplored duplicity and weakness and could become very angry when watching the news on television and seeing how many people did not share his beliefs. I admired Dad; even if I wished, in our more stressful times, he might have been just a little softer and warmer with me.

I began to suspect that something was amiss between Mum and Dad in November 2008. Three months after Beijing, I was invited to the University of Northumbria to receive an honorary doctorate in civil law. I had missed my university graduation ceremony in 2002 because I was competing in the European Championships. A return to Northumbria, as Olympic champion, should have been a day of special pride for the whole family. Yet, sitting in the back seat of Dad's car, as the atmosphere up front turned icy, I was at a loss. Why were Mum and Dad acting so damn weird?

'It's nothing, Lou,' Mum said. 'Let's not spoil your day.'

I told Dad, in the first draft of my long letter to him once I finally learnt the truth, that it felt as if he had spoilt our whole future as a family. There were many other words, accusing and angry words, but they looked wrong on the page when I re-read my letter. I knew I could not send it in such overheated form. It would have to be rewritten after I had taken time to calm down and remove the worst of my spleen. Everyone else was a little ahead of me, even Scott, because they knew how badly I would take the news about Dad. Mum confided first in Scott, which was a sign of how much she had come to like and trust him, and he confirmed what she already knew – I would be better off knowing the truth.

Mum phoned me at home. She tried to break the news to me gently but it was not really possible. Mum was sixty years old and I could hear the crack in her voice as she told me that she had found evidence of Dad's infidelity. It was as achingly predictable as an email confirmation of a hotel room booking.

My mum, Pauline Pendleton, is a bit of a chatterbox like me, and she's lovely. Yet such sweetness cannot mask her strength. She immediately confronted Dad and asked him a piercingly straight question: 'Max,' she said, 'are you having an affair?'

At least Dad did not try to wheedle his way out of trouble by telling any more lies. He confessed immediately. Mum thought he was shocked into the truth because he had also been shaken by an accident he'd recently had on the road. He had been cycling on a Saturday morning when a van, which was transporting horses, attempted to overtake him on a bend and forced him onto the grass verge. The driver did not stop and Dad, on reflection, realized how close he had come to the rear wheel. If there had not been the grass verge for him to fall onto, the outcome could have been fatal. The experience had a profound impact on him.

Dad told her the whole truth. He said to Mum that, although he still really liked and cared for her, he no longer felt the same kind of love. It turned out that he hadn't loved her with quite the same intensity ever since Alex and I had arrived and turned the house upside down. Consumed by the need to care for three small children, including twins, Mum had switched her focus from Dad to us.

'And so that was it,' Mum said sadly to me down the phone.

Dad had strayed from her then. He was now sixty-three years old. As a woman of twenty-eight I didn't want to think of my father in those terms – and, even more clearly, I didn't want to think of the double life he'd led away from Mum and, also Nicola, Alex and me.

My brother and sister, at twenty-eight and thirty-three, were equally stricken. They didn't want to talk to Dad any more. I was different. I wanted him to know how I felt. I knew I could not bear to meet him yet, or even talk over the phone, but I needed to express my feelings on paper. I needed Dad to read my words.

So, as upsetting as it remained, I rewrote my letter. I left out the rage and disgust and tried to draw a distinction between the dad of my childhood and the man who had disappointed us all. I began by telling Dad how difficult I found it to get my head around what he had done to Mum. But I wanted him to keep reading and, as it was also the truth, I told Max that he had been a great dad. I meant it. The words came easily as I remembered how Dad had flown kites with us and always taken us racing on the grass tracks of our childhood. I told Dad he had often been great fun. When Dad was in a good mood, I wrote in the voice of the young girl I'd been, there was no-one better in the whole wide world. I thanked him for bringing us up, with Mum, and for making us happy and giving us such a good start in life.

'I still love you, Dad,' I wrote, 'but I'm not happy with what you've done.'

He answered my letter but it seemed to me as if he had written it quickly. It did not read like a second draft. Instead, it implied that I didn't really understand everything that had happened and that Mum had turned us against him. He sounded hurt and angry.

Mum, in contrast, was extraordinarily calm. Dad still lived with her but she knew it could not last. She wanted him to move out. I thought that, deep inside, she was a little frightened about the future. But Mum was not going to succumb. She told me she was fed up with being overweight – for that was an accusation that Dad, a very fit man, had often levelled against her. She planned to get into shape and, once Dad had gone, she thought she might get an allotment. My uncle Phil had an allotment. Phil had got on with his life, despite the death of his wife, Mum's sister. Mum said she would do the same. The only difference was that Dad was still very much alive. Only the idea of him, the idea we had all once believed in so fervently, had died.

*   *   *

My entire outlook on life darkened for a while. Scott and I were happy, living together in Wilmslow, but it was hard to absorb the continuing accusations of treachery made against us at the velodrome. Jan still felt we had betrayed him. But my dad had betrayed my mum during thirty-five years of marriage. I could not compare their sobering break-up to the farce surrounding me, Scott and track cycling.

We had some strong allies and supporters. Dave Brailsford seemed relaxed about our relationship but we were bolstered more by Steve Peters and Chris Boardman. They were unshakeable in their backing. Chris Hoy, or Sir Chris as I teasingly called him every now and then, was also cool. I sensed that other riders felt differently and they resented my presence and Scott's absence. Gradually, people stepped away from me.

I did not want to be the reason why so many cyclists were deprived of Scott's input. It made me feel guilty. Yet I wished that those with negative opinions could understand the far deeper guilt that seeped through me every morning as I prepared to leave home for work. Scott would have already returned from his 6am stint with a section of the GB swimming squad. He was now working as a consultant to British Swimming and he followed his early morning work with late afternoon sessions which began at 4pm. A good chunk of a busy day was behind him as he sorted out my breakfast and whipped up one of his barista-style coffees for me. I'd look at him and my heart would shrink a little. This brilliant man I loved, a scientist and an analyst, had given up so much for me. He was keeping my sanity in good working order. Yet it was not what he was meant to be doing. Scott was meant to bring all his intelligence to bear on the development of elite sprint cyclists.

We discussed the options of him moving elsewhere. I was ready to emigrate to Australia. It was a fantastic country, and it was Scott's home. We were due to go on holiday in Tasmania after the 2009 World Championships. I told him, sincerely, that I would be happy to leave all the strife behind and settle down with him, and become a domestic goddess at home in a city like Sydney or Melbourne. I could live easily without cycling. As long as I had him, and he was doing the work he loved, I would be fulfilled. I could see myself being absorbed and happy in raising a family – and cooking and baking and making clothes and gardening and doing DIY just as I had done all those years ago when I was a small girl staying with Alf and Mabel Viney, my granddad and nanna, when they looked after me during Alex's battle with leukemia. I'd always been a homely girl and, especially with the imminent break-up of Mum and Dad, it felt important to make a strong start to my life with Scott.

He believed me; but I remained the Olympic and World champion. The 2012 Olympic Games were going to be held in my own country. Scott was certain I needed to be there. He had found work in other sporting environments, but we both agreed that it would be better if he did not accept any full-time positions. Flexible consultancy contracts would allow him to concentrate on supporting me emotionally and practically for the next three and a half years. Scott was willing to make the sacrifice, for me, but he was understandably reluctant to become too heavily involved in my training programme. We both felt it was better to try and keep some distance between the strife of my work and life at home in Wilmslow.

One of the many public mantras of British cycling had long been that the competitor should take responsibility for his or her own programme. I was ready to assume that role. It was plain to me that neither Jan nor Iain felt any real desire to coach me any longer. And, even if that situation had been different, I was not sure how much more they could help me. I had won six World titles and an Olympic gold medal. I also had a degree in sports science and a wide range of past coaching experiences. If I needed reassurance about my programme I could also turn to Scott, the man I believed was the pre-eminent sports scientist in sprint cycling.

My heart still shrivelled a little whenever the time came for me to close the front door and leave Scott for the day. Our fate seemed almost unbearable then. I wondered if my critics at the velodrome ever paused to think what our lives were like. They might have missed Scott – but did they ever think how much Scott might miss his work?

The velodrome became a very lonely place. I would love to be a coolly mysterious person; but I'm the opposite. Everyone can tell whether I'm happy or sad. I cannot easily conceal my emotions. And that means I'm hard work sometimes. Instead of being neutral or emotionally evasive, my feelings are always obvious to the outside world. And so every morning, besieged by guilt and anger, I walked into the velodrome and everyone knew I was churning inside. So I did not make it easy for Shane and Jan and Iain. I was not about to be hypocritical and start kissing them on both cheeks and making wisecracks. There was a distance between us and I withdrew still more from them.

When I did broach the subject I was told that it was 'all in [my] head' and that I was being 'too emotional' about everything. The problems were down to me and my erratic state of mind.

At the same time, they also seemed to intensify the division. They maintained a veneer of icy politeness where more was stated by their silences.

'Morning,' Jan said.

'Morning,' I replied.

We didn't bother with any of the usual stuff – 'How are you?' or 'Did you have a good weekend?' It was best we just got down to business.

'What are you doing today?' Jan asked, knowing that I had already mapped out my training routine for the week. Iain stood quietly next to him, waiting for my answer.

'I'm doing flying ones this morning,' I said.

'Oh ...' Jan said, sounding just a little surprised.

'Why?' Iain asked.

'I'm working on my speed,' I replied. 'That's why I'm using small gears.'

They both looked at each other and seemed to shrug. 'OK,' Jan said as he turned away to talk in much more detail with the men on the sprint squad.

I was soon on my own, hunched down next to my bike, checking the gears and mulling over everything in my head. They obviously thought it was a bad idea, me working on my flying one hundreds, and I wondered if they were right. Maybe I was doing something wrong? Perhaps I should be doing something else? I felt suddenly uncertain and worried. And so there were times when I lost confidence in my plan.

It took a real effort to compose myself and remember that I was in my seventh full season as a professional cyclist. I had been the world's best women's sprinter for the past five years. During that time I had learnt much about training and racing. I surely knew what I should be doing on an ordinary weekday morning at the velodrome? Yet the nature of my personality is such that I do so much better when I am being validated and supported by others. I am less equipped to deal with doubt and sniping.

The cheerful banter of the men around me made me feel even more isolated. My separation from everyone else was accentuated by the fact that I could no longer sit on one of the plastic chairs which we lounged around on in the middle of the velodrome both before and after training. I used to slump terribly and my back suffered. It was already creaking under the strain of training. My physiotherapists advised me that, during my training breaks, I should sit on a stretching mat. It would help me to avoid slouching so much. But the process of laying out my mat, and sitting on my own on the floor, only served to heighten how detached I had become from the rest of the group. As I fiddled with my diary, or simply looked around me on the mat, I could not ignore the sound of everyone else making each other laugh as they rocked on their chairs. More than ever, even when I first began training at the velodrome as a shy and inse-cure teenager, I felt like a girl alone, a woman apart.

I would return home at night and feel so upset and angry that, after dinner with Scott, I'd write reams of letters which I longed to send to the disapproving individuals. But I knew I couldn't send them. It would not help my career if I showed my harshest feelings towards my situation at work. I wrote about how they all made me feel as if I was immoral – and yet I had not cheated on anyone or set out to hurt a single person. I had just fallen in love. What gave them the right to judge me for that? Did they feel they were morally superior to me? The questions tumbled out of me and it helped to set them down on paper. It was like the first draft of the letter I wrote to my dad. I had not been able to send that either. But I did post him my toned-down second draft. Yet even that option was denied to me here. I understood that it was better to suffer in silence than confront them again on my own.

I tried again to talk to Shane and Dave but, once more, they made me feel that I was being paranoid and over-emotional. I was, in short, being a bit of a girl about it all. 'It's just your chimp,' they'd joke, before stressing that they, as well as Jan and Iain, were all willing to work with me. They told me to forget the past and just get on with the job. But I could not blank out the way in which the coaching team behaved towards me. I could imagine their disdain.

As always, I relied on Steve Peters. Calmly and rationally he listened to me and reassured me. Firstly, what had happened

205

between me and Scott, as a twenty-eight-old woman and a thirty-two-year-old man, was perfectly natural. The reaction of those around us was more unbalanced. Steve tried to help me understand the breakdown in communication. I was troubled most by Jan's hostility. We had once been close and now it felt like he could barely tolerate being in the same area as me. I asked Steve why he thought Jan felt so 'betrayed' and 'let down'. Steve was typically thoughtful.

We all valued Jan and appreciated his qualities. Yet it was plausible that he was hurt more by Scott's failure to trust him. He might not have expected me to talk openly to him – but he would have wanted Scott, his flatmate, to speak honestly. Steve said Jan might be feeling so bruised because one of his closest male allies, a trusted friend and colleague, had apparently gone behind his back. That's why it would take time for the wound in Jan to heal.

It made sense; and I felt just a little better. I was also a loyal person. Early in 2009 my agent, Chris Evans-Pollard, found himself in crisis. I had begun working with Chris in 2007 – soon after my triumph at that year's World Championships. Ironically, I asked Shane Sutton to be with me when I first met Chris at a restaurant in Hitchin. Shane, naturally, told Chris that I was like a '*daw-ter*' to him.

I liked Chris and respected the way in which he stayed out of my sporting world and concentrated purely on my commercial prospects. He understood that training, for an elite athlete, should always be the priority. But Chris looked worried when, just as I was feeling at my lowest after the Olympics, he revealed that he was on the verge of leaving the agency where he had also looked after Matthew Pinsent and Tom Daley. There had been a parting of the ways, in both philosophical and business terms, and Chris hoped to set up his own company: Three60 Sports Management. But Chris didn't have a single client.

'Well, you've got me,' I said encouragingly.

Chris looked both hopeful and disbelieving that I would leave an established agency and stick with him. 'Are you sure?' he asked.

'Absolutely,' I stressed. 'You've been great with me. Why would I leave you?'

It was that simple but the relief which flooded through Chris was quite touching. He had a wife and two very small children, as well as a mortgage and bills to pay. But at least Chris now had a business, with one client, me, for starters. We would plot a way out of the mess because I believed in Chris much more than an otherwise faceless agency. I trusted his judgement and appreciated his friendship. It would have never entered my mind to walk away from him just because he was working on his own in a small office.

Chris, however, had to endure my gloomy moods. There were many weeks when he could not even talk to me as I didn't answer his messages – beyond telling him I was having a bad time and needed space. It was impossible to think about sponsor meetings or endorsement opportunities when I felt like shit. Chris would have to wait for me to recover from the mauling and the bruising I'd absorbed.

He hung on. Chris only told me later how hard it had been. His only client seemed to be in the midst of a minor breakdown. She was at war with her feelings towards her coaches and her father. She was hurting and grieving. She was not the sparky and smiley Olympic champion he was hoping to market and promote.

Chris did not say it to me then, but the same thoughts kept churning though his head. 'What the hell is going on with Victoria? Is she ever going to get out of this slump?'

It was just as well he didn't voice those questions out loud. I would not have been able to give him the positive answers he needed to hear so badly. I was still lost in the storm.

Pruszków, Poland, 26 March 2009

Jan van Eijden, silently and calmly, held me up on my black bike that Saturday evening. I remained equally quiet on the start line of the women's sprint final. We had only spoken in restrained sentences throughout the World Championships which had begun two days earlier. There was no obvious animosity between us; and no more accusations were hurled my way by Jan. We were just scrupulously clipped in our communication. There was not much left to say either about my races or our situation.

Tension was etched on our faces. To our left the Dutch rider Willy Kanis, whom I had defeated in the Olympic semi-finals, was supported by her coach. I doubted they would have experienced the kind of conflict that now defined my relationship with Jan. But the intimacy of the sprint start remained as Jan propped me up on my bike. My arm rested on his shoulder and our flanks touched. Jan must have been able to feel me breathing as I looked straight down the track. The usual last few words between a sprinter and her coach were not uttered this time. We stayed locked in our separate worlds, waiting for the moment when Jan would roll me down the wooden boards behind Kanis. Despite all the problems between us, I would attempt to win my fourth world title in the individual sprint.

Earlier that week we had arrived in central Poland, landing in Warsaw, and travelled the short distance to Pruszków, which was just outside the capital. Our focus was distracted. Dave Brailsford had been all over the newspapers in the preceding weeks as, in late February, he had announced the start of, in his words, 'an epic story'. He confirmed that Rupert Murdoch's Sky were about to pour millions of pounds into the creation of a British road cycling team. The new Sky outfit, headed by Dave and including Shane Sutton as one of its key coaches, epitomized the fact that cycling was now big business in

Britain. It seemed to me as if all the money coming the way of the road team stemmed directly from the Olympic cyclists' success – from the pursuit riders and sprinters like me and, especially, Chris Hoy. We would not share in Dave's new dream and, instead, faced a dilution in the previous concentration of attention that underpinned our earlier achievements.

I understood and respected Dave's passion. His past had been steeped in road cycling. It meant that his latest venture was built on sincere foundations. He was also honest enough to admit his time would have to be split. But Dave believed that he and Shane had created a network of younger coaches which would ensure the seamless continuation of our supremacy on the track. I wouldn't have minded going public, with my questions, to ask how senior management planned to resolve the standoff between me and their coaches. But Dave was consumed by his belief that Sky would produce a winner of the Tour de France within the first five years of its existence. I had the distinct feeling that my races in Poland figured low down the list of Dave's priorities. It didn't matter much to me, as Dave had always been peripheral to my training and performing. As long as I had Scott, Steve Peters and Mark Simpson, and Team Pendleton remained intact, I could cope without much input from Dave, Shane, Jan and Iain.

I also heaped new pressure on myself. I'd announced, with just the tip of my tongue in my cheek, that I intended to target four medals at the Worlds. It would highlight the fact that women sprint cyclists were still battling to convince the IOC to offer us more than one event on the track. Yet cracks were beginning to emerge in the IOC's planned scheduling and there were rumours that the team sprint or keirin might be added to the women's programme at the London Olympics.

On the Thursday, during day one of the Worlds, I had won bronze in the first of my four events – the 500m time trial. My time of 34.102 was decent enough but it remained outside my personal best for a race that had never been a speciality of mine. Anna Meares beat me to silver, but we were both blown away by Simona Krupeckaitė who blasted her way around the Polish pine in a new world record of 33.796 seconds. 'This medal is special in its own way because I've never won one in this event at the Worlds before,' I told the press. 'I've been close but this time I've done it. I'm dead chuffed.'

In the women's team sprint the Australian pair of Meares and Kaarle McCulloch showed, just as Krupeckaitė had done, how hard they had worked since Beijing. Meares was still not ready to ride against me in the individual sprint, and had entered only the first two events and the keirin, but she was in rollicking form. The Aussies finished easily ahead of me and Shanaze Reade in qualifying and we knew we needed to go at least a tenth of a second quicker in the final. We did; but Meares was like thunder and lightning on the first lap and clocked an impressive 18.692 which was half a second ahead of Shanaze.

According to Richard Moore in the *Guardian*, 'Pendleton produced a stunning late surge, closing the gap to just two-tenths of a second by the finish – not quite enough to overhaul the Australians whose resurgence, across the board, has been as obvious as Britain's apparent decline. "We're obviously both disappointed but the Australians did a better job than us," Pendleton said. "That's sport."'

I knew it would be disastrous, rather than just another example of sport's great capacity for causing surprise, if I lost my sprint title. Meares might have chosen to avoid facing me, but Krupeckaitė and Olga Panarina of Belarus had both been quick in qualifying with their respective times of 11.134 and 11.176. I went out last, as world champion, and rode almost as fast as I had done in Beijing as I dipped under 11 seconds and seized the top slot in 10.971. I then beat the local girl, Poland's Renata Dabrowska, in the first match sprint, won both heats against my old rival Yvonne Hijgenaar, and then did the same to McCulloch to ease into the semi-finals.

It was relatively straightforward defeating Panarina in two races while Kanis was too quick for Lyubov Shulika, the sturdy and powerful Ukrainian.

Before the final Jan and I waited stoically for the signal to start, our silence growing ever more serious. The Sky name was already emblazoned across my blue, white and red lycra. Jan was dressed less like a billboard in a white short-sleeved shirt and dark blue tracksuit bottoms. Kanis wore the traditional orange of the Dutch national team. Her head cocked to the left as if, staring at us, she was puzzled by our strained relationship. But Kanis knew nothing of the dissent in our camp. She was set to ride the race of her life.

At last, we began. Kanis led us out in heat one of the 2009 World Championship final. My black and white helmet hardly moved as I tracked her steadily around the first lap. As we crossed the start line a second time I moved up to ride above Kanis. She veered and twitched back at me and our speed increased. We were soon racing side by side, close together as we began the final lap. Kanis edged ahead on the penultimate turn but I came at her hard on the outside. She ducked her head low but I made a last spurt and drew level before the line. And then we were over. I was millimetres ahead of Kanis; and needing just one more win to retain the rainbow jersey.

It was my turn to lead us out in race two. Kanis rode close to my back wheel and, on lap two, watching her over my right shoulder, she suddenly darted to the inside and overtook me. I veered up the boards. I would gain more momentum by racing back down at her when we neared the sound of the bell. Kanis, however, was up at the top with me in a flash, her bike just ahead of mine. She held a small advantage as we flashed down the back straight. Kanis rode strongly and I struggled to close the gap. As we came out of the last turn she was a wheel and a half ahead of me. I tried desperately to reel her in and we both dropped our heads low as we flew for the line. The distance between us had shrunk; but not enough for me. Kanis had won race two. It was 1–1, with the decider to face.

I took to the rollers and went through the same old draining preparation. This final now felt as hard as any series of races I'd faced before – and not just because Kanis was riding so confidently. All the dissent and fatigue had drained me. It was hard to know if I had anything left.

Jan was polite and helpful and I knew how much he still wanted me to win. We were both racers, in the end, and victory mattered. But we still didn't talk much. I had moved beyond language. I was in a much darker and more stifled place. It would soon be just me and my bike.

I stood up, feeling the heaviness in my legs but forcing myself to walk to the track for race three with a snap to my step. My eyes were covered by my racing goggles; and I was relieved. I wanted Kanis to think I was blank and powerful and the world champion sprinter who had beaten her so many times before. I felt less certain on the inside. On my bike I held on to Jan, and we both stared straight ahead, anticipating the drama that was about to hit me.

Kanis led the way in race three and we settled into the old routine. I held back at first, allowing three bike-lengths of space to open up between us. Kanis, on lap two, made the first move. She climbed the banking slowly. I followed her, even more slowly. The gap between us widened still more and the English-speaking trackside commentator noted, with relief, 'Kanis and Pendleton decide to ride more regularly now.' We had picked up speed but Kanis was far ahead of me. I knew I needed to ensure that she didn't get away from me. This was no time to make the mistake of an amateur sprinter.

'The distance is now seven metres,' the commentator boomed as we both began to turn our legs still faster. And then, suddenly, changing the stretched-out pattern of my tracking, I flew down the banking with a whoosh! – a sound matched by the crowd, as my bike slipped into a more customary place on Kanis's rear wheel. As the bell echoed I went back up to the outside, riding hard as Kanis stayed ahead of me, pinning me close to the rail even as we zoomed around the track.

We took the next turn, with just a thin sliver of pine separating our parallel rides. She was fractionally ahead but, on the back straight, I worked as hard as I had ever done. We almost bumped but I edged to the front, only for Kanis to come back again. Kanis led us out of the last turn and into the final hurtling straight. I went low and hard, flattening my back, pumping my legs as if my life depended on them. Kanis stayed strong. She was still in front as we both accelerated to the line.

'*Kanis … Kanis …!*' the commentator shouted.

We were over, with my surge turning his cry into a wordless exclamation. It was a sound of disbelief, as if the man with the microphone did not quite understand what he had seen. He just knew it had been excruciatingly close.

The photographic proof was almost instant. 'It was …' he shouted before reaching for my first name. '*Vicky!*' he hollered. He didn't say Pendleton. 'It was … *Vicky!*'

I had won. Incredibly, I had won. The rainbow jersey, despite everything, was still mine.

The tears came, in a deluge, as I slid off my bike. My visor and the helmet were gone. As if I was naked, my face cracked open. I began to cry more deeply. I was not just weeping. I was almost sobbing, my face crumpled and broken. Jan put his hand on my shoulder, to console me. I saw Jamie Staff next. I liked Jamie. He was a great rider and a good man. Jamie enveloped me in his arms and I cried still harder.

Everyone thought I was crying out of sheer relief. They thought I'd been driven to the brink by a World Championship decider. I had; but these were tears I had stored inside for eight months. They were tears for me and Scott, for my mum, and even my dad. They were tears of discord and strife, of pain and separation.

The press wanted to know why I was so emotional. I felt like telling them the real reasons; but I didn't. 'I'm so relieved I can't explain,' I said, wiping my eyes, and concealing the truth a little longer. 'It's one of the greatest achievements of my career, because going straight back into training and racing after the Olympics was one of the hardest things I've ever had to do. I was aware that, after Athens in 2004, no Olympic champion won the World title the following year. And that made the pressure greater.'

The men around me nodded sympathetically as they looked up from their scribbled shorthand or their tiny recorders. I tugged at my sleeve, as if my heart was truly there. My voice quivered and I murmured my last words before disappearing into the cold Polish night.

'I couldn't imagine not wearing this,' I said, touching the rainbow jersey, as tears rolled down my face again.

I also cried the next time I saw my father. These tears were more contained, if no less heart-felt. I was still angry with him for leaving Mum. But Max remained my dad. He'll always be my dad. The force of that feeling struck me when, to my shock and dismay, he offered to return my first rainbow jersey. I had given it to him for his sixtieth birthday, framing with my own hands the world champion's skinsuit I had received in 2005. Dad thought I might want to take it back – after everything he had done to Mum.

'No, Dad,' I said. 'I gave that to you.'

'I'd understand if you want it back,' Dad said miserably. 'It might be better ...'

'Don't ever say that,' I answered. I needed Dad to realize how much it meant to me that he kept that jersey of mine. He had done so much to make me a world champion. Whatever had happened between him and Mum could not change this different truth.

'I want you to keep it, Dad,' I said. 'Don't throw it back at me.'

Dad looked at me, nodding his thanks. He knew it was about more than a framed jersey.

'OK,' he said simply. 'Thank you. I do want to keep it. You know I do.'

So much had changed, between me and Dad, but these pure and simple facts prevailed. He was my father; and I still loved him.

'I know, Dad,' I said, as we prepared to say goodbye again. 'I know ...'

Life became busier off the track. Chris Evans-Pollard was much happier as I was in regular contact again and ready to return to commercial work. I appeared in *Vogue* and went to the Chelsea Flower Show where I was invited to present a rose which had been created especially for me. It was even named after me and I smiled demurely while, wearing a red dress, I held the rose close to my face. The bloom was yellow – which was the closest the horticulturalists at Harkness Roses in Letchworth could come to producing a golden rose.

I was also thrilled when, out of the blue, The Prodigy sent me a framed gold disc of their album, *The Fat of the Land*, with a mounted plaque which said: *To Victoria, congratulations on the gold medal. We were all right behind you. The Prodigy Boys*. I had mentioned in various interviews that *The*

Fat of the Land was one of my favourite records, and that I played it again and again whenever I was struggling. The Prodigy had heard my comments and tracked me down. Liam Howlett, the band's leader, had also written a personal note behind the glass. It said: 'To Victoria, well done, respect. Liam, The Prodigy.' Keith Flint, the tongue-studded singer, the man who sang about being the original 'twisted fire-starter', also wrote: 'To Victoria, buzzed to see you win. Keith.'

I was just as buzzed. In a similar way I loved going backstage and attending a show Stella McCartney put on for Adidas at London Fashion Week. I had signed deals with Adidas and Gatorade and also become the face of Hovis. My mum could not quite believe it. In a deliberately nostalgic photo call, I was dressed as a delivery boy. I wore a flat tweed cap and a waistcoat as I pushed an old-fashioned bike up Hovis Hill while delivering my morning loaves of bread.

More controversially, I agreed to become the first woman athlete to appear on the cover of *FHM* magazine. I took off most of my clothes and posed in swimwear. I refused to pose in the sheer frilly undies the designer had picked out but I did wear an even more revealing swimming costume and high heels; and a black bustier and matching knickers.

Plenty of people criticized me. But I was happy. I went on public record as saying I thought it was a tasteful shoot but, yes, I was thrilled that I looked 'pretty hot'. Those were my words and it made a change from me feeling grim and miserable and at war back at the velodrome. Just as I had done with the naked *OSM* cover, I thought I would be proud to look back at myself in later years.

Chris Hoy sounded sceptical. 'Vicky's one of the few athletes that does really thrive on that,' he said. 'She loves the media spotlight and I think she measures her success by how much attention she gets – which is crazy because she's the best in the world at what she does. That's one of the things I always try

There's always less glamour inside the pits. Here I am – trying to get my mind ready to race while listening to some music.

The wait is finally over and here I am . . . racing.

Life both on and off the track was fraught in the wake of Scott's departure from British Cycling. In our different ways, this was a tense moment for both me and my coach Jan van Eijden. It was taken at the 2011 world championships in Apeldoorn, Holland, where, for the first time in five years, I would lose my individual sprint title.

Scott, my fiancé, introduces me to the two new additions to our family –
Mr Jonty and Stella, our Doberman puppies.

Steve Peters, the team psychiatrist for British Cycling, has provided amazing support
to me over the years. Here Steve is, again, at the 2011 world cup in Manchester,
getting me to laugh during the strain of competition.

My lovely mechanics, Ernie and Mark, do enjoy making me laugh as well. They added this Queen Vic sticker to my bike because, having supported me through so many trials and tribulations on the track, they know that I don't often feel very regal.

At the European championships in Apeldoorn, in October 2011, I endured one of my most difficult competitions. My training was meant to bolster my strength in time for the London Olympics but it meant that, in 2011, I had to sacrifice my form and my speed. I lost in the individual sprint and felt desolate as I left the velodrome that night. The next day I forced myself to find fresh resolve and won the keirin against the expectations of many.

It's not easy to race against your team-mate – but I have occasionally had to compete in the individual sprint against Jess Varnish. Here we are, from an overhead view, as Jan van Eijden gives me a push at the start while Shane Sutton does the same to Jess.

One of the pleasures towards the end of my career has been the team-sprint partnership I've forged with Jess Varnish. In February 2012, at the Olympic Velodrome in London, we were thrilled to set a new world record.

At the 2012 World Championships in Melbourne, Anna Meares and I produced another epic series of races. In the first race of the semi-final I fell on the track. 'She hit hard,' Meares said later when she was asked about my crash. 'I saw it, I heard it, I felt it.' I obviously lost that first encounter but I came back to beat Meares in the next two races.

Overcome with emotion, I simply lift my hand to acknowledge my sixth world title in the individual sprint in Melbourne in April 2012. It was my ninth world title in total – and a fitting way to end my very last world championships.

While Scott and I are hard at work, getting ready for London 2012, Mr Jonty and Stella chill out at home.

My last day at the velodrome – saying goodbye to the gang.

At the 2012 London Olympic Games, in the final of the individual sprint, Anna Meares and I engage in battle one last time.

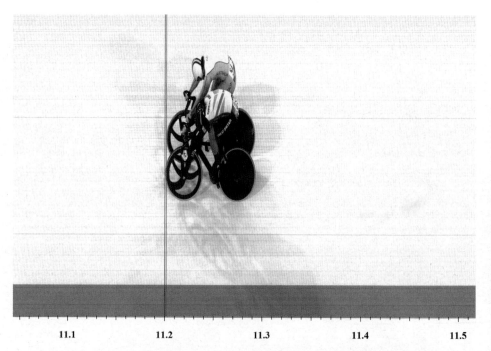

| 11.1 | 11.2 | 11.3 | 11.4 | 11.5 |

This is how close our rivalry was when it mattered most – at London 2012.
I just beat Anna Meares to the line . . . only to be devastated minutes later when I am relegated. Another gold medal was lost in the cruel and often senseless tangle of cycling officialdom.

I did the right thing and lifted Anna's hand in tribute. She was my greatest rival and we pushed each other to extraordinary heights.

In the end, Anna Meares and I smiled and hugged each other. We also happily set aside our rivalry and spoke about wedding dresses. It was a lovely and very girly end to such a long and bruising struggle for supremacy.

After I won Olympic gold in the keirin at the London Olympics, I met Scott at the barrier. We had been through so much to finally reach our point of release and freedom. I felt happier than I had ever done on the track as Scott said, 'We've done it, beautiful, we've done it.'

As I waited for my gold medal I cupped my hands into the shape of a heart. I looked straight at Scott and my family. And then I pointed at them all – telling them how much I loved them.

If luck had gone my way I might have won three gold medals at London 2012. But a disqualification and a relegation meant I ended up with silver and gold. Yet my victory in the keirin, with a gold medal in my hand, provided the happiest moment of my cycling career – and my enjoyment of the medal ceremony made an exhilarating change from the emptiness I had felt on the winner's podium four years before in Beijing.

And, finally, I get to say goodbye ... happiness and relief surge through me with the knowledge that, at last, it is all over. I can walk away into a new life.

to say to her: "Enjoy your success." If you could say to her four years ago that this is what you're going to achieve she'd be over the moon. But she measures her performances against her public recognition.'

I respected Chris's intelligence; and he almost got it right. I do strive for public recognition so that I can be accepted as an equal to my male counterparts in track cycling. But acknowledgement from my team-mates, and peers, for my performances matters more to me. It was a subtle but important distinction.

Life was also different for Chris. Injury meant he could not be in Poland to defend his World titles; but he was still Sir Chris and his significance to British cycling was obvious.

Without Chris, and after I, in total fatigue, failed to make the keirin final, GB finished third in the World Championship table. We won nine medals in total, just one behind Australia, but with only two golds, for my sprint and the women's team pursuit – won by Lizzie Armitstead, Wendy Houvenaghel and Jo Rowsell. Australia, with four golds, and France, with three, were ahead of us. The British domination of the previous two years had disappeared.

Chris had been off his bike for the longest time since he was seven years old; but he was still revered everywhere. I felt like a comparative unknown – a fact endorsed for me when, while shooting a commercial for Sky with Elle Macpherson, she was amazed to see that I could ride a bike so well. The supermodel had no idea I rode one for a living. She was not alone – and I admitted my exasperation to Emma John when, again in *OSM*, she wrote a follow-up a year on from Beijing and charted the relative failure of various Olympic gold medallists, including me, to transform our lives.

There were more opportunities, undoubtedly, but it still felt as if I was pedalling in obscurity. 'I've pretty much done everything I can and I'm still an unknown,' I said to John. 'Never mind, it wasn't what I set out to do in the first place. I know what I'm doing next. I'll get down to training, do my job.'

A different battle, for female parity on the Olympic track programme, ebbed and flowed throughout 2009. In mid-August the IOC announced it would not be changing its schedule. Instead, at London 2012, it would adhere to the same structure of seven events for men and three for women.

The Olympics Minister, Tessa Jowell, promised to meet Jacques Rogge, the IOC president, in Berlin in an attempt to force a rethink. Yet British Cycling's president, Brian Cookson, was worried about the men. 'We would be very concerned about the possibility of the loss of any men's events,' he said. 'The IOC should think very carefully before reducing any men's events. Longer term our objective is for equality in men's and women's events.'

I was regularly asked about the glaring lack of equality. 'Sir Chris Hoy won three gold medals,' interviewers would say earnestly, 'but you only had the chance to win one. How does that make you feel – only winning *one* gold medal?'

It sometimes wore me down that this became the perennial 'angle' about me in the media. My own sporting story was apparently less interesting. I had been the overwhelming favourite to win the individual sprint; and I had duly succeeded. Where was the story? It became more intriguing for interviewers and reporters if they could depict me as a raging suffragette. I was passionate about equality and, yes, I would have liked to compete for three golds in Beijing. I admitted the truth on both counts. Yet I was rather reluctant to have the 'spokeswoman' tag foisted onto me.

The campaign to overturn the IOC ruling gathered momentum. On 26 September the UCI [International Cycling Union] president, Pat McQuaid, was voted back into power for another four years and he said, 'I can confirm that I was mandated to work out exactly how we are going to achieve parity within track cycling for the 2012 Olympics – and it is a matter we are looking at with some urgency.'

In October, I won my seventh 500m time trial title at the British Nationals. It was my first competitive ride since the World Championships in Poland. The following night I picked up my eighth successive National sprint title ahead of eighteen-old-year Jess Varnish and seventeen-year-old Becky James. I had just turned twenty-nine; but I was not done yet.

The track cycling programme at the London Olympics would end in August 2012, six weeks before my thirty-second birthday. Time was beginning to race past. The pressure soon intensified. On 9 December 2009, the UCI announced that the points races and the men's madison would be axed in favour of a women's team pursuit and the omnium event for both sexes at the next Olympics. The individual pursuit titles for both men and women, won by Bradley Wiggins and Rebecca Romero in Beijing, also would be dropped from the programme at London 2012. In their place two new sprint events for women were ratified – the team-sprint and the keirin. I would, like Chris Hoy, have three medals to chase.

I heard a few snide whispers around the velodrome, 'be careful what you wish for' being the most obvious. But everyone else was warm and supportive.

It was a time for me to be measured – if still honest. 'I was as surprised as anyone that the UCI actually made such radical proposals,' I said. 'Having the opportunity to compete in more events in 2012 will be amazing. But I'd be extremely happy to repeat what I achieved in Beijing by winning just one.'

11 | TATTOOS AND MONSTERS

Ballerup Super Arena, Copenhagen, 24 March 2010

The truth came and found me on an ordinary Wednesday afternoon in Denmark. It snuck up and took hold of me with such surprising force that, as if it was an old friend who had suddenly appeared and started tickling me from behind, I laughed helplessly in its grip. Yet there was more amazement than joy in my laugh. I felt like a blind woman who could finally see again.

During a 40km points race I stared at the surreal sight as dozens of cyclists whirred around and around the wooden track in endless circles. On the opening afternoon of the World Championships the utter madness of professional cycling seemed a comic affair. I cackled to myself in a small room. It was such a joke that the alternative would have been to weep at the sheer folly of it all. But I didn't feel like crying. I was happy laughing out loud at the absurdity.

A bunch of people riding round on two whirring wheels, in multi-coloured lycra, was the epitome of pointlessness. They didn't even ride from A to B. They left point A and completed a lap which ended right back at A. And then they did it again, and again. At least on the road a cyclist usually rides from one town to another, grinding up the side of a mountain and then flying down the other side. A road cyclist braves the heat and cold, the sun and the rain, against a changing landscape.

On the track, in an airless velodrome, our cheeks might blow and glow with the gruelling routine, but we look about as intelligent and interesting as hundreds of little rodents pedalling on their wheels in a cage.

'This is so stupid,' I said aloud, when I stopped laughing. I spoke more to myself than anyone else because I was in the midst of an epiphany. How could such a ridiculous business leave me feeling so stressed and strung out? Some days it seemed to be a matter of life and death and yet it was the complete opposite. It was an exercise in futility. We rode around like crazy people on bikes without any brakes. We did nothing else but pedal, churning and turning our legs in quiet desperation.

Laughing at track cycling was liberating. If I could chuckle at such a ludicrous way of earning a living I could stop feeling so intense about it. I could just give it up. The beautiful freedom of that thought was exhilarating. I imagined myself walking around outside, in the pale sunlight of a Danish afternoon, looking up at the sky or at ordinary people going about their everyday lives and doing much more meaningful work than me. I might see doctors and teachers, architects and engineers, chefs and nurses, soldiers and builders – professionals who actually helped others or did something useful for a living. There had to be some kind of work where I could live a more fulfilling life.

I no longer wanted to ride around in circles. I no longer wanted to be with some of the people who surrounded me in British cycling. I no longer wanted to put myself through the hopeless trauma of racing.

Instead, I wanted to walk away. No-one could stop me now. I was no longer answerable to my dad. I owed nothing to the track programme. They were moving into a bigger and better world with their gleaming Team Sky dream. Jan van Eijden and Iain Dyer would be relieved to see the back of me. A few others in the squad would hang out the bunting. We would all be relieved.

The certainty of my decision filled me with a delicious calm. I would compete hard over the next four days of the World Championships and I would give my all – because I would never race for GB again after my three events. These would be the last four days of my turbulent racing career. I was so happy that I simply smiled at the sweet clarity of my thinking.

I was free. I really was free.

In my last ever team sprint I partnered Jess Varnish. She was only nineteen; but Jess was a gifted and tenacious rider whom I liked and respected. We got along from the start and she had begun to understand that, with me, she could be herself. I really wasn't a strutting world champion. Jess saw that I could be as nervous as a teenager like her. We also chatted happily about everyday life – away from our mundane professional world. Jess had no idea I was on the brink of quitting and it was best that I spared her the truth. We would just ride our hardest.

Jess and I weren't going to win in Copenhagen, as she was still learning the art of starting a team sprint, but I sensed that she could be a future champion. She would not be ready to win the individual sprint or the keirin at London 2012, but four years on, at the age of twenty-six, I expected Jess to be at the peak of world cycling. She would not have despaired yet of a brainless activity.

Jess and I finished fourth in qualifying. Kaarle McCullough and Anna Meares were quickest and, in the final, they beat the Chinese duo of Jinjie Gong and Junhong Lin. We lost the bronze medal race to Lithuania's Gintare Gaivenyte and Simona Krupeckaitė. Yet I could praise Jess, sincerely, and tell her how well she had done. She had a bright future in cycling.

I felt deep contentment that my own future had shrunk to just three more days. In the pits, I was calm and utterly professional. No-one knew of my decision, but I was determined to bow out as a world champion. I had been cycling professionally for almost eight years and, despite its farcical nature, it was important I departed on winning terms. Four out of the last five World titles in the individual sprint had gone to me. I liked the idea of a fifth championship on my very last weekend of racing.

There was a pleasing look to the number five. One day I would be able to tell my children how I had spent my twenties. They would open their eyes wide at my strange past – but hearing that I had been a five-time World sprint champion, and an Olympic gold medallist, might make them feel a little proud. But I would be glad not to have wasted any more years tearing myself to pieces over such a silly sport.

On Friday 26 March 2010, a long line of women prepared themselves for the individual sprint qualifying time trial. As the defending champion I would be the last of the twenty-seven riders timed over a flying 200m distance. Jess would go out as number fifteen but my old rivals – Meares, Guo, Krupeckaitė and Kanis – were much closer to me. I felt almost nostalgic as I watched Meares and Guo, in particular, begin their warm-up routine. We had been through so many battles against each other that, even if I would not miss them, I'd never forget them. They had been part of my life for the past eight years and, especially in the solitary and bruising examination of the sprint, we had learnt so much about each other.

I had begun to relax and become reflective, perhaps a little too much, for I qualified only seventh fastest – behind Guo, Meares, Panarina, Krupeckaitė, Kanis and Clara Sanchez. My time, 11.135, was considerably slower than Guo's 10.918 – but I didn't mind. I had ridden faster than Guo and Meares in the past and I knew I could do it again. I was certain I was more than a match for them in the cruel psychology of match sprinting. The problem of mental and physical fatigue had been resolved by The Decision. In deciding to give up cycling forever I had assured myself of one last burst of desire and intensity.

'Are you OK?' Jan asked me as I sat down in the pits after my qualifying ride.

'Yeah,' I said. 'I'm good. You know me, Jan, I'm not really a time trialist.'

Jan smiled. I might have qualified fastest in plenty of major competitions but, essentially, I was better at outsprinting my rivals rather than just racing against the clock.

'I know you can beat every single girl out there,' Jan said simply.

Shane Sutton cocked an eyebrow at this relatively warm exchange between me and Jan. 'Looking good, Vic,' he said in his Aussie drawl. He sounded impressed by my cool resilience. But it's easy to be cool and resilient when your ordeal is almost over.

The top twenty-four riders went through to the knockout rounds. I was drawn against Jess. It felt like the old and the new, Pendleton and Varnish, the past and the future of British cycling colliding in the present. There was still a divide between us. I knew I would defeat Jess. And so I rode within myself and was the fourth quickest of the twelve winners. So much more remained inside me; and I was ready to pour out everything as I took my leave of the track.

I beat Sanchez in the next round and the draw for the quarter-finals that evening made familiar reading:

Guo vs Panarina; Meares vs Vogel; Pendleton vs Baranova; McCullough vs Krupeckaitė.

I wondered how many times I had raced against the seven other women. Now, into the last rounds of the World Championship sprint, I could only race three of them. After Baranova I hoped for Meares and Guo. It would be hard, but true, to slip away after facing my two most consistent rivals for the last time.

That Friday night, in front of a noisy and enthusiastic Danish velodrome, I beat Baranova comfortably in both our heats. I was through to the semi-finals – as was the expected trio of Meares, Guo and Krupeckaitė. Even their races had conformed to the archetype. Guo and Krupeckaitė won each of their heats but Meares needed a decider against Vogel after she was relegated from the second race for illegal riding. I was pleased she made it through to face me in the semi-finals.

I left the arena that night in a quiet but settled mood. I was ready for one last crack at the individual sprint.

Ballerup Super Arena, Copenhagen, 27 March 2010

Anna Meares and I slipped back into the old routine. In the waiting area I looked straight at her, as if saying goodbye, before I slid a new black visor down my face. I settled into the dark quiet as we waited for Guo and Krupeckaitė to race first. The acrid tension rose up from my gut to my throat. I swallowed hard. Meares would be suffering even more than me – unless she, too, was on the verge of retirement. I could not imagine, however, Meares walking away from cycling for years. It defined her more than me.

Krupeckaitė beat Guo in race one and, even before that slightly surprising result could register, Meares was out of her seat. I followed her to the track. Jan was already waiting for me, with my bike.

Meares had drawn the lead-out role and, stealthily, I tracked her for our first slow lap and a half. There was a smattering of applause as I banked up to the right. Meares watched me closely and as we passed the finish line, a lap before the end, a cry of '*Aussie ... Aussie, Aussie, Aussie ...!*' rang out.

We both climbed out of our saddles, on cue, and began to race. Meares was four lengths clear at the bell but I held my nerve. I raced hard and tilted my bike low as we arrowed round the turn before the back straight. The gap between us melted away magically. We raced around the next bend and then, with a surge, I overtook her on the last straight. It was simple. It was almost easy. 1–0 to me.

Guo struck back in race two and evened the score after a photo finish against Krupeckaitė. 1–1; with a decider to follow.

I wanted something much cleaner and more persuasive. Wearing a red, white and blue Sky outfit, I led Meares out. I was determined this would be our last dance, and it seemed right I should take the lead. Let her test me again. It felt like the right way for us to part.

Meares stuck close to my rear wheel. She was all over me. Meares shimmied to the left, as if she might take me on the inside, but we were so near the edge of the track she had to back off.

She shadowed me relentlessly even as, deep in lap two, I began to ride harder. Meares kept pace, ensuring that only centimetres separated us. She looked deadly and impassive because she could not afford a mistake against me. I played with her, just a little, as I twitched my bike to the right, as if I was heading for the upper banking, only to steer back on course. I did it again, and she held firm.

I watched Meares over my right shoulder but, as we completed lap two, she managed a successful dart on my inside. She came out the other side, just ahead of me, on my left. Meares forced me up the track, right to the railing, as if she was going to try and pin me there in parting. But then she peeled away and sped down the steep curve. Meares had opened up a small lead.

At the bell we were out of our saddles, in tribute to each other, and racing one last lap together. She looked strong down the back straight and I could not overtake her. But, as I flew out of her slipstream when we approached the final turn, it was as if I had been catapulted forward on her outside. I was nearly alongside her as we entered the last flat stretch of track. She hunched as low as she could, straining with every fibre of her being to stay ahead of me.

I was lost in my sprinter's world. There was no time to think, just time to open myself up as I hurtled towards the line. I took the lead at the very death, in the last split second of our race. I knew I'd won even before the '1' shone next to my name on the board and the commentator whooped: '*Pendleton!*'

Up and away from Meares, I headed for the sanctuary of the curved rim. I was in the final, and would never have to race Meares again. As we neared each other again I stretched out my hand to her and, generously, Meares gave me hers. We clutched hands for a few seconds and then we were gone. I wondered how relieved she would feel when she heard that, in another day or two, I was out of her life.

Meares would just have to face down Guo then; a less complex woman than me. Guo was still a great rider and, in race three of her semi-final, she snatched another photo finish from Krupeckaitė.

I had the perfect ending – Meares and then Guo – and just an hour to prepare myself for the final.

Jan made a few tactical pointers as we got ready for Guo. I was much less twitchy than normal and I could tell how everyone had noticed. If only it could always have been this serene, I thought, while knowing that my serenity stemmed from the certainty of my decision.

In race one of the final, Guo, wearing a white skin and a red helmet, rolled away first. We pedalled slowly around the track and cruised past the tables where, in the middle of the velodrome and away from the pits and the media area, corporate diners drank wine and tucked into their main courses as they watched us at work. Guo, riding a red bike, scrutinized me more closely. I was content to wait for my moment.

The TV cameraman on his motorized uni-cycle struggled to ride as slowly as we did on lap two. I waited and waited, doing little to disrupt Guo, until she began to pedal faster and faster. Like Meares before her she carried a decisive lead into the last lap but, again, I ate up the track with relish. I drew level with her and, on the penultimate turn, riding alongside each other, I edged in front. Then, almost effortlessly, I raced ahead of Guo to seal the win.

Race two was different. In the lead-out role, and intent on keeping Guo's mind occupied, I decided to stretch us by taking us up the banking. But I had hardly begun to climb, turning to the right, when my front wheel suddenly skidded and buckled. I was thrown violently off my bike, somersaulting to the left and towards the oncoming bike of Guo. My arms stretched out helplessly as if I was trying to cling onto the handlebars.

I smashed down into the track, landing heavily just before Guo drew level. She was past me as I rolled in agony to the bottom. I lay in a crumpled heap next to the inner railing and tried to work out what had happened. My bike, for some reason, had just slipped from underneath me on the rising track. The pain in my leg was searing. I didn't want it to end this way; but I knew it could be all over.

Jan was there first, with the paramedics and other members of British Cycling behind him. I could see the concern in their faces as, gently, they lifted me off the track.

I could not allow my left leg to take any weight and so they had to support me as I limped away from my overturned bike. The businessmen and women looked up from their meals in surprise, applauding me politely as I was helped to the pits.

Jan and Shane were unsure I could continue. Yet I was resolute. 'I'm OK,' I said. I told them I'd made a mistake. The track was a little dusty and on that steep part of the track I had turned my wheel too fast and the tyre had lost its grip.

I could feel the adrenalin spiking through me as I insisted on heading for the rollers. It felt important to shake the shock out of me.

On the rollers I spent as much time regulating my breathing and pulse rate as turning my aching left leg. I would forget the pain as soon as I was racing again. But I needed to regain the composure that had helped me throughout the sprint. I breathed and pedalled, pedalled and breathed.

It was soon time to go again. The crowd rose to me as I walked gingerly towards my bike on the track. I nearly smiled as I thought: 'Typical … drama right to the very end.'

Jan held me up and I leaned against him. I wanted this to be the final time I would need to be propped up at the start of a sprint.

In a re-run of race two it was again my turn to lead us out. I kept to the lowlands this time, venturing no higher than the middle of the track. For most of the first two laps, I hugged the pale blue ring circling the bottom of the pine boards. At the bell, I was a bike-length ahead of Guo.

She came at me early, anxious to seize the initiative and force my battered body into a third race. We jostled for half a lap, almost touching each other as we battled for supremacy. At turn three she seemed to surge ahead but I had the perfect line on the inside. I was past her as we came round the bend. I felt speed rather than pain as I aimed for the finish.

I was half a length ahead as we raced the last few metres of track. The end was in sight. It was mine.

I flew over the line a decisive winner. I raised my arms above my head. My left fist, on the side where I had fallen, was clenched. But I opened my right hand to stretch five digits to the rafters. I was a five-time world sprint champion.

After my warm-down, the British pressmen were waiting. They reminded me that I had now won eight World titles, with two in the team sprint and an additional in the keirin, which was one more than Yorkshire's legendary Beryl Burton. She had won five World titles in the pursuit, and two on the road. Her first had been won in 1959 and her last in 1967 – thirteen years before I had been born. I was proud; but I did look a bit of a mess and limped heavily on my damaged left leg. There were few tears this time – unlike in Poland the previous year when I had sobbed inconsolably.

'It was difficult at last year's Worlds,' I told the reporters. 'I didn't want to be in the same position again. I did too much after the Olympics. It takes over your life and I really struggled.'

I didn't want to talk about my future, and so I praised Guo instead. 'She's getting stronger,' I said. 'I have absolutely no doubt that she will have more World titles than me when she retires.'

Someone asked if I would be fit to ride in the keirin, with the heats beginning early the following morning. 'I enjoy the keirin,' I said with a smile. 'I managed to have another go on the rollers after tonight's final. It hurts all right but I will see how it feels in the morning. I'm sure I'll be OK and I'll give everything I've got left in my legs. I'd like to go one more time.'

I was stiff and sore on the Sunday morning but I won my first heat in the keirin to set up a killer line-up in the semi-final: Meares, Guo, Kanis, McCullough, Welte and me. I won again and Guo, Kanis and Meares finished in the bottom three places which meant they were out of the final. My fairy-tale ending seemed suddenly possible.

It would, of course, have to be tumultuous to the last, and I drew the bum place. I was drawn as the lead rider behind the derny – and would be left open to attacks from the rear. I got on my bike for the last time. One more was left for me; one more victory to chase.

'The keirin,' Krupeckaitė said later, 'is not like a race. It is more like a war.'

We went to war, Krupeckaitė and I, and in the lurching dash for position on the last lap she moved out of the sprinter's lane and impeded my attack. I put my head down and had another crack at her. It was not enough. Krupeckaitė sneaked the gold. I had silver as my ending.

I felt disgruntled and, after consulting with Jan and Shane, we lodged an official protest against her riding. Race footage was examined while we waited.

'It's over for me, anyway,' I said.

'Not yet,' Shane insisted, thinking I was talking about the result of the keirin, rather than my life in cycling.

Yet it really was over for me in the keirin. My protest was overruled and the result was ratified. I spoke one last time to the reporters – some of whom had followed me my whole career.

'I hope they are going to be a bit tighter on the rules,' I said to the press. 'I am a rule-abider and as long as everyone else is, I will be happy.'

I answered some ritual questions about taking pride in winning gold and silver and looking ahead to London 2012. I agreed that, as a team, we had done competently. Chris Hoy had lost in the sprint, for once being outsmarted, but GB had won three golds, four silvers and a bronze in the Olympic events.

'We're in the mix,' Dave Brailsford said as he followed me into the media area. 'Vicky is looking good in the keirin, she won the sprint again, and we're in really good shape, across the board, in depth. This was another big step towards London.'

Jan, Iain, Shane and Dave came over to congratulate me in our meeting room after the competition had ended. I thanked them as they praised my attitude throughout four days of racing. I then asked Jan and Iain if I could speak to them alone.

In a corner of the room my two official sprint coaches looked happily down at me. 'You were pretty amazing this weekend,' Jan said. He thought my mentality had been perfect – calm yet resourceful. And, physically, I had raced with impressive force.

'There's a reason for that,' I said quietly. Jan and Iain waited for me to continue and then, at last, I told them the secret I had stored inside of me for five days. 'I'm giving up cycling.'

There was silence in our section of the room. It was as if they had not quite heard me. 'I've had enough,' I said bluntly. 'It's over. I don't want to do this any more …'

Steve Peters was soon called into action. He and I talked late into Sunday night in Copenhagen. The shock of my announcement, and the certainty with which I had spoken, meant that Steve was instructed to speak to me with real urgency. Of course, being Steve, he had listened first as I explained the reasons for my departure. He nodded thoughtfully as I outlined the extent of my epiphany the previous Wednesday afternoon. I was weary of the surreal circling of a track but, more deeply, I felt worn out by the negativity of the environment at British Cycling. I was tired of going into the velodrome every day with a sinking feeling in my stomach. After eighteen months I was tired of feeling lonely.

I knew how much Steve wanted to fight for me. He spoke more personally than he usually did in one of our routine sessions. Telling me how sorry he would be if I chose to walk away and not fulfil all my potential, Steve reminded me how much I meant to him and how he had once introduced me to his students as his 'greatest success'. That accolade meant as much to me as any of my world titles, for it proved how hard we had both worked to ensure my fragile psyche could not only survive but flourish in the unforgiving world of competitive sport. Steve urged me to reconsider. Leaving cycling just two years away from my home Olympics seemed the wrong ending for me.

'You owe it to yourself to finish in London,' Steve said.

He didn't mean to do it but Steve made me feel as if I also owed it to him to continue. I would be letting Steve down, disappointing him, and that sadness clouded my certainty. But it was impossible to continue. I would make myself ill if I was forced to put up with another two and a half years of strife and turmoil.

'Two years is not that long,' Steve said quietly. 'You can do another two years … I know you can.'

'I can't,' I said for the umpteenth time that night, as the clock ticked towards midnight.

Steve told me a story about his own difficult years as a medical student. He was essentially a country boy and he found it desperately difficult to study in a big city. Steve felt he was stuck in a rut and judged unfairly at medical school. There were some lecturers who made it seem as if they might dislike you on the basis of your appearance, and fail you for that simple reason, and he'd briefly considered quitting. Just like me, he wanted to escape a harsh environment. But, in the end, he reverted to logic. Steve worked out that if he could withstand another five years at medical school he would emerge with the degree that would then allow him to live the life he had always wanted – a life in which he helped people like me. Yet he had to survive those five years first. He was grateful now that he had not given in to himself.

'I did five years,' he said. 'You can easily do two years …'

I refused and insisted on quitting. And so back and forth we went, over and over again, with the gist of Steve's argument being that it all hinged on London. If the 2012 Olympic Games were going to be held in any other country on earth he would accept my reasons for abandoning cycling. But he understood me so clearly. He knew the competitive urge that burned deep inside me, beneath all the layers of complexity and vulnerability. Steve believed I would never forgive myself if I pulled out of London.

'Just think about it,' he said as I hung my head low. Scott and I were on our way to the Maldives for a long-planned break. Why didn't I wait until we got home before I made any dogmatic decisions? 'Don't give up yet, Vicky,' Steve said softly. 'Not yet …'

It took more than a month after we returned from holiday before I said the words out loud. 'Two more years,' I groaned. 'How can I go on for two years?'

Scott, who had made it clear that he would support any choice I made, shook his head in sympathy. He knew me well enough to understand that my question was also a statement of fact. After much deliberation I was going to carry on, despite everything I had thought in Copenhagen. 'It's going to be hard,' Scott said. 'But you'll do it.'

'Two more years,' I repeated, almost in disbelief at the choice I had made. 'Two more years …'

* * *

One late afternoon in May 2010, not too long after I had agreed to carry on, Steve invited Scott and me to his house for an informal meeting. We would have a coffee and a chat and work out how best to proceed over the next two years.

Soon after we had arrived, and said our hellos, Steve turned to me and asked a strange question. 'Are you ready?' he said.

I did not know what he meant. Was I ready to continue training? Was I ready for 2012? Was I ready for life?

But before I could say anything the kitchen door swung open and two adorable Doberman puppies bounded in and jumped up at me.

'You're a mum now,' Steve said.

I was speechless. 'Do you still want them?' Steve asked.

I nodded helplessly and Steve simply smiled at my stunned reaction. We both loved dogs and had discussed the possibility of my getting a couple of puppies in the past. Steve knew how much I liked Dobermans, and so he and Scott had decided to take the plunge. Steve was certain that it would help me find a new life for myself by becoming responsible for two lively Dobermans.

I was smitten. It did not take long for us to settle on their names – Mr Jonty for the boy and Stella for the girl. We were a family now. Scott, me, Mr Jonty and Stella.

Steve was right. The dogs ripped through our small house like a wonderful whirlwind. It was daunting at first, and it felt as if we really were looking after two hyper-active toddlers. Yet it was also invigorating to think about something happy and healthy and panting, with lolling pink tongues, rather than all my problems at the track.

'We're going to be busy these next two years,' I said to Scott as we gazed at our babies.

*　　*　　*

The night before I turned thirty, on 23 September 2010, I won the twenty-eighth National title of my career when I beat Becky James in the final of the individual sprint at the Manchester Velodrome. It was my ninth successive British sprint title – to add to the collection I had also won in the keirin, the team sprint and the 500m time trial. Becky, who rode well and beat Jess Varnish in the semi-final, was only half a wheel behind me in our second race. But it was more sobering for me to think that she had only been nine years old when I won my first National sprint championship. Becky called me 'The Queen of Sprinting' – which made me feel old rather than venerable.

Yet the emergence of Jess and Becky highlighted some progress for women. Anna Blyth had switched to endurance events but we now had three sprinters capable of competing at the highest level – and life seemed different at the velodrome. Even though I had more than ten years on both of them, and their lives were much less complicated than mine, they helped me feel less lonely. It was no longer just me and the men. I had Jess and Becky and they were starting to push me. I liked that sense of competition and it felt good that I'd been tested harder at a National championship than since my days as a raw novice.

They were still in an invidious position in regard to the Olympics. Only one slot would be available to a British rider in the sprint and the keirin and, for all my reluctance to continue riding, I had won gold and silver in the Worlds in Copenhagen. They did not have much time left to dislodge me before London 2012. Jess had resolved to nail down the starting position in the team sprint, alongside me, as it looked unlikely that Shanaze Reade could be wooed back to the track. Shanaze's views of track cycling politics, at least for sprinters, were about as flattering as mine. She preferred working in the simpler world of BMX riding. I didn't blame her. If I'd had Shanaze's skills I would have made the exact same choice.

Jess and Becky kept saying, 'Woahhh! You're going to be thirty!' as if I was about to receive a telegram from the Queen for turning 100. I had enough going on in my life without worrying about my age. I liked the look of thirty. It was a clean, round number, with the symmetry of a milestone.

As I reflected on my turbulent twenties I decided I had done alright over the last decade. I had achieved a lot, even if cycling often headed my list of meaningless activities, and I was proud of the way I had overcome the isolated trauma of Switzerland and found such happiness with Scott.

We decided to make 24 September 2010, my thirtieth, a special day. I settled on a facial in the morning, a tattoo in the afternoon and dinner with Scott in the evening. The facial and the dinner were my usual style. A tattoo was different. But I needed to mark the occasion with something more personal and lasting.

I considered having Scott's name inked into my skin. But I wanted something more, about us, on my right arm. It was only when I listened again to one of our favourite albums, *Siamese Dream* by The Smashing Pumpkins, that I found my answer. We both loved the record, and each track meant something to me. But the song which touched me most was called 'Today'. Whenever I thought of our giddiest early days, and Scott and me falling in love, 'Today' echoed through me. It was our song; and the song I had heard on the rollers in Beijing, just before I won the Olympic final.

The opening line, I decided, would be printed forever on my arm, in honour of Scott and me, of the day we fell in love, and of all we had been through the last two and a half years:

Today is the greatest day I've ever known

It also meant a lot to me because my twin, Alex, had introduced me first to The Smashing Pumpkins. Alex loves a sing-song and whenever we were in his car it seemed as if he was singing along, word for word, to the Pumpkins. So my tattoo would remind me of Alex and the Olympics and Scott.

The tattoo artist in Wilmslow was an impressive beast of a man. His flesh was covered in inky-blue tattoos, right down to his knuckles, and he played an old video of *Withnail and I* as he went about his work. He had no idea I was an Olympic champion. I was not about to tell him either because I would have hated to have said, in a hoity-toity voice, 'Do you know who I am? For I am Victoria Pendleton, MBE.'

The pain was disappointingly slight. I expected something more testing but it hardly seemed to hurt. I surprised the tattooed man, who decided that I was tougher than I looked. He could have used his needle and black ink to stencil the next few lines of the song into me. They would tell the world that I can't live for tomorrow and that I'll burn my eyes out and tear my heart out. Instead, I keep it short and sweet.

I'm being chased by a monster. The monster occupies a dark and malevolent shape. It's some kind of faceless killer, a cold murderer, intent on hunting me down. Closer and closer it comes; and harder and harder I pedal and run. I can't get away but, somehow, it can't quite catch me either. The hunting of me feels unending.

With a stifled scream, I sat upright in bed at home. I was suddenly wide awake, my flesh crawling and my heart racing. In the darkness and the silence, Scott slept peacefully next to me.

Another night, another nightmare.

It was the same old nightmare. It had begun a few months before my birthday and not even the new maturity of being thirty could take the edge off it. Each time it was raw and unsettling.

I had always experienced vivid and gory dreams. I'm not sure where they come from, because I don't watch horror movies, but they involve me being chased and then fighting off some kind of fiend. Dreaming about being chased by a killer was normal for me. But these nightmares were different. They were darker.

Scott looked mildly disturbed in the mornings when I told him about my recurring nightmares. But I reassured him. I understood the stress and tension of my life.

'I'm fine,' I told Scott demurely. 'It's just my conscious and subconscious having a little chat.'

One of my reasons for carrying on, for not just succumbing to my strongest instinct, hinged on Scott. Every day I was with him reinforced my awareness of how much he had given up for me. I could not easily reject cycling at the Olympics when he had made such a sacrifice for me. It would have felt as if the last two years had been wasted if I did not continue in pursuit of all we had planned.

Yet, in early October 2010, a letter for Scott arrived from the UK Borders Agency. It informed him that his visa to work in Britain had been revoked. As his situation at British Cycling had changed he was now without an official sponsor to support his work in the UK. We were already engaged but, still, Scott was instructed that he would have to leave the country by 31 October 2010. Scott had ten days to inform the Home Office of his exact departure date – which would have to occur within the next twenty-eight days.

The letter was delivered just before I was due to go into training. I was distraught.

The next few days passed in a blur. Scott established that he could not hope to overturn the ruling. He would have to return to Australia and reapply for a different visa on the grounds that we were engaged. We would need to supply detailed proof of our relationship over the previous two years, offering up love letters and bank statements to prove that ours would not be a marriage of convenience.

I had to continue training at the velodrome every day, despite our worry and hurt, and it was then that Jason Kenny unintentionally added to my distress. Jason spoke harshly to me. Without knowing what had happened to Scott and his visa he said that, if I insisted on looking so miserable, I might as well just quit. Jason missed Scott. He was angry that, because of me, he had lost the expert scientific analysis Scott had brought to assessments of his training and racing. Jason wished Scott and I could swap places.

Slowly, I undid my training shoes. I started to cry and then, slowly, I stood up. I walked away from Jason and everyone else.

Later that morning Jason came to find me and apologize. He had just heard of our visa strife and he said that he hadn't meant to speak so coldly to me. I accepted his apology but his words lingered in my head. He had simply said aloud what he and various other people in the velodrome seemed to think of me and Scott.

I was not quite sure how I would cope without Scott; but it would have been worse for him if I had just taken the easy way out and quit cycling. Scott remained passionate about elite sport, and he was already working in new consultancy roles. He also believed, if I shrugged off the doubts around me, I could produce something special in an Olympic year.

My concern over his visa situation escalated. So many obstacles had been placed in front of us, it was difficult to believe that luck would finally turn our way. But I would keep going to the velodrome, at least until we discovered Scott's fate. If he was refused entry back into Britain then I really would escape cycling and the country for good and go and live with my future husband in Australia.

Such domestic drama had a sad echo in Stotfold. Dad had finally moved out of our family home. My mother was relieved and I was impressed by her courage. She had lost three and a half stone, without going crazy on a diet, and had lived up to her promise by taking on an allotment. In her early sixties, it was difficult to start all over again but at least she had Nicola, Alex and me. They were still not talking to Dad. My own contact with him was minimal, but Dad knew of Scott's visa problems and my unhappiness at work. He tried to be support-ive but he also understood that, after all that had happened, he could say a limited amount to me. For so many years, anyway, he had only asked me about cycling and training rather than me and my emotions. It would take time for us to rebuild even our stilted relationship of the past.

My whole world, just before I turned thirty, was beset by flux and uncertainty. All I could do was hold on and hope that a rough ride would soon flatten out into a smooth stretch of life.

Scott flew to Australia the day before I travelled to Poland for the European Championships. A taxi picked me up early on the morning of Monday 1 November 2010. I looked bleakly out of the rain-spattered window as we sped through Wilmslow towards Manchester Airport, where I would meet the rest of the GB squad.

I could hardly believe how Scott had been treated at the airport. He had been due to fly on 30 October but the plane from Manchester was severely delayed and his flight was pushed back twenty-four hours. The airline announced that they would accommodate all the passengers in a nearby hotel. Scott explained that he lived just a short drive away. He asked if he could spend the night at home, with his fiancée, instead of in a bare hotel room.

Scott was made to feel like an illegal immigrant or a crimi-nal on bail. He was threatened and told that he would be arrested and deported permanently if he failed to return to the airport on time. We had to remind each other that a decision on his new visa application would be reached within twelve to sixteen weeks. His suitcase was crammed with as much information as we could find to prove the seriousness of our commitment and love.

Scott's rescheduled flight finally took off, with him on board, and I knew he would still be in the air as my taxi sped to the airport. In late November I would travel to Australia, to race and hopefully be reunited permanently with Scott in the sunshine. Before then, I faced three weeks without him and I already felt heart-sore.

At least Jess Varnish would soon be with me, as my team sprint partner; but an unglamorous championship loomed. It seemed a fittingly downbeat symbol for a barren period without Scott.

I had much work to do, however, in a bid to make up for all the time I had lost over the previous two years during my stand-off at the velodrome. It was vital I spend the next year building my strength. I was ready to sacrifice some of my speed and dedicate myself to a carefully structured training programme that would enable me to withstand the rigours of pursuing three different Olympic disciplines.

There would be fewer medals and victories during the next year, but I was prepared for that dip in my performances. Rather than chasing win after win I would make myself stronger and more resilient. It would be difficult, in my thirties, especially with my back suffering after eight years of flat-out racing, but I was ready to take the hit.

I decided to sidestep the Commonwealth Games in Delhi and compete in the Europeans – where I would ride only in the team event and the keirin. My chances against Meares and Guo over the next year would be affected but everything, hopefully, would be redeemed by performances of strength and quality at the 2012 Olympics. It was a calculated risk; but if I had remained on the same training routine I had used before Beijing I would be ruined long before London. So Scott and I resolved to stick to our plan. We needed to be brave and determined.

In Poland, in the familiar setting of Pruszków, Jess and I were fastest in team qualifying in 33.381 seconds – marginally quicker than our time earlier that year in Copenhagen. We were improving. Yet we were still inconsistent and, in the final, we were considerably slower. Our time of 33.586 gave the title to the experienced French duo of Clair and Sanchez. Our qualifying time would have been enough to win the final and so we could console ourselves with the thought that, when we rode properly, we were the best in Europe. But we'd still lost the race that mattered most in Poland; and we knew how far we lagged behind the Australians and the Chinese. We had time, though, and belief in each other.

My confidence in Jess also grew as, sitting on the sidelines during the sprint, I was impressed as she qualified second fastest in the individual sprint behind Olga Panarina. She was ahead of established riders like Krupeckaitė, Kanis, Shulika, Sanchez, Clair, Vogel and Welte. Shulika beat her in the second round but Jess won the repechage ahead of Welte and Baranova. She then lost to Panarina in the quarter-finals but was sixth overall. Jess was a serious competitor.

I raced in the keirin. I won my first heat, came second to Krupeckaitė in the next round but made a tactical mess of the final. Riding at the rear I hung back far too long, over-complicating my strategy by attempting to be too wily, and had far too much track to make up round the last bend. I finished fifth – behind Panarina, Krupeckaitė, Shulika and Clair – and left Poland without many regrets. It had been one of the most subdued championships of my career.

12 | VANQUISHED

An old year raced towards its end; and we skidded through the same old battles. On 1 December 2010, the day before the Melbourne World Cup, I was called into a showdown with Shane Sutton and Jan van Eijden. They thought it appropriate to force a face-to-face clash on the eve of my racing Anna Meares on her home turf. Our meeting ground on for an excruciating six hours.

My happy reunion in Australia with Scott had already been clouded by another dispute. Dave and Shane had decided to race me in the match sprint – despite my two-year Olympic training programme being tailored specifically to avoid the event in the immediate future. I wanted to focus on strength rather than speed and, also, step up my experience in the keirin and the team sprint. Shane, however, instructed me to earn more World Championship qualification points for the team by racing in the individual event.

In trying to justify my enforced participation they compared me to Theo Bos – the champion Dutch sprinter who had not raced much before the 2008 Olympics. He'd bombed in Beijing and quit the track soon afterwards. I knew Bos better than Shane and Jan did as we had often trained together at Fred Magné's academy. We could hardly have been more contrasting:

a confident Dutchman and an insecure Englishwoman. Whatever had happened to Bos had no bearing on my future.

They then suggested that, if I didn't learn to lose, the trauma of an unexpected defeat much closer to the Olympics might knock me off track. I looked at them like they were crazy.

'You shouldn't fear losing,' Shane said.

I wasn't afraid of losing; but what was the point of racing in a competition for which I had deliberately chosen not to prepare? Meares had worked hard for this event and had tapered her training perfectly. A win would boost her confidence after her failure to beat me once during the previous five years.

They also both knew that I had severe back pain. At first they thought it had been caused by the long flight but, without a GB physio in Melbourne, it became more worrying. I had to stop all weight work in the gym because I could not even do a squat with an empty bar.

Our emotions became increasingly heated and I made them revisit the fallout from Beijing. I turned to Jan. As we were in the midst of baring our souls maybe he could explain why he'd felt so 'betrayed'?

We went over the same old ground, going nowhere new. Jan wanted to return to our old happy routine, but he was still hurt by the way he had discovered the truth about me and Scott. Our deadlock remained.

I then challenged Shane – for he had forced his disastrous showdown with me and Scott in Beijing. Had he deliberately sabotaged my happiness as a new Olympic champion?

Shane launched a withering attack on Scott. He painted a grim picture of the man I loved.

'Don't you think this really hurts?' I asked Shane at one point, between the tears.

'You know I love you, Vic,' Shane said before resorting to the ritual standby: I was just like a '*daw-ter*' to him.

I was relieved not to be his real daughter. My deepest frustration stemmed from the fact they seemed to completely misunderstand my real character. It was as if they had no concept of my strengths and weaknesses. They were making a catastrophic mistake in forcing me into the match sprint – and it felt to me as if they would end up undermining my confidence. Strung-out and exhausted, I remembered how clearly I wanted to quit cycling earlier that year. The same bitter desire rose up in me again.

Shane's anger matched my own. He threatened that if I retired from cycling before the Olympics then I would be internationally blacklisted and no-one would ever want to work with me again. I had apparently, and single-handedly, created all the fuss about there being only one sprint event for women in Beijing. The hoo-hah had forced a seismic shift in the Olympic track programme. I would be ridiculed if I now shunned cycling and the London Games. It was time I just got on with my work and stopped whining.

We all felt wrecked at the end; and, as if obeying Shane's instruction, I got up and walked away from them in silence. We had hit an all-time low.

The Australians had their own strategy. Anna Meares was allowed to miss the team sprint and ride instead in the 500m time trial. It was a non-Olympic event but she loved it. And so, on 2 December, Meares and McCullough were missing from the list of team sprint starters.

I was reeling from the previous day's six-hour pummelling but Jess and I finished second in qualifying – behind the Chinese but ahead of France, the new European champions. In the final, Jinjie Gong and Guo Shuang beat us to the gold medal. It was still a useful experience – in contrast to the individual sprint where I had so much to lose.

The following morning, I recorded the third quickest time in qualifying behind Meares and Guo. It was Meares's first sub-11 time – 10.985 seconds. She was approaching the form of her life. I, meanwhile, faced an exceptionally tough first round match against Krupeckaitė, which I won, while Jess beat Yvonne Hijgenaar.

In the quarter-finals I lost to Jess for the first time in my career in heat one; but I came back strongly to beat her in the next two races. My lack of preparation, however, was evident. I also had the harder draw in the semis – up against Guo while Meares had the clear beating of Vogel.

Guo and I had hardly begun to race in our opening heat when she crashed and broke her collar bone. It was a distressing sight. I felt even more unnerved as I took my place in the final.

I was drawn to lead us out in heat one. Yet, with my head in a mess and my body unprepared for sprinting, there was little surprise when Meares steamed past me on the home straight to win by two lengths. The second race was better. I pushed her hard, but Meares held on. She was ecstatic to have beaten me for the first time since a World Cup event in Sydney in 2005.

'Victoria has dominated this event for the last five or six years,' Meares said, 'and it's been a long time between sprints for me to get a win over her. To be able to do it in front of my home crowd is extra special – but I don't think Vicky was quite at her best tonight. But a world champion like her is often scarier when she is not at her best because she has a habit of drawing on the emotions she needs to win.

'Tonight she couldn't do it and, honestly, it's huge for me to know I can still beat her. I haven't had that feeling for over five years. It's a massive psychological boost for me. It will give me a whole new approach every time I line up against her now. It gives me the fuel to make sure it continues to happen.'

We had handed Meares just the incentive she needed. 'Yeah,' Shane Sutton grunted. 'Maybe I made the wrong decision there ...'

I looked at him for a long time. 'Shane,' I eventually said, 'don't ever do that to me again.'

That Christmas, in 2010, marked a sad time. I arrived home in Stotfold on 24 December and, on Christmas Day, Mum and I went to see my granddad Alf. After a few months in hospital, he had deteriorated markedly. Mum had suggested I take in my medals to show Granddad – we thought it would help to remind him that, as he'd always promised me when I was a girl, I had become a 'champ'.

Granddad did not even recognize me. I held his hand and kissed him as he slid in and out of consciousness. Remembering all the days I had wasted in tangled disputes, I wished I had made the time to visit Granddad when he would have been able to talk to me. I slipped out of the ward and cried in the hallway.

Alf Viney died on Boxing Day – and I only smiled when Alex pointed out late the following afternoon that Arsenal, Granddad's football team, had just beaten Chelsea 3–1.

His beloved Gunners, Alex said, had given Granddad a three-gun salute. I cried again then; but my tears fell through our laughter.

A Monday morning in February, on a cold and rainy day in Manchester, offered another snapshot of the downbeat mood between me and my superiors at British Cycling. After three days of competition at the velodrome, during the last round of the 2010–11 World Cup series, Dave Brailsford was splashed across the national newspapers. His comments about me had unleashed predictable attention.

'Vicky has work to do for sure,' Dave had said when asked to assess my performances. 'She is where she is. This weekend was a true reflection of where she is at this moment. Compared to where she was in the build-up to the last Olympics she has more of a fight on her hands this time round. As is the case with everyone; if you want to be an Olympic champion you need to roll up your sleeves and get involved.'

The implication was that my sleeves were rolled down in prim and diffident fashion. They covered pale and demure arms which, presumably, were folded in a sulky stand-off as I declined to get stuck in alongside my hardworking coaches and colleagues.

Dave was effusive about Anna Meares. 'She has stepped up and you've got to admire the way she rides and conducts herself,' he said of my arch-rival. 'Meares is setting the pace. She's the woman to beat. She's got strengths in all three sprint events.'

Meares, galvanized by her victory over me in Melbourne two months earlier, had won gold in the team sprint and the match sprint at the World Cup in Manchester. I had won three medals – one silver and two bronze. Yet Meares had beaten me in two straight rides in the individual semi-final. She then overwhelmed Guo Shuang in the final while I defeated Olga Panarina to secure bronze. Jess Varnish and I, on the opening night, had lost the team final to Meares and Kaarle McCullough. But I thought it significant that Jess had broken the 19 second barrier for her starter's lap for the first time in her career. It felt to me as if we were on the path to some-where new.

I'd continued to concentrate on strength work in training because, for a long time, I had been unable to lift any weights in the gym. All the CT and MRI scans had confirmed that I had inflammation of the facet joints in my back. It was due to wear and tear after nearly ten years of professional cycling. I had lost all my power and form; and my training numbers were down.

It was essential that I remained committed to a conditioning programme meant to help me reach optimum condition in the summer of 2012 rather than the winter of 2011. My race strategy focused on the team sprint and the keirin; and so I was prepared to step back and even neglect the individual sprint for the next year. I knew I would absorb some big hits in the process.

Even a great sprinter like Chris Hoy was subject to setbacks. At the World Cup he won the keirin but was beaten in the semi-final of the individual sprint by Jason Kenny. His younger rival had edged ahead of him in the race for the sole British place in the match event at London 2012. Kenny still lost the final in Manchester and he, Hoy and Matt Crampton were beaten by France and Germany in the team sprint.

Shane Sutton professed his concern. 'People believe that we can just rock up and win medals,' he said of the contrast between public expectation and our own dip in performance, 'but it doesn't work like that. It is a cold, heartless business. The idea of going for everything could be the biggest mistake we ever make. You need to identify which medals you can win and give those events everything.'

Chris was bent on repeating his Beijing hat-trick in London, even though he would be thirty-six in August 2012. Then, I would be a month away from my own thirty-second birthday. Time was closing in and my body kept reminding me how many years had slipped away.

We had begun the Olympic countdown. On 21 February 2011, the day Dave and Shane were quoted in the newspapers, just over seventeen months remained for me and my fractured team to rebuild a sporting dream. It was difficult, but I still believed there were three medals for me to chase in London. I was not about to give up on them when determination surged deep inside me.

Irony, meanwhile, underpinned all the talk of rolled-up sleeves and tightly focused targets. Dave was immersed in Team Sky after a disappointing debut in the previous year's Tour de France. The road cyclists were under pressure. As the head of Team Sky, Dave himself was subject to intense scrutiny.

The track team's golden haul of medals had delivered a £24 million four-year deal with Team Sky for Dave's road riders. They were paid salaries, unlike us, and wherever they travelled they did not deign to sleep in ordinary hotel beds. Specially designed and portable Team Sky beds were laid out every night to ensure the road cyclists were well rested. There were no such fripperies for the track team.

Shane could not help himself. His sheer enthusiasm for Team Sky meant that he regularly pointed out their sleek and stylish kit, their smart Notebooks and fleet of new support cars. He also told us about the road team's outstanding chefs who cooked food as tasty as it was healthy. Shane did not mean to do it, but his extreme positivity for Team Sky felt negative, at least to me, to all of us on the track.

It was also notable that, within the track squad, Dave and Shane showed a definite allegiance to the pursuit riders. And, amongst these, Team Sky's Brad Wiggins was king. I was a Brad fan – but it was hard not to smile knowingly whenever he showed up for a rare session on the track. It had become a standing joke after one occasion when, as soon as Brad's session was done for the day, the clank and clunk of the boiler being shut down resounded. Presumably, as sprinters, we were considered hardy souls who could train in the cold.

On the train from Manchester Piccadilly to London Euston that Monday afternoon, staring at the green fields and grey skies flashing past my window in a bleached blur, Shane's words echoed in my head. He was right. We worked in a cold and heartless business. I knew the months ahead would be even more testing.

They called it the 'Pringle'. Yet the Olympic Velodrome was so elegantly beautiful, a smooth and curving architectural master-piece, that it seemed ridiculous to compare it to a mere crisp. The swooping symmetry of its design meant that some people believed it resembled the sleek saddle of a bike, or the steep banking of the track inside. Others praised its artistry by comparing it to a Stradivarius violin. To me it was just a gorgeous building.

Where else, but here, in London, would I want to ride my last races?

The Velodrome was officially opened on the morning of 22 February and, alongside other members of the GB squad, I was allowed to ride around the track. Before then, of course, Sir Chris was nabbed by Boris Johnson and Sebastian Coe while I tried to duck out of answering the same old questions over and over again. I did not have much luck. I must have done thirty vox-pop interviews with television, radio and newspaper reporters. The same four questions made a square pattern of recurring predictability.

'Are you excited about competing in an Olympic Games at home?'

'How are you coping with the pressure?'

'What would it mean to win a gold medal in London?'

'Can you match Sir Chris Hoy this time?'

I stuck to my stock answers. I was 'very excited – obviously'. The pressure was 'quite hard – but I'm trying not to think about it!' It would make me, in my own personal quest for the quote of the day, 'super-duper excited' to win another gold medal. As for the last one: well, Sir Chris was 'a legend ... you can't really keep up with a legend, can you?'

In an effort to make my answers sound droll I laughed a lot when I said them out loud. I had to do something to turn myself into a sound-bite machine.

That same afternoon I did a fashion shoot for a woman's magazine. It was not quite as glamorous as I'd hoped. They applied my make-up in a portakabin tucked away down a side-street in south London and then, all afternoon, in the February cold, I trudged up and down a path in a park, pushing a bike and doing my best to look pretty, while the photographer became agitated as the winter sun faded from a sludgy sky. Young mothers stopped hurrying home and, pausing with their prams and friends in the park, watched me strut my stuff. I could tell that most of them weren't quite sure who I was or why I was holding onto a bicycle with a smile of fixed intent.

'A couple more,' the photographer urged.

'Of course,' I said with a professionally cheerful lilt in my voice.

Secretly, after three days of bruising competition in Manchester and a morning inside the Olympic Velodrome, I was shattered. I also missed Scott, Mr Jonty and Stella. Scott had been allowed back in the country, as my fiancé, and he was in Wilmslow, looking after our two big Dobermans. I longed to be back home again with them all – stretched out on my sofa and dreaming of not moving for a very long time.

There was no respite. Training was cranked up in the gym and on the track but, still suffering from my back injury, I could not undertake the concentrated strength programme I needed. I lost so much muscle that I knew my hard work would be of no direct benefit during the World Championships that began in Apeldoorn on 24 March 2011. It would take much longer for my muscle-mass to return and for any real gain in strength and power to emerge. In the meantime, watched closely by my rivals and coaches, I had to withstand the agony of competition.

If it was left to me, in a dream world, I would train and avoid racing. I am the opposite to many of my contemporaries in elite sport. For many sportsmen and women, especially those approaching the end of their careers, the hard grind of training is the most hateful aspect of their work. They moan about the draining tedium every day. Competition, instead, is a release – a battleground where they feel alive and exhilarated. But I was sick of racing. I was tired of the nerves and the stress. I wished I could just work in the gym with Mark Simpson, my friend and strength-and-conditioning coach, or at the laboratory at the English Institute of Sport where Jonathan Leeder and Paul Barratt were lovely and uncomplicated. They churned out the scientific data which, with Scott's help in analysing the stats, encouraged me to believe I would eventually become more resilient. I might have complained, almost every day, that I was 'rubbish' – but Scott and the EIS numbers told me I was wrong. I just needed time to rebuild my muscle. Once that was achieved I would, steadily, get better and stronger.

On the track, most of my training was geared to the keirin and, especially, my partnership with Jess. We worked together effectively and, out of the three events, the team sprint intrigued me most. I had begun to believe that, in the next year, we might challenge for the gold medal.

Apeldoorn is sixty miles southeast of Amsterdam. Jess and I shared a hotel room and I was struck again by her maturity at nineteen. She was motivated, yet contained, and I knew I could rely on her.

On Thursday 24 March, Jess recorded the best start of her career with an opening lap of 18.992. Meares was quicker, at 18.698, but I could make a little time back against most second riders. I rode my lap in 14.364, benefiting from the momentum of following Jess rather than beginning from a standing start, while McCullough clocked 14.664. I had eaten into their lead but Australia qualified fastest. We were behind them, but ahead of China and France.

We both rode quicker in the final, with Jess recording another PB. Australia still beat us. They had won their expected gold but we had established ourselves as the next best team in the world.

Iain Dyer, as our sprint coach facilitator, rightly hailed Jess's improvement as 'a fantastic trend of progress which is very linear and very strong'.

My own progress, after nine years as a professional track cyclist, was inevitably more complex. It certainly wasn't 'linear' because side-steps and backward steps were also entailed. I was prepared for both as we moved into Friday's individual sprint. I qualified sixth behind Panarina, Meares, Shulika, Guo and Krupeckaitė. I soon felt sharper. Having beaten Baranova and Becky James in my first two knockout heats, I moved into the quarter-finals. There, I dispatched Shulika without needing a deciding third ride. It had been a relatively calm day.

It was meant to be the final but Meares and I were drawn, instead, against each other in Saturday's second semi. Krupeckaitė needed three rides to defeat Panarina, having lost the first heat. I would have to try and follow a similar route after, in race one, Meares surged past me on turn two of our final lap and chalked up a dominant victory. She had won the last five races between us – ever since, fifteen weeks earlier, Shane and Dave had forced me to compete in the sprint against her in Melbourne.

Meares, after five barren years against me, had regained her belief. She no longer avoided eye contact as we waited to race at trackside. It was as if she had finally discovered her taste for battle again. On the rollers, Jan and Shane urged me to fight back and impose myself. I nodded, but their words drifted over my head. A silent resolve took hold of me. I could not easily bear the thought of a sixth straight loss.

Race two was close but, when Meares hesitated briefly, I gained a significant jump on her. I clinched the win in straight-forward style. 1–1.

I hoped Meares would crumble. It helped that she led us out and watched me over her shoulder in heat three. I could wait until the moment I shot out of her slipstream. Meares, however, drew me up to the railing and angled her bike to a near stand-still. It was a tactic she had used effectively against me in Manchester. I was not about to surrender this time. She rolled on a little further and tried again. We stood tall in our clamps, legs and bikes quivering as we waited to see who would crack first.

Meares was denied, and denied again. Incredibly, she tried for a fourth time and, eventually, she got me. Meares later admitted, 'I was so nervous – my foot was shaking on the pedal and I couldn't steady the stance. On the fourth attempt I finally got her to take the front. It's always nerve-wracking doing a standstill in front of a crowd like this, but with so much hinging on that race it was a case of do or die. I knew that I wanted to be riding from the back, and yeah, it worked.'

I cursed silently as I was forced to slide past her and take the lead. We weaved this way and that and, again, she was happy as I led her back up the ramp. It was a tactical error because it offered her the chance to suddenly dive under me and produce the burst of acceleration that gave her the lead as we made the last frantic dash for the line. There were only millimetres between as we flashed across the line. Meares had edged it; but I should have won.

Meares then beat Krupeckaitė in two straight rides in the final. Rather than my fifth straight World sprint title in a row,

Meares had her first individual crown. It was her seventh rainbow jersey in total – after three each in the time trial and team sprint – but she was thrilled to have finally won the race that mattered most. 'In ten years in the senior ranks,' Meares said, 'I've been a silver medallist, been a bronze medallist, been fourth, been not even in the picture on occasion. We've worked on every little aspect we possibly could to make this happen tonight and it feels so good. I looked at that race as if it was my final. I tried to bring out everything possible to beat her.'

I joined Meares and Krupeckaitė on the podium, having defeated Panarina in the bronze race, and tried to look gracious as the new champion waved jubilantly. For the first time since March 2007, exactly four years previously, I was devoid of my World title.

The doubts and queries rolled in and I struggled to deflect them. I hate making excuses, and there were just too many complicated troubles to explain, and so I just about held myself together after Apeldoorn.

'I think for me the Olympics are now so big,' I told the press, 'that I find it hard to get up for the World Championships. It's like this one doesn't matter – it's all about 2012. I feel like everything has moved down a rung. The Worlds feel like a World Cup. The World Cups feel like the Nationals and the Nationals might as well be Thursday track league. London 2012 is so off the scale it's quite difficult to get as geed up for these competitions.'

At the same time I sent out a reminder. 'I made a commitment to a two-year programme. I'm sure it was right. I did a lot of strength work and it did take away my speed. I knew it would but you have to step back to move forward. I'm very confident that what I've gained this year will come through. I've done it before and I can do it again.'

I was asked, increasingly, about Anna Meares. 'She didn't beat me in my best form,' I said. 'I'm definitely under par and she's in the form of her life so it's difficult to compare. I'm not really focusing on Anna's performance.'

Meares had also won the keirin in Apeldoorn, while I finished seventh, having been reduced to victory in the 'B' final for those riders outside the top six. Her clean sweep matched my achievement in Palma in 2007. There were widespread predictions, as much in the British press as the Australian papers, that Meares had my number – and would inevitably assume my Olympic role in 2012.

We had reached such an impasse at the velodrome that something had to be done. The loss of my world title had shaken the coaching establishment. Dave, Shane, Jan and Iain met to discuss what they might do next. Someone suggested they bring back Scott. Shane was dubious. He said that Scott had caused all our problems in the first place by breaking the rules of protocol which are meant to keep a necessary emotional, romantic and sexual distance between a coach and an athlete. But they knew, in a grudging admission, that we had to restore some of our lost balance as a team. I missed Scott and, most of all, I needed Scott. If he returned I would be able to work with them again.

A climb-down was agreed and negotiations were brokered. Scott would work for British Cycling on a part-time basis with the express purpose of helping me prepare mentally and physically for the London Olympics.

It represented a significant moment – and my mood was boosted further as Mark Simpson received some new belt-squat equipment that enabled me to return to the strength work I had been forced to abandon after injuring my back in Melbourne.

Scott wanted to ease me slowly back into racing, and to concentrate on building my strength, but Shane insisted I return to sprint competition. I was equally sure that I needed training, rather than match-sprinting, and so a compromise was reached. Instead of riding in all the World Cups I would concentrate on the European Championships – as victory there would guarantee my place in the next World Championships.

As the seasons changed, and the temperatures plummeted, fate relished the cruel trick of sending me back to Apeldoorn for my next test. In a quirky twist of scheduling, the 2011 European Championships were held in the very same velodrome where I had lost my World title.

So, in late October, we returned to the same sleepy Dutch town and the exact same hotel. Jess and I could have sworn we were assigned the same room we had stayed in earlier that year. At breakfast they still paraded the same sign which offered a choice of 'Cheese' or 'Old Cheese.' They meant 'mature' rather than old cheese, we guessed, but we ate in a separate enclave where we were provided with a more suitable breakfast choice.

The track team budget, however, still did not extend to the perfect Team Sky beds that followed the road racers around Europe. Jess and I lay on our soft and lumpy hotel beds and got set for a *Downtown Abbey* extravaganza. We'd brought the box-set with us and, at night, we planned to devour one episode after another as if tucking into a girly box of chocolates. It was one way to beat the boredom.

On our third night, the first of competition, Jess and I raced together. It made for an unusual opening because, due to a technical problem with the gate, they needed to resort to a hand-held start in Apeldoorn. Rather than bursting out of the gate, Jess initially held on to Iain Dyer. And then, at the gun, she had to push away from that strange position for a team sprint. The painted lines on the track were slippery and it was a struggle not to skid behind Jess's wheel on her lead lap. Finding some grip, eventually, we qualified fastest ahead of Lithuania, Russia, Germany, Netherlands and France – who all included more renowned riders than Jess.

It was easier in the final. Jess was not far behind Ukraine's formidable Lyubov Shulika on the opening lap and she presented me with the perfect platform to outsprint Olena Tsos and win in a time of 33.276 seconds. We had won our first major title together and Jess, rightly, smiled with pride.

I thought I had done 'alright', the phrase I used to describe my lap to the media, but I was far happier discussing my team-mate: 'Jess has progressed massively,' I said. 'She's very mature and she astounds me every day. When I was her age I was a mess. But Jess has committed herself 100% to this role – which is to be the lead-out rider in our team. When someone is that focused and driven they're going to be a force to be reckoned with. I think the time we rode could have won us a World Championship medal.'

We were just outside Australia's winning time in Apeldoorn earlier that year but, significantly, we had entered Meares–McCullough territory.

On the podium, Jess and I were presented with gold medals, tulips and a pair each of small wooden clogs. We celebrated in more obviously English fashion, after an 11pm meal at the hotel, by watching another episode of *Downtown Abbey*. I could have done with another, to help me switch off, but I needed to at least attempt to sleep before a long day in the sprint.

We woke early on an icy cold but sunlit Saturday morning. Getting out of bed I looked pale and concentrated as I stared at myself in the mirror. The pattern was set: another day, another shattering series of races. I would not have to face Meares or Guo; but the pool of talent ran deep. The east Europeans would be flying. Chatting to the French and the

Germans and the Dutch, we always speculated why the women from the east seemed to do better at events when drug-testing procedures were more relaxed.

Jess and I ate breakfast with the rest of a muted team. It was no time for deep conversations or witty repartee. Chris Hoy, in particular, felt grim. He was suffering from flu and did not look as if he should be riding; but trailing Jason Kenny in the pecking order he could not afford to show any weakness.

As we caught the small bus to the velodrome, Chris said he would try and ride through the lurgy. Jason and Jess were with us as we sped through the deserted streets. We were let off near the entrance and I walked behind the others. A black beanie covered my head and, wearing a GB tracksuit and carrying a backpack, I looked ready for another day at work.

I drifted past some familiar faces – a writer and a film crew I knew – but kept my head down low. My gaze was fixed instead on a corridor that led like a dingy artery into the heart of the velodrome. At the end of the passage, up the stairs and out into the arena, I headed straight for the rollers in our corner near the track. The beanie disappeared and I slipped on tinted racing glasses. I climbed aboard the stationary bike.

Slowly, with my tiny earphones plugged in, I began to pump my legs in the old warm-up routine that had eaten up so many hours of my life.

In a half-empty velodrome my face felt drawn and tense. It seemed to show the darker stories of my life.

Shane Sutton watched me from a distance. After a while, he came over to talk to me.

'Just go through the process,' Shane said as he stood alongside the rollers. 'Don't get anxious.'

'No,' I murmured.

'You're going well enough,' Shane suggested.

'Yeah,' I nodded.

'Last night you looked really good,' Shane said. 'That last lap you looked real good.'

I kept quiet and pedalled a little harder.

'This ain't the time to get anxious,' Shane said.

'Yeah,' I said flatly.

The silence stretched out between us. 'You'll be fine,' Shane promised, as I deliberately looked away from him. 'Feel good.'

I knew that Shane and all the men on the team still could not quite understand how, over the past seven years, since first becoming a world champion, I could be so successful and so vulnerable at the same time. They kept saying the same set of words to me: 'Don't get anxious ... Feel good,' or 'Just get on with it, Vic, what's all the faffing about?' It was difficult for them to fathom how desperately upset I became whenever I failed and how negative I remained about my performances.

Chris and Jason didn't appear to suffer from insecurities; and, even if they did, they would never expose themselves to Shane or anyone else. They kept their doubts to themselves. In Apeldoorn I felt the usual response. The team didn't admire me for revealing my vulnerability. I think they saw it as a weakness.

Jan told me that, in being so honest, I gave my opponents an advantage over me. He advised me to stop being so candid. I shrugged and said, 'If only ...'

As always, the individual sprint began with a time trial to determine the seedings for the knockout rounds. I finished fourth quickest and in round one I easily beat Gabriele Jankute from Lithuania. But a superior Lithuanian, the redoubtable Simona Krupeckaitė, loomed. It was hard to face her so early in the competition – at a stage when only one race would decide who'd qualify automatically for the next round.

Jan led me out onto the track. I climbed aboard the black bike and wrapped my left arm around Jan's broad shoulders. He could sense the tension churning through my body, which pressed against his, and so he spoke almost tenderly to me. 'I'll give you a big push from the back again,' he said softly, as if I had never done a sprint before in my life. 'Let me do the work.'

'Yeah,' I replied, hearing the blankness in my voice.

'You'll be alright,' Jan said, trying to reassure me in those last fraught moments.

I nodded slightly as my hushed voice echoed the same old word: 'Yeah.'

We went back into battle and, despite rising early out of my saddle in an attempt to find more power, I could not hold off Krupeckaitė.

I was miserable – even though I could remain in the competition if I won one of two repechages for losing riders. As the winners relaxed there was no other option for me but to stay on my bike. I rode round and round, my incessant circling taking me right past the press tables and my most stringent critics.

Dave Brailsford and Shane Sutton, on top of their usual perch of a mobile staircase in the middle of the velodrome, watched closely as Jess and I prepared for our repechage. We occupied opposite ends of a golden era for British cycling. I represented the ground-breaking past, but Jess, alongside other young riders like Becky James, Dani King and Laura Trott, symbolized the future.

I stayed strong and beat both Varnish and Miriam Welte to reach the quarter-finals through the back door. It was not quite the entrance expected of a five-time world champion.

More trouble lurked in the squat shape of Shulika. We had defeated her in the team sprint but an individual match seemed different. Shulika sauntered around the pits, as if calling me out for an early scrap. Her legs and rear rippled with power.

I pulled on the black helmet again, feeling the weight of it on my head. As I rolled down the visor I was aware that my mouth looked much more delicate than Shulika's grimace.

I led us out. Shulika hung a long way back so that I was almost craning my neck to keep track of her. The white flash running down the middle of her helmet acted like a beacon. Shulika didn't mind. She was happy to keep me occupied. Slowly, the tension ratcheting up with every lap of our cat-and-mouse prelude, I increased the pace. And then, half a lap before the bell, I began to race. Down the back straight, I heard the guttural sound of her coach, a hulking man, as he gave Shulika the signal to attack. He barked like a big old seal: '*Hup … hup … hup …!*'

Jan's voice also reverberated above the crowd, but I couldn't react quickly enough. Shulika was out of her seat first. She drove hard. Her blue and yellow top hurtled towards me on the final lap.

Shulika was soon on my shoulder. As we approached the final turn I should have been in my element for, over the last twenty-five metres of track, I normally want the win more than any opponent of mine.

But, almost inexorably, Shulika closed the gap. '*Hup … hup … hup …!*' the Ukrainian seal bellowed. Shulika drew level. And then, in a blur, she powered past me. Shulika won by centimetres.

Needing to win the next two races, I returned to the rollers. I pedalled and pedalled, trying to convince myself I could come back.

A few metres away, Jan and Shane consulted quietly. 'I think Vic is just starting to dip,' Jan said.

'Is she?' Shane asked, even though he already knew the answer. He looked at me as I kept my head down, lost in post-race fatigue.

'She can do this,' Shane said with urgency to Jan. 'You've got to get fucking into her. Get into her.'

Jan walked over to me once I was back in my chair. 'Come on, Vic,' he said as he tried to turn my attention to the next race. 'You ready for this?'

He was a sensitive man and, gazing at me, he understood that there was no point in letting rip with a big speech. Jan patted me on my leg when I didn't answer.

'C'mon,' he said gently, 'I know you want to.'

I looked up at him and smiled wanly. It was my way of telling him I would try again.

We opted for a slightly higher gear against Shulika. It was risky but, at the death, I would have something hard to press down against. I needed to do something out of the ordinary to compensate for my lack of sprint training.

Shulika led us out in race two. She had clearly watched Meares against me in the Worlds for she brought her bike to a standstill. Shulika wanted me to assume the lead. I denied her. She tried again about ten metres later. Again, my legs were strong enough to lock my bike to a stop behind her for fifteen seconds or more. Finally, she conceded and accepted the lead.

I waited and waited and, at the penultimate turn, I was in a perfect position, tucked just behind Shulika. I switched to the outside, bang on course to nail her on the last straight. I worked hard but a big chunk of my speed was missing. Shulika just held me off. She had beaten me in successive rides.

As we circled the track on our warm-down lap, Shulika waited for me. She leaned across and, in a gesture of sympathy for a former champion who had been vanquished again, Shulika rested her left hand briefly on my right shoulder. She gazed down at me and, through my dark visor, I nodded.

In the pits, I felt wretched. Jan spoke gently to me. 'From a tactics point of view that was really, really good,' he said as he tried to find something positive amid all my pain. 'I'm really pleased with that ...'

I knew Jan was not used to complimenting me in defeat. 'It just didn't work,' I said bleakly. 'I just didn't do it right.'

The indignity was not yet over. Three hours later, having briefly escaped to the hotel, I was back again on the start line for the humiliating ride-off to decide places five to eight. We looked a decent quartet – Krupeckaitė, Vogel, Clair and me – but I was the worst of us. I had nothing left. I finished last.

Shane Sutton found me. He spoke some words that I didn't really hear about picking myself up.

'I hate this,' I said simply.

'You don't, Vic,' Shane argued. 'Not really.'

I looked up at the coach with whom I had shared so much, good and bad, for so many years. Shane knew I meant it. He could see my suffering.

I pulled on the black beanie. I zipped up my GB top. I wanted to escape.

Apeldoorn had caused me such grief in 2011. I had lost my rainbow jersey there; and on that same track I had fallen to a new low. I wondered if my rivals would laugh at my European results.

I may be vulnerable, but I am also intensely proud. On the frame of my black bike, in a jokey tribute to that pride and my regal reputation, my mechanics Ernie Feargrieve and Mark Ingram had attached a sticker of their name for me: *Queen Vic*.

There was nothing regal about me as I added another layer and pulled the hood up over my head. My eyes glazed with tears, I left the arena on my own, disappearing into the night like a vanquished champion stripped of her power.

At the exit I saw a familiar figure. Daniel Gisiger, who had been the UCI's endurance track coach at the academy in Aigle, when I had fallen so hard as a young girl in Switzerland, could see the hurt etched into my face. He had always supported me in Aigle; and he did so again in Apeldoorn.

Daniel spoke softly to me as I drifted past: 'You'll always be a great champion and a role model – whatever happens. Remember this.'

His words rang through me and, as a small thank you, I nodded to him. But the pain ran so deep that I could not speak as the cold and the dark of a winter night enveloped me.

Apeldoorn, Holland, 23 October 2011

Courage was needed that lonely Sunday morning. In my hotel room I sat up slowly in bed, knowing it would be the start of an unyielding process that had to end with me climbing back on my bike. I just wanted to be with Scott, but he was still banished from the team. Scott stayed at home with Mr Jonty and Stella – our Dobermans. He was still in the doghouse.

Even the thought of going downstairs for a hotel breakfast felt hard. But I braved my team-mates and exchanged a few words with Chris Hoy. He had been forced to withdraw midway through the previous day's sprint programme. A chest infection had since been diagnosed. Chris waved goodbye to us all.

Hunched over a small bowl of fruit I wished I could catch the same plane back to Manchester. I forced a few more small segments of orange into my mouth. I chewed dutifully and talked to Jess. Everyone felt deflated because not one British medal had been won the night before.

I needed to be strong even though I felt so wounded. Scott, on the phone, and Steve, in person, had both attempted to boost me. The truth remained. I had to try and salvage something from the wreckage.

We returned to the track in Apeldoorn one last time. The keirin was often a lottery – but I needed to use it as a way of changing my luck. I had to break the pattern of negativity and defeat.

Fourteen riders were divided into two heats of seven. In my heat, scanning the list of riders, I knew I should only feel concerned about the electric pace and experience of Krupeckaitė – the 2010 world champion in the keirin. But my confidence was minimal, my expectations muted. Only the first two riders would qualify automatically for the second round. Everyone else would be condemned to the repechage.

Krupeckaitė had demolished me in the match sprint twenty-four hours earlier but I calmed myself. The keirin, being so unpredictable, was different. I had as good a chance as anyone as long as my mind was right and I stayed out of trouble. I resolved to attack early and control the pace of the race from the front.

I slotted into second place from the opening lap and, glancing coolly over my shoulder to monitor the movements of the five women behind me, I held my nerve until the derny peeled away. And then I raced hard. I won, using strength and power rather than pure speed. Krupeckaitė was edged into third place by Spain's Tania Calvo Barbero. I could relax during the repechage heats.

In the semi-final I was drawn once more in heat two, with Krupeckaitė, Varnish, Vogel, Kanis, Baranova and Streltsova. I moved quickly into second place and maintained my position for the next four-and-a-half laps. Once the motorbike left the track I switched on the burners. Baranova snatched the win on the line but I was ahead of Krupeckaitė. All three of us were safely through.

In the final we were joined by Vogel, Sanchez and Clair. My luck seemed to have run out. I was assigned the last position in the draw. There was little I could do but ride and wait. We followed the little man in the helmet as his pedal-powered motorbike led us round and round the track in a stately cavalcade. Music blared and the Dutch commentator barked out our names over the trackside speakers: *'Baranova ... Vogel ... Sanchez ... Krupeckaitė ... Clair ... Pendleton ...'*

We held our position until finally the motorbike slid across the pale blue ring and off the track. As if some kind of magic took hold of me, my legs began to pump effortlessly and rhythmically. My bike surged forward into fourth place. When we hit the back straight of the second last lap I was out of my saddle and just behind Baranova and Vogel. I raced within myself for another lap and then only Vogel remained between me and the lead.

The commentator sounded excited: 'Pendleton is coming ... Pendleton is coming ...' he roared. At the next turn I was level with Vogel, on her outside, with Sanchez chasing us in third place.

The bell rang for the last round. I was away, showing all my old velocity and snap. They were never going to catch me. I looked in another world as the others strained over their handlebars, their helmets down, while my head stayed upright. I gazed straight ahead as I flashed across the line, a decisive winner.

'Pendleton!' the commentator cried again. 'A big win ... *Pendleton!*'

Shane Sutton was waiting as I entered the pits on my bike. He said one word twice to describe my ride: 'Beautiful ... beautiful ...'

Jan simply smiled and patted me on the back. I was whisked away to meet the British press.

'I didn't expect that,' I confessed. 'But I just tried to relax. Yesterday was hard because I wasn't ready. And it's never nice, when you're used to winning, to get knocked out like that. But I knew my training was perhaps better suited to a longer event than a shorter, more explosive one. I just kept thinking, "Have confidence and try to enjoy it."'

The reporters grinned as I smiled at that rare use of the word 'enjoy' in relation to my racing. But my eyes welled up as I spoke a little more: 'Yesterday, I wondered whether I had what it takes to compete here with the training I've done. I was annoyed for letting myself down. So I told myself: "Today's a new day." I was determined that this time I would take courage in the work I've been doing.'

For a moment I could not talk for fear of crying. But I gathered myself. 'You know, Shulika beat me in two rides and I just thought, "Aarrghhh … focus on tomorrow. You can't go back." The sprint is sometimes like a toss of a coin. Sometimes it's heads, sometimes it's tails. Yesterday I had a lot of tails. Usually it doesn't go that way – so hopefully I've got some heads-credit.'

Someone asked if my win marked a turning point. 'I think so,' I said. 'It hasn't been great lately. I didn't conclude the season in the form I wanted and it was a knock to my confidence. The worst thing you can do is to start doubting everything. As soon as you do, you start spiralling down. I'm an emotional person, you know, and it happens a lot.'

The tears fell then, but they were streaked with relief and, almost, happiness. I had done it. I was on my way back. I was still a champion. 'This year hasn't been my best year but, you know what?' I murmured, my voice almost cracking before I answered my own question with conviction. 'I'm going to try my damn hardest to make sure 2012 is my year.'

13 | THE COMEBACK

The battle at the Manchester Velodrome softened and turned. Apeldoorn had changed everything in 2011. Losing my sprint title at the World Championships was a hard blow; but agony and defeat during the sprint at the Europeans had unsettled British Cycling still further. The old team – Iain, Jan and Scott – needed to click back into place in an attempt to lift me up. We all knew there had been too much hurt to rekindle exactly what we'd once had. But we were professionals and, gradually, we found a new way of working together.

Jan and Scott gelled and my loneliness ebbed away. It became possible again to discuss race tactics with Jan and to feel a semblance of unity in our camp. I even began to laugh inside the heart of the velodrome. After Jan and I sprinted against each other on the track during training we would join the rest of the team in the inner ring. We'd crowd around Scott's laptop and there was amusement whenever I claimed, yet again, that I had been 'rubbish.' Scott's stats and numbers disproved me most of the time. I was growing stronger; I was getting faster.

There were still moments of sadness and anger. It irked me that essential backroom staff received no real recognition of their contribution to the success of the team. I was devastated when, in December 2011, British Cycling lost Mark Simpson, our head of strength and conditioning, to a new role in the NBA with the Oklahoma Thunder. Mark had been a real friend, and one of my closest allies, and I always regretted that his work had never been fully acknowledged, simply because it took place during the private rituals of training.

They did not fight hard to keep him. Instead, there was more concern that I hung out in the office and nattered away with some of the administrative staff – like my friend Denise Yarrow. We were reminded that it was 'not appropriate' for athletes and staff to forge friendships. A draconian rule was imposed: Denise and I were banned from chatting together during lunchtime. My workplace was not quite as warm and flexible as some might have expected.

I knew it was best to turn away and get back to work. Jan, Scott and I were trying to build something between us again. We were a team. We were on our way. We were trying to regain everything we had lost since the Beijing summer of 2008. We could, at last, look ahead to the biggest year of our lives.

The Olympic Velodrome, Stratford, London, 17 February 2012

The noise was ridiculous. It was crazy. It was good. Jess Varnish and I looked at each other and, wordlessly, we communicated. 'This is what it's going to be like, Jess,' my gaze told her, imagining the London Olympics. Yet, to ease that intensity, I offered a small, encouraging smile. 'Relax,' my look silently reminded Jess. 'Breathe. Concentrate. You're ready. We've done the work. Let's go.' Jess smiled nervously but, also, with a flicker of intent.

We had reached the team sprint final in the London World Cup – which doubled as the first test event at the Olympic

Velodrome – and were minutes away from racing Anna Meares and Kaarle McCullough. The velodrome was bursting with a Friday night crowd. They were roaring even before we reached the track.

Jess's name was said first and, then, it was my turn. Amid the bedlam I had to resort to my own hushed reminder: '*Relax. Breathe. Concentrate. You're ready. We've done the work. Let's go.*'

Meares and McCullough were ready. Six hours earlier, during qualification, they had torn around the Olympic track at speed. They not only set the fastest time of the day; Meares and McCullough smashed the world record by completing the two-lap team sprint in 32.828 seconds. They were building towards a crescendo in an Olympic year – and the cycling experts were convinced it was all over. Meares and McCullough were unstoppable; and Meares would be just as crushing in the individual event.

Jess and I, meanwhile, were quietly pleased with ourselves. We were happy to be in the final, having recorded a time of 32.966. It was, at least, the fastest we had ever ridden and, therefore, a British record. We were also quicker than the Chinese and the French; and the chance to race in an evening final was the marker we needed to measure ourselves against the three-time world champions.

Meares sounded even happier. 'This is the best possible outcome we could have hoped for,' she said. 'An Australian–British final is the closest thing to the Olympic Games in terms of atmosphere – so win or lose we will get a lot out of this.'

We operated in starker terms. 'It's shit or bust,' I had said to Jess and Jan an hour earlier as we'd pondered how we might match the Australians. I knew we had to gamble. We had experimented with gears in training but, during qualifying, we'd reverted to type. But a normal routine was never going to unhinge Meares and McCullough. We needed something dramatic.

'Why don't we try it?' I said, after it was suggested that Jess should gear down a little while I geared up in a big jump. When Shanaze Reade and I won our first team sprint World Championship in 2007 I had ridden a 92" gear. I was ready to gear up to a 96". The deficit in gear size between Jess and me would be huge. She would start so much more quickly than me. My big old clunky 96" would take much longer to wind up. But, once up to speed, I would have so much more to press on.

'Let's do it,' Jan said.

'Cool,' I'd murmured. But I didn't say out loud the thought that suddenly reared up in my head: 'God, please let me get on Jess's wheel. Please ...'

At trackside, in our seats, just minutes before the final, I blew on my hands, trying to dry the liquid chalk so my grip was optimal. My fingernails had been painted bright red. I clenched my fists, readying myself for the moment I could stamp down on the 96" monster.

The same pleading phrase echoed again in my head: '*God, please let me get on Jess's wheel. Please ...*'

Jess often worried about disappointing me; and I felt the same acute responsibility. I knew how hard she had worked for this moment. Every start she made in training at the velodrome was from the gate – and she had made over 500 starts in preparation for this ride. I could not bear the thought of letting her down.

I felt edgy as we walked to the track. We were unsure whether the gears would work, but we hoped we had much more to offer in the final – as long as I could crank it up fast enough while Jess flew ahead of me.

My mind was diverted from both divine beseeching and gearing technicalities by the raw noise. The crowd was even louder as we climbed aboard our bikes. Deep in my gut, right inside my bones, the noise invaded me. I knew it was a force. It could be a force for good, if it strengthened my resolve. But it could be a malevolent force if it made me crumble inside.

On the opposite side of the track to us Meares and McCullough clenched hands, briefly, in a defiant display of good old Aussie mateship. Jess and I were more reserved. We were the British girls, after all, and expected to be a little less bullish. Yet Jess and I were fighters. We had fewer muscles and smaller expectations, but we were just as gritty and determined as the world champions and world record breakers.

I was held higher up on the track, Jess to my left, her back wheel locked in the starter's gate. We were alone, but for the noise and tumult.

On their side of the track Meares and McCullough were alone, too, but for the noise and tumult. McCullough was on the outside. Meares, as the starter, was in her gate.

Jess and I were dressed identically in blue, red and white GB skins. Only the colour of our helmets was different. Jess wore white, streaked with red and blue. I wore pitch black, with the visor lowered over the top half of my face.

The countdown began. I saw the 15 second mark.

I swallowed hard. I could taste my tenacity. I could relish its briny tang in my dry mouth.

Jess was already out of her saddle, muscles clenched and ready to launch her from the gate.

Five seconds. The noise flattened into the beeping of a machine that would soon stop. There would be nothing then but the empty white hum of racing.

Beep ... beep ... beep ... beep ... beep.

Jess was out of the gate and away, her teeth gritted and her face a rictus mask of pain and desire. She had to ride faster than she'd ever done before in an attempt to give me an opportunity to catch McCullough.

Soon, we felt quick, bloody quick. But I was concentrated rather than elated. I was on it. I really was on it. The big old 96' gear was already biting and racing.

We flew out of the first lap, Jess peeling up the bank in relief at her fantastic ride. I was racing then.

Unknown to me, up in the BBC commentary box, our final was described on live television. 'Australia are quickest at the moment,' Hugh Porter said. 'They've really got the bit between their teeth ... but so has Victoria Pendleton. Pendleton powering away, around the rim of the track.'

It was smooth, it was powerful, it was quick. The track flashed beneath me and I rode like I hadn't ridden for a year or more. I could sense it. I was closing on McCullough. I rode faster and faster.

The crowd stood as one and bellowed. 'It's going down to the wire!' the BBC man screamed into his microphone.

I was lost deep inside myself. I was back where I belonged.

Ten metres beyond the finish line, and outside my blank gaze, Jan crouched and urged me on. He was bent low, bellowing almost as loudly as the crowd, all the hurt and confusion of three years and more gone from him. 'C'mon, Vic!' Jan screamed. '*C'mon* ...!'

I came on like an express train. The 96' gear, feeling so much lighter than I'd expected, churned with a power I could barely believe.

'Oh, look at that,' Porter yelped as the 96 express flashed over the line like a speeding bullet. 'A fantastic contest!'

It was over. The race was done. We had done our best.

I looked up. I wanted to cry out loud. I wanted to holler from right on top of my black train: '*Wooahhh!*'

Behind my visor I blinked hard. I needed to check that my eyes were really working. They told me the truth again.

The number 1 gleamed next to our names. In yellow little digits of computerised colour, a great big wonderful '1' really shone alongside the Varnish and the Pendleton.

We had won. Fuck me. We had done it.

I looked again. Two new digits were up on the board. They spelt out the letters W and R.

WR. We had just broken Meares and McCullough's brand new world record with a new time of 32.754.

Iain Dyer leapt around at trackside like a deliriously happy school kid. Jan van Eijden simply pumped his fists. Shane Sutton and Dave Brailsford embraced and laughed. Steve Peters, slightly apart from everyone else, stood and smiled at me. Scott was up in the rafters somewhere. I could feel him looking down on me. Scott had got me back. I really was getting back to where I belonged.

There was little time to think. I circled the track, searching for Jess. I could see Jan wagging his index finger at me. But it was no longer the finger of rebuke. It was a finger which said number 1. He waved it at me while his face looked as if it might split open beneath the width of his smile.

Jess and I were reunited. We were off our bikes and in each other's arms. We babbled and laughed as we were surrounded by photographers. The noise and the joy took over. I gave into it and the release was euphoric. I had not felt such bliss since Palma and winning three world titles on one amazing long weekend on a Spanish island in 2007.

Usually, winning brings just blunted relief, a sigh that it's over. This was different. This was unrestrained delight and excitement. Jess and I stood together, beaming as we held the Union flag that had been shoved into our hands. And, for once, the celebrations were real rather than forced. I felt happier on the track than I had done in five years.

'The crowd … the noise …' I said in a breathless trackside interview, 'I could just feel it shaking through my body. I carried it right through.'

Shane Sutton hugged me; the brief hug of old friends who know what it's like to fight and hate each other and then try again. There was no need for words. I turned next to Dave, who also swallowed me up in his arms, telling me how well I had done.

The television cameras and the interviewers were soon on top of me – but I was ready to talk. 'I'm really happy this year,' I said. 'When it became 2012 I thought, "Oh my gosh, what an amazing opportunity." I just want to go out there now and enjoy every race.'

As I watched Jess soak up the plaudits and the euphoria, I realized again how much the night would help her. Disappointment and failure can drive you to work harder; but so can triumph and jubilation. The value of all our hard work could not have been shown in a more visceral and exhilarating way. Jess looked as if she wanted much more of the same in an Olympic summer.

We wouldn't get to sleep for hours and so, after we dumped our bags and medals in our hotel room, Jess and I went out for some noodles around ten o'clock that night in Canary Wharf. Of course, as we were mere sprint cyclists, no-one came over to congratulate us or tell us how we rocked their world with our surprising result. We didn't care. Jess was buzzing; and I was buzzing off her. It was just sinking in that she had gone under the 18.8 second barrier for a start lap in a time of 18.792; and her best-ever speed had set me up. I had broken the imposing 14 second mark with a world record second-lap time of 13.962. We could hardly believe it; but we were exultant.

It seemed strange to remember that once, when she was a girl in Bromsgrove, in Worcestershire, Jess had stuck a poster of me on her wall. She had been born in 1990, when I was already ten, and it usually felt as if we belonged to different cycling generations. But, on a winter night in London, having just set a world record together, we were a team. It felt as if we might do something still more extraordinary.

In between blathering away to each other, Jess swapped texts with her dad, Jim, a keen amateur cyclist who had been instrumental in her emergence on the bike. Jess had not had the same fraught relationship with her father as me and my dad; but watching her, radiant with happiness, I thought of Max. Nights like these made all our unforgiving Sunday morning rides on the roads of Bedfordshire seem worth it. This was another race I had won for Dad; and for me.

Dad would be at the Olympic Velodrome to see me in the sprint, which I knew would start twelve hours from then. So much had happened, and changed, since those girlish days when I was in thrall to Dad in Stotfold. But I still wanted to make him proud of me. That feeling would always remain deep inside me.

We might not have been recognized in a noodle bar on a Friday night in east London, but Jess and I were splashed across the front pages of the Saturday morning broadsheets. It was another taster of what might await in August 2012. But we could not afford to linger over the coverage; not when such a serious day of sprint racing loomed.

It did not take long for the list of starters in the qualifying time trial to arrive. I was out ridiculously early; at number eight in a list of forty-seven riders. Meares and Guo were drawn, more respectably, next to each other at forty and forty-one. Jess was at thirty-five.

In the end the four of us were in the top five and joined, in second place, by a talented young sprinter from Hong Kong called Wai Sze Lee. Meares was quickest in 10.939 while I was fourth fastest in a uniform if slightly disappointing time of 11.111.

I was drawn in my first match against my Russian namesake Viktoria Baranova. We had raced often in the past and I had few qualms on the start line. In the end I was right; and my win took me into the quarters where, after our celebratory night, I faced Jess.

It's difficult to race against your sprint partner but I beat Jess in both races. I was safely through to the semi-finals where, yet again, while Guo met the inexperienced Wai Sze Lee, the same old match-up caught the eye.

Meares vs Pendleton.

Between us, we shared fifteen World titles, two Olympic gold medals, a few crashes, a whole heap of bruises and festering acrimony. We felt like two boxers coming out for a title fight, with my walk to the track being accompanied by the doleful chimes of Big Ben. The crowd went crazy.

I was in my usual Team GB kit, with 191 pinned into the lycra skin. We were both on black bikes – Meares having ditched her old colour of Wallaby gold.

Chris Boardman, commentating for the BBC at trackside, told the viewers, 'There's a lot of emotional background for both these riders. They've both won and lost to each other. There's been a lot of heartache and despair and elation. It's going to be closely matched again tonight. Meares was obviously quicker in qualifying but Victoria Pendleton went on to show she's got real sharp acceleration at the moment.'

A surprise victory in the team sprint had felt significant; but defeating Meares in an individual match, especially so early in my revamped training programme, would represent a seismic shift in momentum.

I had the advantage of following her in the first heat. We went round in familiar circles, our speed slowly gathering pace on a track that would shape the outcome of our lives in August 2012.

At the bell, as I tore at her, Meares held the inside line, bolting shut any possible opening. I had to try and come around her on the outside. We were both quick but Meares would not buckle. She held the line, and the lead, with iron control. Meares had done enough to seal the win in a strong time of 11.325 seconds.

The odds had swung heavily towards Meares. She'd looked impregnable and I would have to adopt my least favoured position of riding from the front.

Before race two, Jan, dressed in a blue British top and shorts, held me close near the base of the track. He said a last few words and, even though they were lost in the din of another capacity crowd, I nodded. I knew what I needed to do – ride out of my skin. I had done it the previous night; I hoped I could do it again. My jawbone jutted as I ground my teeth in readiness.

I led her up the incline early and, for a few moments, as my bike paused and almost halted, it looked as if I was about to challenge Meares to a standstill. But, as if to keep her guessing, I rolled slowly down the banking. Meares followed me at a distance for the next lap and a half. She was clearly gathering herself for a big rush at me. Still, she waited, and I pedalled faster, eager to hear the bell.

Meares, however, had anticipated its pealing chimes before me and, in a flash, she was on my wheel. As the bell tolled she powered past me on the outside. Meares was gone and, soon, two clear bike-lengths separated her from me.

'I tell you what, this is looking dangerous,' Hugh Porter roared in the commentary box. 'Pendleton's got a lot of work to do now.'

I could see the gap and the work ahead. I could see the whole race in my head. And so I remained cool and held my nerve. I just needed to have a wheel to aim at over the last half-lap.

Turning on the gas, and feeling instant relief at its presence, as my bike shot forward at the urging of my legs, I shut down the distance between us. I was on Meares's wheel as we approached the turn, her slipstream increasing the rush of my acceleration.

'Go, go, go …' I said silently just before I made my strike.

We were level and Meares knew it. She twitched her bike this way and that, as if trying to unnerve me while we brushed shoulders. But we had done the same old dance so many times that I simply pedalled faster. I went over the top of her and took the lead. The race was already mine. She came back at me but I had the win. It was tight; but it was still clear-cut and, in a time of 11.183, even quicker than race one.

1–1; and ten minutes from the decider.

I rested briefly in the pits, sitting quietly, while, not too far away from me, Jo Rowsell and Laura Trott, the pursuit girls, chatted happily. They were in a different world to me. I was in agony, suffering from stomach cramps, and locked in an epic struggle with Meares. There was hope, however, in the certainty that Meares would be suffering just as much. After our team sprint showdown the night before, and with little sleep in its aftermath, Meares would also feel like she had just been run over by a bus. Entering our seventh race of the day, with more to come, we were trapped in an unremitting schedule.

It would be different in the Olympics. Each morning in August we could rest and we'd never have to sprint more than two rounds a day. But the World Cup was brutal – for both of us – with hardly any time to recover between races.

In our last year of competing against each other after a decade of bitter racing, we were both sprinting near the height of our powers and the limits of our resilience. Meares would not succumb. I needed to dredge up another momentous race from deep within myself.

I was drawn again in the lead-out role. Yet I had ridden from the front and then come from behind in race two. I could beat her again. The cramping in my gut eased as my mind was consumed.

Meares hung back for the whole of lap one and a big chunk of the second. It would not last. She was soon stalking me, riding close to my rear wheel. The bell encouraged her to race high and hard, and I watched her climb above me.

It only took an instant; but I missed it.

In a flash, Meares steamed down the banking again and took me on the inside. It was audacious. It was brave. But it was also clear that she came off the bottom of the track as she sped past me. The race was lost in that moment. My body was not quite strong enough, yet, to come back at her again. Meares had sprung a surprise and, after one last surge with her head lowered, she clinched victory in 11.243 seconds.

Meares tapped her handlebars in rapture and waved a finger in the air. Behind her, I pointed instead at the mark where she had left the track while overtaking me. I was not about to detract from her win by lodging a protest but it felt appropriate to gesture to the spot. Meares looked straight ahead, away from me, but she then stretched out her left arm. Her hand hung in the air, waiting for me.

I closed the gap between us and, just as she looked back, I stretched out my right arm towards her. Our hands clasped and Meares lifted mine to the rafters. That shared tribute pleased Hugh Porter on the BBC. 'They sportingly acknowledge each other's fine skills,' he purred.

It felt the right moment to clasp hands with Anna. We had just ridden the three fastest races in the history of women's sprint cycling. We had taken chunks out of each other and, once again, pushed each other to new extremes. Once more we were like battered fighters at the end of another ferocious contest.

Meares said afterwards that she had never known sprinting like it; and had never been driven so hard. 'You couldn't hear it but down the back straight I was going "Hhuggghhhhhnnnn!"' she exclaimed as she attempted to voice the almost primeval effort we had both produced against each other. Meares laughed wryly: 'I was just trying to get everything out because I knew she was coming.'

I was disappointed but I knew I could beat her again. 'It was a tough draw,' I said afterwards. 'We both kicked the shit out of each other. You could see she felt the same today. They were very tough races.'

Guo, meanwhile, had cruised through her two routine heats against Lee in the second semi-final. Yet neither Meares nor I had much left for the medal races. Six minutes after our decider, I went out against Lee in the bronze heats. Meares and Guo followed us immediately afterwards in the final.

'That's nasty,' Meares said of the scheduling. 'That's nasty in anyone's book.'

I still won the first heat against Lee in 11.556. It was a quicker ride than Guo's win over Meares in 11.972. But I felt drained and empty when Lee took the next. She won the third race as well to claim bronze. Meares had already lost 2–0 to Guo by then. She had to settle for silver, while still relishing her defeat of me, 'the toughest girl in the field'.

After ten races in one day I didn't feel tough any more. I felt exhausted and wounded. But not beaten; for Meares and I were closer than ever.

We went at it again early the next morning. It took three rides in the keirin, because I went down the scenic route of the repechage, but I reached the semis. Only the first three would qualify from an exacting heat. Our names were barked over the public address: Sanchez, Clare, Kanis, Lee, Meares and Pendleton.

Somehow, I won. Meares was second and Lee third. Three other riders were already waiting for us in the final: Shulika, Guo and Krupeckaitė.

Meares was in worse shape than me late that Sunday afternoon. She finished last. I was fifth and the win went to Krupeckaitė.

I felt as if I could barely walk to the obligatory media interviews in the mixed zone at the far end of the velodrome. And so I wheeled myself over on my bike. Jan caught me. He hunched down next to me. 'Well done ...' he said softly. And then, as if remembering that I was out of the meaningless medals, he said, simply, 'Forget it ... well done ...'

An hour later, after Chris Hoy added the keirin title to his earlier victory in the sprint, the venue emptied. There were just a few kids waiting for autographs and some enthusiastic British supporters gathered together in a tight knot at the bottom of the stand near the finish line. I could see my sister, Nicola, and Scott amongst them. Nicola was beaming and waving. Jess's parents were also there, waiting for us. Inside the main ring only Jess, Simona Krupeckaitė and I were left. We walked Simona slowly towards the exit. Simona was an old rival but we chatted happily as, still clutching her winning bouquet after clinching the keirin, she congratulated us on our world record in the team sprint.

In six weeks we would do it all over again, at the World Championships in Australia, before returning to this very velodrome for the Olympic Games. Jess and I walked across the track where we had done battle with Meares and McCullough two nights earlier.

After I had signed lots of programmes and had my photo taken on countless mobiles, it was time at last to see Nicola. We embraced and laughed because her big bump stopped us getting too close. Nicola was seven months pregnant.

As my hands covered my sister's swollen and healthy tummy, and we marvelled at the fact that she would soon become a mum, and I'd be Aunty Vicky, a life beyond the track suddenly felt real. New life stirred inside my sister. One day, I hoped, after everything on the track had slipped away into the silence of memory, Scott and I would be just as happy as we started our own family.

Scott put his arm around me and, feeling weary and hungry, I leaned against him. I would never have to ride another World Cup again. I felt strangely happy.

We were down to the last two events of my career – my eleventh World Championships and my third Olympic Games. The end, at last, was in sight.

They loaded the same old question with new ammunition every time. On Tuesday 3 April 2012, two days before the start of the Worlds in Melbourne, the media had me in their sights. Wheeled out to face their barrage, I smiled thinly. I knew what they were doing. They were relying on me to stoke up my rivalry with Anna Meares. There seemed little need – for our riding in London had commanded respect. But they were desperate for a few choice new quotes to heat up the battle.

They always came to me because, on the sprint circuit, Anna and I held contrasting reputations. I might have been disliked by some, and dismissed as temperamental or too right-eous, but no-one had ever accused me of riding unfairly. Everyone in cycling had seen the opposite way in which Anna competed to me. I could afford to speak more openly for I'd never tried to ride illegally or push anyone off their bike.

My position was also unusual. Unlike Meares and the over-whelming majority of my rivals, I had not striven to become a professional cyclist. I had fallen into the sport by chance. It was one of the main reasons why my coaches, especially Shane and Jan, found it so hard to relate to me. They could not really understand me. I liked riding my bike but I did not have the passion for racing that they shared with my fellow sprinters. They all seemed to live for the moment that they could enter a race environment. I was very different.

In the press conference I waited for each question, hoping I might be surprised by a changed tangent, but every time it was like a ball-machine drilling a serve out wide to my backhand on a hot and sweaty practice court. The query would, in a slightly altered set of words, repeat the same question I had just answered. Everything boiled down to a seeming obsession: 'Why don't you like Anna Meares?'

Sometimes the ritual question would look like a serve with additional slice on it, or a bit more kick, but I was compelled to play the same old backhand defensive block. I couldn't say exactly what I thought but I was not about to lie. Every question was returned with an attempted smile and a softer caveat. But of course most newspapers only printed the words that suited them. And even when I was quoted more fully the big juicy headline deliberately highlighted the apparent controversy.

I started out by saying that Anna was a formidable rider, my greatest competitor and a woman with whom I'd once been relatively friendly. More questions were loaded and fired my way. 'There's no animosity on my behalf towards Anna,' I said politely.

Back they came again, suggesting that she, at least, thought differently. 'I'm really sad to think that she might genuinely feel that way towards me,' I said.

Surely I was aware of her antipathy? 'It's kind of happened and I don't even know how. I've heard her make some comments about how she dislikes me or I dislike her, and I'm not entirely sure where it's come from, because we used to be quite good pals.'

A new question, with the same intent, was on its way. I stressed again that 'Anna and I are contrasting riders. She's someone who kind of likes to push the rules and I definitely don't. But there's nothing wrong with that. It's just slightly different styles and how we approach the same event.'

They probed the source of my discontent and I re-lived the way she had deliberately ridden into me during the World Championship keirin in Bordeaux in 2006. 'That really shocked me because she apologised for doing it afterwards, saying, "I'm sorry I hooked you, I didn't mean it to be dangerous." I was like, "Well, OK then, you might do it, but I wouldn't." I haven't come from a background of sprinting where contact is expected. So we've got very different backgrounds in sprinting and that's all it is really. We're just really different.'

Could I imagine sitting down and enjoying a beer with Meares after the Olympics were over? 'I hope so,' I said, 'but I don't think she'd want to have one with me. That's sad because this isn't war. This is sport. I respect her achievements and I hope that she respects mine. I don't want to have any bitter rivalries. Rivalries are good. Bitter ones aren't so good.'

The Australian papers had their headline – which had our names added for some real punch. Pendleton: 'Meares likes to push the rules ...'

In Britain it was even harder-hitting. *The Daily Telegraph* ran this headline: British track cycling star Victoria Pendleton fuels war of words with Australian rival Anna Meares. The *Sun*, obviously, went for a more hysterical headline – Vic: Push Off, Anna!

It was strange to see sprint cycling in the *Sun* but they liked the story: 'Victoria Pendleton accused Aussie rival Anna Meares of "pushing the rules" in a bitter cheat row. Olympic champion Pendleton warmed up for next week's World Championships in Melbourne by claiming that when she pipped Meares to gold in the individual sprint in Beijing in 2008 it was revenge for an incident two years earlier.'

After Meares took her turn to meet the press, a typical report ran in *Cycling News* the following day: 'Embarking on a war of words with arch-rival Victoria Pendleton was never going to be Anna Meares' style, following the Brit's attack on the reigning sprint, keirin and team sprint world champion with the Australian adamant that her battles would be fought only on the track. Meares denied Pendleton's claim on Tuesday that she is a rider who not only "likes to push the rules", but had snubbed her friendship. "No, I think that's incorrect," Meares responded when asked if there was any lasting bitterness from her side. "I've always had respect for Victoria. I've never said anything to the contrary.

"Sometimes with great rivalries you can't have a great friendship because there is so much riding on the line for those involved. It's an uncomfortable situation to try and be able to switch off and open yourself up to that person when you do need to beat them on the track. I think it's fair to say that all sports people push the limits, myself included. The people who judge you on that are the commissaries."'

The *Sun* preferred to run a story from Kaarle McCullough which, this time, carried a Pendleton Scared headline. 'Victoria Pendleton has been accused of running scared of her Aussie arch rival on the eve of the World Track Cycling Championships in Melbourne. Meares' team-mate Kaarle McCulloch said: "I think Vicky's a bit scared. Anna's on her way to achieving three Olympic gold medals – and I'm going to put my money on Anna winning those golds. I see what she does in training every day and, if I was Vicky, I'd be scared as well."'

On the Wednesday morning of 4 April, with Jess and me due to race against Meares and McCullough in the team sprint, we left our room and headed for the hotel foyer. Waiting for the rest of the team to join us on the bus ride to the velodrome, I stood quietly to one side, lost in thought. An Australian woman who worked in the hotel came over to me. She was not hostile or even unfriendly – but she spoke bluntly: 'You're the one that's been bitching about Anna Meares, aren't you?'

I was surprised but I looked her full in the face. I didn't go into a long explanation about the workings of the modern media but I responded as simply as I could. 'Well, no, I haven't, actually ...'

It was a cloudy start to another day in sunny Melbourne.

The mood was no less overcast when we returned to the hotel that evening. After the elation of London, and blitzing the world record, Jess and I had come to ground with a dispiriting bump. Little went right for us together in Melbourne. Shortly after we'd arrived, almost two weeks earlier, Jess had picked up a heavy cold. She had yet to shake its lingering hold on her.

Our qualifying ride disappointed. Jess and I had both expected her to complete the opening lap more quickly than the 18.855 seconds it took. Meares scorched her with a blistering time of 18.450. There was too much for me to claw back. If I had known the pace Jess was on, I would have left myself more of a gap on the run-in behind her wheel. My time of 14.086 was faster than McCullough – who rode 14.302 – but Australia were still ahead of us in 32.752. They had broken the world record we'd set in London.

It did not last. Germany's Miriam Welte and Kristina Vogel took first place in qualifying after a scorching time of 32.630. They were both experienced and talented riders and so I was surprised rather than shocked. It was the first time that everything had clicked perfectly for Welte and Vogel on both laps.

We qualified fourth behind Germany, Australia and China. Jess was full of apologies and determination to improve in the bronze-medal ride. But dejection had set in and she was slower in 19.088. I rode more quickly than in qualifying but we couldn't catch the Chinese. We were out of the medals and forced to watch as the Germans set another new world record, 32.549, as they beat Meares and McCullough to gold. It was a brutal reminder that the heavily hyped talk of a shootout between Australia and Britain meant nothing. We were down to fourth in the world.

In our room at the hotel, I felt for Jess as her apologies began. 'I'm so sorry,' she said. 'I let you down.'

Worry and regret etched her young face and I felt almost maternal. 'Jess,' I said firmly, 'you have nothing to apologize for.'

She looked at me doubtfully. 'Listen, Jess,' I said, 'don't ever, ever apologize again. You're not the kind of person to ever do anything less than your absolute best.'

Jess nodded, a little less miserably. 'If we've got to let one go,' I said of our World Championship let-down, 'then I'm far happier it's this one.'

We still had August. We still had the Olympics, on the track where we had both been so happy just six short weeks before. 'OK?' I said.

'OK,' Jess said with a small smile. 'OK ...'

Anna Meares was on fire. In qualifying for the individual sprint she set another world record of 10.782 seconds for the 200m time trial. I was slower, finishing fifth, in 11.076, and I could do little but watch as the Meares bandwagon rolled on. She was a machine, apparently, an indestructible powerhouse.

I tried to ignore the Meares momentum and kept riding, beating Yvonne Hijgenaar, Lin Junhong and France's Virginie Cueff to reach the semi-final. My Easter date was set with, of course, Anna Meares.

*　　*　　*

Good Friday was meant to be a day of resurrection. For me, it began as a day of introspection. I had the morning to myself. It was a time to pause and think. I had raced well the previous two days but I was still struggling. The heats against Lin and, in particular, Hijgenaar, had been close. Meares, in contrast, was in world record-smashing form; and I knew I didn't have such a ride in me in Melbourne. I was still far from my peak, for we were four months and one day away from the Olympic sprint final.

Meares had been almost three-tenths of a second faster than me. Three-tenths, to a sprinter, is like three blocks to a suburban walker. I was that far behind Meares. She was at the top of a long road and I was at the bottom. Unlike Meares, I had never been a great time trialist. A match sprint, with its cruel test of a rider's psychology and her natural burst of speed, suited me slightly more. Yet if I had been on her bike, with such a gap in my favour, I would have approached our showdown with unshakeable belief. Meares clearly thought the same.

She had looked formidable in the time trial; and jubilant after her ride as, in her rainbow hooped jersey, she'd waved to her adoring home crowd. Meares was obviously ready to make me pay for the words I had said on the eve of the championships.

I needed a fresh strategy. In the quiet of my hotel room I thought about risk and opportunity. In training we'd often experimented with different gears and, benefiting from my strength and weight work, I had become increasingly adept at riding some of the big numbers. I had never tried anything so drastic in a match race. And so I was unsure if I had started to go crazy. But the longer I sat alone in my room, the more the thought of a 98" gear lodged in my head.

In 2008, when I beat Meares in the Olympic final, I had ridden a 92" gear. I would never have thought then that, for a woman, it was possible to sprint on a 98" – that was a man's gear to me. During the keirin I used a 96" as a way of winding me up to speed over a gradual two-kilometre race. I'd also ridden with a 96" during my team sprint win with Jess in the World Cup in London. A 98" gear in a match sprint sounded scary; but I needed something scary against Meares.

By the time I met Jan, I was even more tempted. I began my suggestion carefully.

'This might make me sound like a bit of a nutter,' I said to Jan, a man who'd grown used to my craziness over five long years, 'but I've been wondering if I should put a massive gear on and just go for it.'

'What do you think?' Jan asked, sounding intrigued.

'No,' I countered. 'You first.'

Jan did not hesitate. 'I think you should go up and ride a really big gear against her.'

'Me too,' I said. 'I was thinking 98 ...'

'Why not,' Jan said quietly.

'Yeah, I can give it a whirl ... I've got nothing to lose.'

I had a World Championship to lose; and defeat to Meares in Apeldoorn a year earlier had been hard. I would not enjoy losing again. But we had little alternative with Meares in such a commanding mood.

'I'll get Ernie onto it,' Jan said, mentioning our mechanic. 'He'll make sure the 98 is ready for you.'

Hisense Arena, Melbourne, 6 April 2012

Anna Meares, on the start line, turned her head to look at me. On my 98"-gear bike, a few feet away from her, I felt the coldness of her gaze. It was one way to take the heat out of the trackside commentary.

'What a night it's going to be,' the Australian man with a mike said excitedly. 'Strap yourself in. First event: the much talked-about women's sprint semi-final. World record breaker, yesterday, Anna Meares is in the form of her life ...'

I shut down then, blocking out every other word and distraction. I let go of Jan, holding me up on my bike as usual, and dropped down onto my handlebars. I would lead her out and then, just round the turn before the bell, I was going to stamp on it. I would not care where she was and what she was planning. Me and the big old 98" would just go for it.

The plan felt simple and good. I led her around the track and, on the last lap, after I had really stepped on the 98", I was a bike-length clear of her. I was out of my saddle, my leg-speed high and my rhythm strong, but I could sense her coming at me. I could feel the surge and hear the noise. Meares was bearing down on me. As we approached turn three her front wheel was level with my rear wheel. She was bent low with intent as she tried to charge me on the outside. I held on, angling my speeding bike as I pedalled like fury.

I came out of the turn, still slightly in front, defying Meares, the battle between us as close as ever. Flying down the back straight I dug in for a long and searing sprint between my black and red sprinting lines. It was already hurting but I was holding her. Meares raced alongside me between the broader bank of track bordered by the red and blue lines.

The gradient of the boards in Melbourne, however, tends to make you drift to your right as you hurtle out of a turn. I could feel the balance of my bike shifting, and tilting up the track. I was powerless. My front wheel shuddered and then skidded at 65km/h.

It happened so fast. I flipped over the red line and came crashing down, almost hitting Meares.

The smash was bad. Meares was long gone, past the next turn and giving an ironic salute to signal that she had not been at fault for me lying in a bust-up heap. The pain in my arm and shoulder, where a chunk of my flesh had been peeled off by the hard wooden track, cut into the numbness that spread through the rest of my quivering body. My legs were still entangled with my bike, my feet clamped and twisted.

I lay very still for a few moments, my eyes open.

Jan ran towards me, his arms pumping and his shaved head rocking as he tried to focus on whether or not I had begun to move again.

He was followed by our team doctor, anxious that I might have smashed a bone or dislocated a shoulder.

I forced myself to sit up and, soon, I was surrounded by the backroom staff of British Cycling. They separated me from my bike and helped me to my feet.

The hurt was there; but so was another thought. '*Shit, I want to win this ...*'

I said little as they led me to the pits, beyond murmuring, 'Yeah ... yeah ...' when they kept asking me if I was alright. I knew where I was headed.

The rollers were waiting. I needed to get on them. I needed to get my legs turning again so that I could shake the shock out of them.

I threw my helmet down and moved to the rollers. A cautionary hand stopped me.

'Richard,' I said, looking at our concerned doctor, 'I'm fine ...'

'I'm sure you are,' Richard said, 'but slow down. Let's check you out.'

Richard knew me well enough to allow me to take to the rollers. As my legs started to churn beneath me, he went to work on my right flank. My skinsuit was torn with a great big hole in its side. Richard gently began to cut it away. I was soon down to my orange crop-top, leaving my midriff bare above my red, white and blue GB racing shorts. Richard looked closely at my wounds. They would have to be cleaned before I raced again.

There was little time left before I went back out on the track with Meares. Richard hustled me away to the closest loo so he could set about my burnt flesh with an iodine-covered surgical brush. The crash was nothing compared to the brush. It felt excruciating as the brush scoured my bleeding skin, dislodging splinters from my flesh. I had to hold onto the sink and concentrate on breathing deeply, and slowly, to contain the hurt.

Yet all the while, as the stinging pain and whiplash made me grimace, I clung on by thinking how close I had come to holding off Meares. I was convinced that, if I hadn't fallen, I might have beaten her. If nothing else I had reminded her again how tough I was in the heat of battle.

My arm was worse than my shoulder, for the stripped skin was a raw shade of bloody pink. I winced as Richard helped me pull a new racing suit over my head. The wounds were covered. I knew it was important I walked out onto the track with my race-face intact. I needed Meares to see my resolve.

In race two, leading from the front, Meares again seemed calm and controlled. All the pain of my fall had gone as I stalked her until the bell.

Then, I attacked from the upper banking. Meares watched me over her right shoulder as she responded with a big kick of her own. I still closed on her wheel and found a perfect position. We were soon racing alongside each other. She rode hard and close, brushing against me in her usual style, our wheels almost touching.

As we came out of the last turn and hit the final straight, Meares rocketed back into the lead. I tried again but she didn't crack. She maintained the gap between us. It was too late. I half sat up with just a metre left as I surrendered to reality. Meares had won, 2–0. She clenched her fist. I was out.

Sliding off my bike, my face blank, I returned to the sanctuary of the rollers. 'Shit,' I thought, 'it was close again.' But I had not been strong enough. I spoke more calmly to myself.

'OK,' I said, 'get ready for the next one.' I would ride against Shulika or Krupeckaitė for bronze. I put my head down and pedalled some more, resigned to my fate.

'Vic,' someone shouted. 'She's been DQ'd.'

I looked up. Three or four people, including Jan, rushed towards me. They were talking about Meares.

'Has she?' I said, sounding almost suspicious.

We all looked up at the screen, replaying the moment Meares had been relegated from race two. It had come near the end, as we raced shoulder to shoulder, and Meares's bike twitched towards mine. Up on the big screen it was obvious. Both of her wheels had crossed the red line and drifted out of the sprinter's lane. She had cut across my line. It was an unintentional illegal move, just like mine had been in race one, but without an accompanying crash.

The commissaries had been strict all through the Worlds and, even for the local favourite, they were not about to waver. I was awarded the race. 1–1.

Suddenly, my mood switched. From the dejection of defeat I felt the familiar spike of adrenalin that follows winning. We were down to the decider.

On the rollers I sat up high and pedalled fast. Only Jan came near me. He spoke firmly and decisively, reminding me of my strengths. Jan pumped his fist and looked intently at me, willing me on to win this last race. I looked at him, nodded, and said my ritual, 'Yeah … yeah.' There was nothing new that Jan or anyone else could say to me. In the depths of my final World Championships I had so many memories I could turn over in my mind. I had been locked at 1–1 so many times before. Yet I had won more deciders than I had lost – even if Meares had taken the previous two clinchers in Apeldoorn and London.

I had won the individual sprint at five World Championships; Meares had just the solitary title from 2011. Deep down, I believed more in me.

Slowly, I walked to the track, 'The atmosphere here is electric,' Hugh Porter said on the BBC to everyone watching back home in Britain. 'Can she do it? Can Queen Victoria win an incredible sixth World Championship?'

In my less favoured lead-out position, I watched Meares closely as we circled the track in the old prelude. It was a slow dance between adversaries, a protracted build-up to the final duel. I tried to keep Meares on my hip so that she would not have the chance to make a real jump out of my slipstream.

Meares shimmied her wheel towards me but I darted back at her, my equally aggressive twitch making her glide to the left. She had decided to take the race on and so I went high up the track. Deliberately, she stayed low as she took the lead.

Only half a lap was left. I stayed in my red saddle, slung low like an arrow, as I tried to maintain the small gap between us and shelter behind her before my final attack.

I pumped my legs, hard and true. Aiming for the inside line, I was blocked.

We approached the last turn and I opened myself up. The gap between us was obvious but, as I chased her, it happened. I began to take advantage of her slipstream and felt myself gaining momentum and speed.

She was on full gas but I was on rocket fuel. I reached her slipstream and felt myself being sucked forward.

I let my legs go in celebration. This was the moment. It was like the moment of coming, a point of no return. 'Yes … yes … yes …' I said silently.

The wonder of my timing was enough to allow a moment to think again: 'You've got her,' I said to myself, amazed that I could string three words together. '*You've got her …*'

I was up close and then out of her slipstream, flying next to her.

The last line of this ending was almost upon us and, in the commentary box, Hugh Porter was beside himself. 'Here comes the reaction from Pendleton – five times world champion from Great Britain. I think Pendleton's got it …!'

His cry melted into the stunned exclamation of the crowd as Meares and I crossed the finish. We were right next to each other and, in that instant, Porter changed his mind. 'I think Meares might have got it …' he said.

I headed up the banking, my mind a haze of colour and speed. As Porter yelped into his microphone I looked up at the board. I thought I knew the truth but I wanted to gaze upon it.

'It's a photo finish,' Porter confirmed. 'But it's showing Victoria Pendleton on the screen … but it was very, very close indeed.'

My legs kept turning mindlessly beneath me as I completed the fastest warm-down lap I think I've ever ridden. I was sure I had won.

Porter, finally, agreed. 'She's beaten Meares 2–1!' he yelped as the camera panned across the track and locked on Jan as he pumped his fists again and whooped wordlessly. 'Look at Jan van Eijden!' Porter shouted. 'Just look at his face.'

I stretched my hand out, looking for Meares. We did something to each other, Anna and me, something which made us produce all that was best inside us.

In the pits Jan was already under control. He knew I was a five-time world champion who had just reached her seventh individual final. We needed to remind Meares that this was not a shock. This was business as usual for me.

There were still whoops and cries as Shane Sutton greeted me with an arm around my less damaged shoulder. He held me as I walked. I headed back to my seat.

They applauded me in the GB pits but my impassive mask remained. I knew Meares would have to go back out ahead of me – in the race for bronze against Shulika.

For me, the final awaited against Krupeckaitė. She had not fallen or needed a decider against Shulika. Krupeckaitė had made it through after two simple rides in her semi.

I was soon back on the rollers, pedalling while Richard taped up my damaged shoulder again. I was good to go. I wanted to beat Krupeckaitė in two straight rides. I wanted it over.

In race one, she pushed hard but I felt serene. I felt strong. 'Pendleton!' Porter hollered at the end. 'She's fired up for it!' 1–0 to me.

Krupeckaitė, however, was a two-time world champion. She was a seasoned pro, and a real sprinter, with the desire to drag me down into the basement of a decider.

In the second heat, we raced hard against each other. Chasing her down, I caught her on the second last turn. We were head to head, neck and neck, shoulder to shoulder. Krupeckaitė came even nearer as we sprinted for an advantage. We were so close we could have crashed but we made it to the final straight.

Porter, on the microphone, was certain. 'This is Victoria Pendleton, in imperious form, showing she's going to win the crown ...'

Yet Krupeckaitė was not yet done. She sprinted on, as I did too, and Porter exclaimed in surprise: 'Oh ... I don't think she's done it! It looks like Krupeckaitė took race two.'

I walked back to the pits and gave my black helmet to Hanlie Fouché, the assistant *soigneur* who always looked after me at major championships. 'My contact lens is stuck on the inside of my visor,' I said to Hanlie, trying weakly to laugh as I spoke, realizing again how dry and tired my eyes had become.

The cameras flashed as I climbed on the rollers. 'That's twenty people taking pictures of me,' I complained to Shane. 'Please go away.'

Glancing at the snappers and TV crews, Shane spoke curtly: 'Just got to ignore them ...'

I put my head down and pedalled, oblivious again, set for yet another decider.

Jan called my name out first. 'Vic! Vic!' he shouted, spreading his arms wide. 'It's over ...'

I turned to look at him in amazement. It was true. Krupeckaitė had been relegated. She had crossed wildly over her line on the second last banking. It was a much more blatant offence than Meares had committed.

I had won. I was world champion again – for the sixth and very last time.

I climbed off the rollers. Hanlie reached me first. She hugged me close. Iain Dyer and I embraced next. And then, as I turned, Steve Peters was waiting for me. Steve, who had saved me so many times before, wrapped his arms around me. 'Six in a row,' he said, conveniently forgetting my loss to Meares in Apeldoorn.

'Vicky!' Dave Brailsford cried out. I hugged Dave as he laughed happily. 'Brilliant,' he said.

I fell to the floor then, buckling with emotion. On my knees, I hunched over. I covered my face as I cried.

Crying less with joy than from the release of all Scott and I had endured since Beijing, I rocked to myself. The sobs ripped through me, feeling more hurtful than the torn flesh and whiplash.

'Steve,' Dave said, calling for the one man in British Cycling who understood me.

Waiting for Steve, the mechanic of my mind, Hanlie leant down and, gently, stroked my back, her blonde hair bobbing in sympathy.

Steve spoke practically to me as I cried. 'Tool up for London,' he said. 'Enjoy your win.'

They pulled me up onto my feet. Shane wiped my face with a towel and Steve steered me to a chair. 'Alright,' he said calmly. 'Alright.'

I sat down and Dave B shouted over to me: 'Vic! You should be smiling! Come on, hey, come on! You're world champ!'

Standing up, I saw Jan. I went to hug him, and to thank him for trying so hard the past year. 'Well done, Vic,' he said softly. 'First rate job.'

I held him close, remembering all that had happened between us, everything that had split our team apart. 'It's not the way I wanted to win,' I said.

'That's just the way it went,' Jan replied. 'That's cycling.'

I was on the rollers, again, when Steve Peters came to find me. 'This is a magnificent win,' Steve said, as I heard the gentle pride in his voice. 'You won it fair and square.'

Smiling at Steve, I nodded. I kept looking for Scott, high up in the stands. Finally, my gaze found him. He was waving at me, his arms making great big sweeping motions above his head. I waved back, counting the minutes until I could feel his arms around me.

There was a hush in the hubbub of the crowd. Anna Meares was being interviewed at trackside. She had beaten Shulika in two straight races to win bronze. But I could hear the tremor in her voice. I knew how much I had shaken her. 'She hit hard,' Meares said as she was asked about my crash. 'I saw it, I heard it, I felt it.'

I wiped my eyes and, in my burnt orange crop-top, I went to find my unsung heroes of the velodrome. I saw Mark Ingham, one of my two mechanics. I hugged him and said, 'Thanks so much for all your help over the years ...'

'You're more than welcome,' Mark said.

Ernie, my other mechanic, was next. 'Thank you, Ern, for all your help,' I cried.

'You're welcome, doll,' he said as he squeezed me tight.

'I really appreciate it,' I stressed.

'You're more than welcome,' Ernie said.

'Maybe just one more hit,' I said, clinging to him and thinking of London. 'Just one more …'

Ernie hugged me back, harder than ever. 'Oh yeah,' he said. 'Oh yeah …'

14 | THE END

The robotic routine consumed our lives. Day after day it was the same. I became a machine. Even as I gathered my strength, fitness and form, the sacrifice ran deep during a twelve-week block of work before the London Olympics. At the end of another grinding day, Scott and I would return to Wilmslow and I'd have no option but to rest. Scott took the dogs for a long walk and then we would make dinner, wash up and get everything ready for our return to the velodrome the following morning.

My ceaseless graft meant that I was hopeless at helping him. He wouldn't allow me, anyway, to rise from my Buddha Bag, a giant beanbag that supported my aching back, until there was food on the table or the last dish had been done. We spoke of little beyond training – and my ever-improving results. We had abandoned our lives but, well, I'd had a couple of track sessions where I went under eleven seconds on a flying 200m. We were on the right path – and my gratitude towards Scott was plain.

It still felt like a barren path. There was no colour and no intimacy as the countdown ticked relentlessly. I did not have the energy, or the inclination, to do anything but recover and prepare myself to do it all over again when Scott and I woke in our separate rooms. Even falling asleep alongside each other, next to the man I loved, had to disappear during a surreal time. Scott did not want to disturb my sleep and we told each other that it would not be for ever.

It was an unusually wet summer, even for Manchester, and most mornings I opened my eyes to find that darkness had given way to yet more drizzle. In the pale and dreary light I reminded myself why I needed to keep on. One day, on the evening of 7 August 2012, it would finally end. But, until then, I would surrender to the old ritual of moulding my body and soul into gleaming shape.

Scott came to almost every one of my sessions during those final three months. We kept to ourselves because interaction with Jan van Eijden, Iain Dyer and Shane Sutton was still strained. The closer we moved to the London Olympics the shorter tempers became at the Manchester Velodrome. You could sense the stress and tension in the building. But it was more important to concentrate on myself and Scott – and to do justice to our training programme.

The speed and resilience I had been in search of for so long was finally there. It was set to burst out of me, in early August, just as we had planned. Even the doubters could be heard murmuring: 'Vicky's going well …' I found reassurance in their muted surprise. Scott and I had not been so crazy after all.

As the days slipped away it became difficult to shake the blurring milestones. The last month became the last week. And the last week shrank down to the last day. I made my final journey to work. After ten years it was almost over. I did my last lab session at the English Institute of Sport, with the guys I liked so much, and went across to the velodrome for my concluding session of training on the piney track that had defined my life. I looked around and saw the faces I knew so well. Some of them, those who would not be travelling to our holding camp in Newport and then on to London, I might never see again.

Diane, the receptionist, had almost made me cry when she'd said, 'Don't say goodbye today … come back after it's all over and say a proper goodbye then.'

I promised her I would, for I had received equally sage advice from Emma O'Reilly, my massage therapist. Soon after she had given me my last-ever training massage, she told me not to clear out my locker entirely at the velodrome. 'Leave some stuff in there,' Emma said, 'so you have to go back. Don't deal with all those emotions now. Do it afterwards.'

Still, I could not hold back the momentous feeling that began to swell inside me. I was so glad it was nearly over; but goodbyes are always difficult. From August 2002 until July 2012 this had been my home. It had not been, in the preceding four years, an especially happy home; but I'd spent more time in that decade at the Manchester Velodrome than anywhere else in the world.

It was hard to stop my eyes brimming as I slipped on my training shoes for the last time and stepped out onto the track for one final stint. Looking around the deserted arena and at the curving banking that had thrilled me the first time I had ridden here as an innocent sixteen-year-old, I sucked in a few deep breaths. I needed to make this last time count.

'OK,' I said softly to Scott. 'Let's go …'

Our holding camp at Celtic Manor in Newport felt like an army camp. The hotel was obviously swish and comfortable but, by the end of our first week, we were all desperate to get out. Staff and riders were offered the privilege of a family day. It would be like the luxury of a prison visit. We were just warned that, unlike some real convicts, there would be no conjugal rights. No family members or friends were allowed in our bedrooms. Instead, we could be visited at the hotel and taken out for a meal before, at the appointed curfew, we returned to barracks.

The day offered sweet relief to many – but not to me. No-one came to visit me. It was decided that Scott would not be allowed to step inside the hotel. As a member of our coaching team, my fiancé could attend my training sessions but he was forbidden from entering Celtic Manor. I wondered if they really imagined we were such a fallen couple that we would not be able to resist making out in the lobby – and publicly humiliate ourselves and the team.

There was an even more ludicrous element to the ban. Jan and Scott were working together, helping me prepare for the Olympics, and they needed to have a meeting away from the track. But Shane would not give permission for Scott to actually meet Jan at Celtic Manor. Scott was initially instructed to pick Jan up and drive him back to his hotel – which was the requisite mile away from me. After their meeting, Scott would return Jan to Celtic Manor without seeing me. In the end, Jan just went to Scott's hotel. It felt like a vicious kind of pettiness.

I was also anxious because, on the evening of Wednesday 18 July, at 9pm, an hour-long documentary was being screened on BBC One. It was called 'Victoria Pendleton: Cycling's Golden Girl' – but I knew that Dan Gordon, the director, had probed beneath the glittering surface. Dan and his crew had followed me for two years, and we had been in discussion about the film for eighteen months before that. They knew the turmoil I had been in at the velodrome and, for the first time, I would speak openly in public about all that Scott and I had endured since Beijing.

My uncertainty escalated. I had cried a lot during some of my filmed interviews. I wondered if, through the tears, I might have said something I had since forgotten. Would I cause yet more damage in our already fraught training camp? I knew that at Celtic Manor, with everyone confined to their rooms, I would fill the hotel television screens.

I decided to watch it just with Jess. I felt safe with Jess. If it all turned out disastrously, at least she would be the only person to see me in close-up.

In the end, as I had always hoped, Dan made a film that was as poignant as it was revealing. Jess and I were both in tears – again – during the final scene, which had me talking of 'happy endings' over tender footage of Scott and me at work in the Olympic Velodrome. Our reaction was not unique. The reaction to the film was overwhelmingly positive and within an hour of it being shown I was trending on Twitter and being sent thousands of messages from strangers who wrote such touching words. I picked up another 15,000 followers on Twitter overnight, and the reviews were warm and generous. It seemed as if people finally understood me a little better.

There was one telling scene in the film where Shane said no-one really knew what I'd had to overcome in my past. Only I could tell that story. Yet the most distressing personal trauma and strife could not be laid bare on national television nine days before the London Olympics. The documentary was just a first step. Scott and I spoke on the phone afterwards to voice our relief and happiness. We had, of course, not been able to watch it together.

Olympic Velodrome, Stratford, London, Thursday 2 August 2012

The Olympic Velodrome looked more beautiful than ever, but its nickname had stuck. On an opening afternoon of incredible noise and tumult it seemed as if the curving lid of The Pringle might pop as soon as Jess and I took to the track. The track cycling programme began at 4pm – with the women's team sprint qualifying. We were drawn in heat four against Australia. It seemed as if the organizers were determined that Anna

Meares and I should see as much of each other as possible. Germany, the world record holders and world champions, were drawn in the last heat against China.

Jess was so keen to race that she almost jogged to her bike in the starting gate. Against a sea of Union flags, I followed her. I climbed on my bike and, in the familiar way, leaned on Jan. Jess hunched low over her bars.

Our red helmets glimmered underneath the hot lights. The cacophony of sound grew still louder. It was incredibly hard to concentrate on the computerized timer. Opposite us, and to my left, Meares and Kaarle McCulloch were in position. We needed to beat them and put down an imposing marker in our first race.

Jess was up and out of her saddle, her feet clamped in their pedals, blowing her cheeks and fixing her stare on the seconds rolling past. Once we were in single digits there was no time to think. We were into the beeps.

And then came the roar and pain of the start. Jess grimaced but she got us away. We were fast, even if Meares was predictably quicker, and I could feel my legs picking up momentum as Jess led me round. Our red-white-and-blue train sped smoothly along the track as Jess gave me the platform I needed. She was over the line, banking away to the right, in a fraction over 18.4 seconds. We were 0.3 seconds behind Australia but, oblivious to the difference, I knew I could take McCulloch.

My legs felt stronger than ever, and the speed they generated was faster than any woman had ridden a second lap in team sprint history. The Siberian pine flashed beneath me as I crossed the line. I had not only demolished the deficit between me and McCulloch. We had smashed the world record.

Our time of 32.526 flashed up on the big screen and I raised my left arm in acknowledgement. We were on our way.

Our world record lasted three minutes. Jinjie Gong rode a blistering first lap and, although Guo Shuang was not as fast as me, China lowered our new mark with an impressive time of 32.477 seconds. Germany were third, and Australia a comparatively sluggish fourth. In the first round we would face the seventh-ranked team of the Ukraine, featuring Olena Tsyos and Lyubov Shulika. The four fastest pairings would compete in the medal races – with the top two racing for gold and silver.

I could sense the crowd's euphoria as Jess and I took a brief break in the pits. Thirty-five minutes separated our qualifying and first round races and we needed to calm ourselves.

We were followed onto the track by the men's team sprinters. Philip Hindes, Chris Hoy and Jason Kenny faced Germany in the final heat. Ross Edgar, my oldest and dearest friend on the team, had lost his place as Man One to Hindes – a promising nineteen-year-old born and raised in Germany – at the World Championships. It was another example of the cruel way in which elite sport ruins the hopes of so many.

Hindes, Hoy and Kenny had been relegated in Melbourne – but British Cycling retained their faith in a trio who had hardly raced together. The organization's collective desire for the men to succeed appeared more obvious than any lasting concern for Jess and me.

They started badly. Hindes could not find any speed out of the gate and he appeared to fling himself onto the track to force a restart. It could have resulted in a relegation or even a disqualification, but GB were given a second chance. They eventually qualified fastest, in a new Olympic record, ahead of France.

Soon afterwards, Jess and I rose confidently for our race against the Ukrainians. Another big ride and we would be through to the final. We did not need to say a word to each other as we returned to work.

Jess was slightly slower than she had been against the Australians but, following hard on her wheel, I could feel my own speed uncoiling inside me. The finish of Jess's lap came closer and closer, and I saw her bike move fractionally to the side. That was my signal. Jess going wide meant I could put my head down and just go. I flew across my start line.

I rode a fantastic lap, rocketing even faster than my earlier world best, and we produced a combined time of 32.567. A stonking 1.053 seconds separated us from Ukraine, and we were faster than Germany and Australia. Only China and Venezuela remained, and I knew we were in the final. Venezuela would come nowhere near our time and the only remaining question was whether China might join us in the race for gold. We enjoyed a minute of quiet contentment, despite the raucous din, and retreated to the pits.

My first inkling of the trouble ahead was framed by a picture of the chief commissaire on the big screen. He looked down at a television monitor as he chewed the top of his pen. Jess and I had never had any previous difficulties with officiating in the team sprint and so I only felt a flutter of disquiet.

It was strange to see the commissaire finally scrunch up his face and shake his head before he walked away. Rather than ending there, the confusion escalated as he went in search of his assistant. The two men returned to the monitor. Dave Brailsford joined them. I was told they were considering the possibility that I had overtaken Jess before she had finished her lap. Jess waited quietly next to me, her face etched with tension. Dave's body language looked ominous and his words appeared to have little impact.

China and Venezuela were already underway and Gong, in particular, and Guo were in the mood. They stormed into the final and, in the process, set another new world record of 32.422. I was still sure we would beat them in a straight race because I doubted they could set a third world record on the bounce.

My more pressing uncertainty wrapped around the depressing picture of Dave being asked to step away. Dave seemed subdued, and the commissaire looked defiant as he bent down to look one last time at our changeover.

I knew that the ruling allowed for some discretionary judgement to be used. We had beaten Ukraine so convincingly that the few centimetres separating my overtaking from the official line could surely be discounted. I asked Shane what he thought of our chances.

'Slim,' he grunted.

That hard word – 'slim' – made my stomach tighten. I felt sick during our seemingly unending wait.

When the public address announcer confirmed that we had been disqualified I was desolate. Our certain silver medal, and a possible gold, had been removed by the unsmiling men in blazers. The official ruling was that Jess had moved above the red line before the change box – and relinquished her lead. It was totally unintentional and I had seen the same minor offence go unpunished many times before. Despite the fact that I had not overlapped her back wheel, it was still deemed an illegal change-over and we were relegated.

I had gained no advantage in overtaking Jess as soon as her bike drifted to the side. If anything I lost a few hundredths of a second by coming out of her slipstream. All common sense seemed to have been tossed away in favour of an inflexible ruling that meant that the clearly inferior Ukrainian team would be pushed up to fourth place. They would race Australia for bronze while Germany took our place in the final against China.

I was almost as shocked by the fact that no-one, apart from Luc de Wilde, our chief *soigneur*, came over to Jess. Luc patted her sympathetically on the leg and told her it would be all right. There was nothing else he could say but at least he had the emotional intelligence to realize Jess needed the most basic form of comfort. I had already wrapped my arm around Jess as I felt so sorry for her. She had sacrificed so much for the team sprint and to have lost the chance to ride in her first Olympic final on a technicality was a brutal fate. I still had the keirin and individual sprint. Jess had nothing. Her Olympics were over.

Yet the attention of Dave and Shane, of Iain and Jan, had switched to the men. Surely one of them could have broken away and just given Jess a hug? As she sat alone I was steered towards the media.

I tried to sound philosophical when talking to the BBC's Jill Douglas. 'We didn't change over in the right zone of the track,' I said. 'It's really hard when you're going at that speed. I was following Jess's wheel. If Jess moves up slightly I just go – that's what happened.'

Moving down the line to the journalists in the mixed zone I said: 'I'm devastated for Jess. In qualification she rode the best race of her life so far. I've no doubt she will be back in Rio [for the 2016 Olympics] and absolutely smashing it. We are talking about one hundredth of a second of a mistake here. Jess moved up a fraction too early, and I just saw the door and went for it, because that's my cue to try to squeeze underneath her as quickly as possible. We felt we were getting into that gold-medal gear.'

I paused and smiled wryly. 'Now and again,' I said, 'rubbish things happen.'

After experiencing the irony that I was the rider selected to go through dope control for a routine test, Steve Peters told me that Jess was with our respective families. We met at the gate and I saw that she was cuddling my ten-week-old nephew, Nathan. Jess has strong maternal instincts, even at twenty-one, and I felt moved when her face softened into a smile as she hugged the baby close to her and whispered sweet words to him. Nicola, my big sister, then passed her new son to me. I also cuddled Nathan. A sense of calm filled me. Many things in life were thankfully still far more important than an Olympic disqualification. One day, I resolved, when he is much older, I will tell Nathan how much he did to restore me and Jess in our lowest moment on the track.

There were few words my mum, Nicola, Laura, Alex and Saskia, his girlfriend, could say to us. But they had worked some magic with Nathan.

The Chinese girls, Gong and Guo, looked even more in need of sustenance from the little man. They won the final against Germany but, within minutes, their rejoicing turned to bewildered hurt as the commissaire also relegated them. Gong was inconsolable as they were forced to accept silver. Miriam Welte and Kristina Vogel looked as if they could not believe their luck.

Jess and I had trained specifically for three races, feeling certain that we were equipped to peak when it mattered most. The Chinese, in contrast, had ridden the slowest of their three rides at the very end. The gold medals, clutched in rapture by Welte and Vogel, should have been belonged to Jess and me.

Hindes, Hoy and Kenny had duly won the men's final, beating the French, and I felt lonely again as we left the velodrome. That hurt and isolation turned to anger when Jess and I were back in the sanctuary of our apartment in the village. We watched the cycling on the BBC's Olympic highlights programme and the almost farcical harshness of our disqualification became more obvious. Jess had already apologized to me for going wide fractionally early. I repeated the advice I gave her in Melbourne. She would never need to make any apology for she had given everything of herself to our team sprint.

We felt more upset when, on television, we saw Jan and Iain running around in jubilation as they celebrated success for their favoured men's team. I did not blame them for being happy; but their joy seemed inappropriate when set against our dejection. If they had prefaced or followed their exultant leaping about by offering Jess a sympathetic arm, their celebrations would have been less hurtful.

Jess looked utterly miserable as she packed her bags for the night. She felt that she would drag me down as I tried to get my head right for the following day's keirin. I only agreed to her leaving, so that she could spend the night with her family, on the condition she returned to the village twenty-four hours later. Jess nodded when I told her that I didn't want her to make my mistake from Athens, eight years before, when I wasted my opportunity to sample the atmosphere of a first Olympic Games. The more time she spent in the village, and watched other sports, the better prepared she would be for Rio in 2016.

'OK, Vic,' Jess said as she gave me a hug goodbye. 'Try and get some sleep …'

My fingers trace the scar on my right arm. I can still see it below The Smashing Pumpkins tattoo that reminds me: Today is the greatest day I've ever known.

Four years ago, in Beijing, I marked myself on the night after I won an Olympic gold medal. In the midst of being lambasted by Jan for falling in love with Scott, I began to cry. I had been a twenty-seven-year-old single woman when I fell for Scott. He had been an unattached thirty-two-year-old man. But British Cycling seemed furiously certain that we had 'broken protocol' and betrayed them.

Even as Scott joined Jan and me in my apartment, the supposedly greatest night of my career turned grimy. As the arguing intensified, my tears became uncontrollable. I was hyperventilating on a sultry night in Beijing, gasping for breath in between my sobbing.

I retreated to the bathroom, in search of a darker refuge. The old feelings from Aigle, from my distressing time at the UCI Academy in Switzerland, took hold of me. They came in a rush, just as they did in my small white-walled room in Aigle, when I felt desperate for another kind of hurt to replace the pain deep inside me.

In the Beijing bathroom I found a pair of nail scissors. I picked them up without really thinking. Holding the small, cold steel implement in my left hand I walked back into the room. The words still flowed in a torrent. I needed them to stop.

Looking away from them and down at my arm, I wanted to bleed. I took the scissors and cut my skin open. Blood trickled from my right arm.

I don't really know why I did it – except that I wanted them to see how much they had hurt me.

'Oh my God,' someone shouted. 'What the hell are you doing?'

I felt calmer and, instead of hyperventilating, I could speak again. I was still crying but I was coherent. 'When will you understand that this is more than I can handle?' I asked Jan. 'It's too much. I'm hurt. I'm really hurt.'

The room was very quiet and I saw the shock on Scott and Jan's faces. I felt sorry; but I had to be honest as the blood ran down my arm.

'Does my physical hurt show you more?' I asked. 'Does this help you understand how I'm feeling right now?'

I had just become an Olympic champion; and I was in love with a special and gentle man they accused of the most awful treachery. What had we done that was so wrong? We had fallen in love. Did we deserve to be treated like criminals?

Jan went back to his own apartment. Scott stayed behind to look after me. I was soon cleaned up and able to tell him everything that I had done to myself in Aigle. I was not proud but, because I loved him so, I knew it was better to be honest. I had lived with this secret for too long. I had to share it with him to help me become better for ever. Scott understood. His feelings for me did not lessen. Instead, they strengthened because he suddenly recognized, with fierce clarity, how much I had withstood to become an Olympic champion.

And now, on an English summer night in Stratford in 2012, I am better. At my home Olympics I have just lost a certain medal, a silver or a gold, but there are no small dramas with nail scissors. I simply feel far worse for Jess than for myself. But I know she will be fine, just like I already am, for there are far better things to have in life than a piece of metal attached to a ribbon. Baby Nathan taught us this tonight. As soon as I saw the look of kindness spread across Jess's face as she held Nathan close, I knew she accepted that truth.

I think of Mum and Dad, of Nicola, Alex and, now, little Nathan too. And I think of Scott and how much I love him, and how much we have endured to reach this point. Tomorrow I will race again, in the chaos of the keirin. I do not feel especially confident; but I know I'm going to try my heart out.

On the track, a few hours earlier, I had felt the sheer rollicking force of my speed. I had never ridden as fast before. So I still have hope; and I still have courage.

As I turn the light off and lie down in my Olympic village bed, I know sleep will not come for many hours. But I also know that, tomorrow afternoon, back at The Pringle, I will race again. I will try again.

Olympic Velodrome, Stratford, London, Friday 3 August 2012

Bradley Wiggins, the new king of cycling, arrived at the velodrome in the afternoon looking like a dead-cool dude. The winner of the 2012 Tour de France and the Olympic Games time trial wore a maroon Fred Perry cardigan. In the stifling heat he soon slipped off his cardie to reveal a pristine white Fred Perry tennis shirt. His shades were tucked between the second and third top buttons and he looked very mod – and very Brad. He was now, officially, the most popular man in

Britain, for he matched his extraordinary year on the bike with his usual nonchalant veneer as he told everyone that he refused to become a celebrity. Brad, instead, had gone out and got wasted, and cheerfully tweeted that he was 'blind drunk'. Everyone loved him all the more.

I understood how driven Brad was on the bike. I also could not forget the encyclopaedic knowledge of cycling he had shown when we sat next to each other on a flight to Brno, and the European Championships, ten years earlier. Then, even in my naïvety and ignorance, I had been certain that Brad would become a legendary cyclist. My gut had been proved right.

It seemed best to trust my instincts again as we entered battle for the keirin. All I needed to do was nail three straight rides. I had resolved to take on each of them as early as possible and dictate the outcome of every race. There was no point hanging around and reacting late. I was determined to ride the keirin in my own style.

Of course Anna Meares and I were drawn together in heat two, right next to each other, as I would lead us out behind the derny. The field was completed by Fatehah Mustapa, Willy Kanis, Natasha Hansen and Lyubov Shulika. Only the first two finishers would qualify automatically for the next round, while the losers would be condemned to the repechage.

It was the first time the women's keirin was being ridden in the Olympics – but Meares had established herself as world champion in the event in both 2011 and 2012. I had only one World Championship keirin title to my name, from 2007, and it has always been my least convincing discipline. But, on the start line, I reminded myself to stay strong. I remained impassive, dragging down my race-face.

My head sank over my handlebars, and I gripped them a little tighter, as we waited for the derny. To an ever-deeper roar the little man on the motorbike trundled down the inside. He looked like he was on his way to pick up a late-afternoon baguette and bottle of chilled Chablis as he pedalled his bike around the track. Meares and I settled into the same leisurely routine as I led us out, tucked right behind the wheel of the derny. Every now and then I looked over my shoulder just to check that the rest of the field were trailing me in an orderly procession. Meares was close behind but, in third place, Kanis had left a small gap. I peddled and breathed, breathed and peddled, steeling myself for the last two laps of racing.

As the derny slipped off the track, Meares came flying past me. Kanis followed her. They were both riding hard and I slipped behind Shulika and Hansen as well. I was in fifth place; but I felt no panic.

At the bell, Shulika took over. She would not hold the lead for long. On the home straight Meares swept past her while, with a burst of acceleration, I overtook the three riders immediately in front of me. Kanis, Hansen and Shulika disappeared as if in a puff of smoke. Meares and I scorched the field in a fiery burst.

I was on Meares's hip as we raced down the back straight. And then, as if to offer her a sharp little warning of how much was left inside me, I gave a venomous kick of speed. I cruised past her.

Brad Wiggins stood up and lifted his hands above his head to applaud. It was almost as if he were telling me, with every ounce of his cycling nous, 'That's how you do it, Vic ...'

In heat two of the second round, I followed the same pattern. I took charge from one-and-a-half laps out and powered home, with Sanchez and Guo joining me in the final. Meares, Lee and Sullivan had already made it safely through.

The Pringle was in uproar. Jo Rowsell, Laura Trott and Dani King had broken their own world record in qualifying for the women's team pursuit. In the men's final, Ed Clancy, Geraint Thomas, Peter Kennaugh and Steve Burke raced against Australia just before I went out for my last-ever keirin. As the four boys flashed around the track like a zooming bullet-train the noise grew. The reverberations invaded my body.

It was impossible to think straight as, in a triumphant phalanx, the GB team-pursuiters rode side-by-side over the finishing line. They had obliterated the world record. I was happy for them, and I sneaked a look at their smitten faces, but it became difficult to regain my concentration. The medal ceremony and the national anthem followed as, all the while, minute by raucous minute, the pressure tightened around me. It felt suffocating.

At last, we were summoned for our Olympic final. In the field of six, four of us shared half-a-dozen world keirin titles between us. Meares and Sanchez held two each; Guo and I had one apiece. Sullivan and Lee were meant to be outsiders but I knew that the latter, the young rider from Hong Kong, was quick. It was going to be hard and testing, and I had to find every last vestige of composure to steady me.

Guo, typically, moved from third in the starting row to the lead-out place behind the motorbike. I was tucked behind Lee, who was second, with Meares in fifth spot. As the tempo lifted I could just about hear the drone of the derny. Stay calm, Vic, I kept telling myself, stay calm.

Once the derny was gone, Meares struck early. She took the lead and I slipped down to fourth with two laps left. After another half-lap, I climbed out of my saddle and turned on the burners. I went past Lee and Guo with a whoosh, and found Meares's wheel. I kept pedalling at a furious rate and simply dropped her as if she were not even there. Meares must have been so shocked that she fell back rapidly.

I flew around the final turn. I had the race won. My heart surged as I raced towards glory and relief. Guo came back at me with one last mighty tilt, but she was never going to catch me. I finished half a wheel in front of her. Incredibly, I was an Olympic champion again.

The noise rolled down towards me and, at last, I raised both arms above my head in celebration. My face cracked open in a helpless smile at my pure racing and sensational victory.

Of course I broke down and cried real tears when I was engulfed by Luc and Hanlie, my *soigneurs*, and Mark and Ernie, my mechanics. Steve Peters held me close, and I accepted the embrace of Jan and Iain, Dave and Shane. They were present in a way that was so different to their absence the night before, when Jess had needed them most.

Compared with Beijing, where I had felt so numb on the podium, I loved the medal ceremony at The Pringle. It meant so much to me that I could see Scott and my family right in front of me. They held a giant Team Pendleton flag and happy tears came again as I gazed at Scott, his sister Isabel, my mum, Nicola, Alex, Laura and Saskia. Jess was with them too. She grinned as she covered Nathan's ears in an effort to block the noise. He slumbered on.

As I waited for my gold medal I cupped my hands into the shape of a heart. I looked straight at Scott and my family. And then I pointed at them all – telling them how much I loved them.

Once I felt the heavy chunk of Olympic gold settle around my neck I sang the anthem and finally understood what you are meant to experience in such a moment – joy, pride and relief all wrapped up in a magical blur of feeling.

I only missed my dad. Amongst the masses of texts and voice-mails and tweets there was nothing from Max. Dad had made me the cyclist I had been in the keirin. I had also ridden all three races like Max Pendleton might have done had he become an Olympic cyclist.

In the quiet of my room in the Olympic village I reached for my phone. I called Dad and, after four or five rings, he answered. He was driving home from the velodrome. I could tell how pleased he was to hear from me. He must have thought I would be too busy to read a text from him.

Dad was thrilled, especially after the team sprint debacle, which he had watched on television. 'That was a rubbish decision,' Dad said, and I laughed. I could have done with Max Pendleton bending the old commissaire's ear.

'I'm proud of you Victoria,' Dad said.

'Thanks, Dad,' I replied. 'For everything ...'

Sleep, of course, resisted me again for a long time. The night before I could not find any rest from all my brooding over the injustice Jess and I had suffered. And then, after victory, I was equally powerless to stop my mind racing in the dark.

Finally, I drifted off before, in the early hours, I woke with a jolt. I wondered if I had dreamt it all. The room was so black that I could not see anything. I dimly remembered having left my gold medal on the beanbag next to my bed.

I leaned over and stretched my fingers out to the beanbag. It would have not been a complete surprise if I had discovered nothing but empty fabric.

Then, and with a small smile, I touched my gold medal. I picked it up in the dark. I still could not see it but I felt its comforting weight in my hand. It was real. At four o'clock on the Saturday morning of 4 August 2012 I remained an Olympic champion.

I had a day to rest before I returned to the track with a vengeance. Super Saturday, as the British media exulted, had seen six more GB gold medals at London 2012. Attention focused on the Olympic Stadium where, in less than an hour, three British victories were confirmed in the heptathlon, the long jump and the 10,000m for Jess Ennis, Greg Rutherford and Mo Farah. It was the greatest night in the history of British athletics. The achievement of the team pursuit girls was just as impressive at the velodrome – for they smashed the world record for the sixth successive race as they won the final with ridiculous ease.

Each one of Jo Rowsell, Laura Trott and Dani King had overcome some form of adversity and deserved their sudden emergence in the national consciousness. But I felt sympathy for Wendy Houvenaghel – for so long a key member of that squad – who was bitter at being denied a chance to ride at least one race and so also secure a gold medal. She complained to the media that she had been treated 'shabbily' by British Cycling. Wendy accused Shane Sutton of being 'vindictive' and picking an unwell rider, Rowsell, in the final.

Lizzie Armitstead, who had ridden brilliantly to win GB's first medal, also expressed some discontent to the press after coming second in the road race. 'The sexism I have encountered in my career can get quite overwhelming and very frustrating,' Lizzie said calmly. 'You just get used to it. There's not much I can do about it now as an elite athlete. But I certainly hope to after my career is over.'

It seemed striking that a smiling twenty-three-year-old silver medallist on the road and a dejected thirty-seven-year-old team pursuit rider should voice the problems faced by women in a male-dominated sport. I was not alone after all – but it was time, on the brink of qualifying for the individual sprint, to set aside our shared concerns.

During the depths of my lost form, and my attempt to concentrate on a training programme to increase my strength, I had lost a lot in the sprint. In 2011, I relinquished my world title to Anna Meares. But the most obvious symbol of my struggle in the sprint usually came in the qualifying time-trial. It had never been my greatest attribute but, at my most dominant, during 2007 and 2008, I sometimes qualified fastest. In Beijing, I had done so in a new Olympic record of 10.963 seconds. Yet from 2009 to the World Championships in April

2012 I had finished outside the top four too often. A low seeding meant I ended up facing Meares in one semi-final after another. This time, I wanted to plot a different way to the final.

I was the third last name in a starting list of eighteen riders. Kristina Vogel headed the standings, in 11.027 seconds, when I hit the track. The noise unfurled in booming waves as I picked up speed. I rode with unerring certainty and velocity as my black bike arrowed around the boards.

Hugh Porter, commentating for the BBC, was also in the groove. 'Here comes Pendleton,' he yelped. 'Pendleton stops the clock in 10.724. That is an Olympic record, a lifetime personal best and a world record. Unbelievable!'

Miriam Welte had ridden marginally quicker at altitude in Colorado two months before. But cycling at altitude provides distorted times. Everyone assured me that I had the 'real' world record – having ridden faster than Meares had done in Melbourne earlier that year when she clocked 10.782. She would have to produce something even more majestic if she was going to be quicker than me in London.

Guo was next in a time of 11.020 while, lastly, Meares made another big sub-11 effort. But she was fractionally slower than she had been in Melbourne, in 10.805, and adrift of me. I had guaranteed myself the top seeding and a route to the final which would avoid both Guo and Meares. During the afternoon session the old haughty strut was back as I completed comprehensive victories in the first two rounds over Ekaterina Gnidenko and Willy Kanis. Meares dispatched Kayono Maeda and Monique Sullivan.

A day later, in the quarter-finals, I beat Olga Panarina in two straight races while Meares did the same to Shulika. We were heading towards our expected final clash.

Olympic Velodrome, Stratford, London,
Tuesday 7 August 2012

We had our storybook ending even if, considering our edgy encounters, my rivalry with Anna Meares carried a darker hue. Over the last decade we had taken chunks out of each other in between winning nineteen world titles – ten for Meares and nine for me. I had two Olympic gold medals to her one and it seemed fated that I should ride against her in my last race.

I'd felt as strong as ever as I beat Vogel 2–0 in the semi-finals while, unsurprisingly, Meares matched that score against Guo.

We were soon summoned again to the track for the final. In race one, I drew the lead-out role and rode steadily for the first lap and a half. There would be no psychological game-playing or tactical bluffing from me. I was ready to back my speed against Meares. She allowed a clear gap to open up between us. But then, as I rose out of my saddle, Meares came for me with intent. I could sense her headlong rush as the crowd screamed and stomped in support of me.

Meares was closing on me and, as we approached the final turn, she was past my back wheel. We went into that last bend shoulder-to-shoulder. As we flew up and out of the curve and into the back straight she leaned across the line. I could feel her left elbow dig into my ribs. It was an old Meares trick of forceful intimidation and my bike drifted out of the space between my black and red lines. I was sucked into her lane for a second before I corrected myself and went for home.

She inched ahead me of as we neared the finish. But, in a defiant lunge, I ducked my head low and found one more desperate kick. My bike surged forward and, on the line, I thought I spurted in front of her. It still felt impossibly close.

The thunderous appreciation subsided into confusion as the numbers 1 and 2 did not appear next to either of our names. I rode around the track, waiting and hoping, as my breathing fell hard and fast. Anna bloody Meares never made it easy – just as Vicky bloody Pendleton made it just as hard for her.

Eventually, the agonizing wait ended. My heart soared and the crowd roared as I got the number I wanted – that beautiful '1'. I needed to win just one out of a possible two final races to complete my career with the most gorgeous and memorable victory of them all.

Heading for the rollers, I felt my conviction. I could win one more race. I just wanted to do it before Chris Hoy won his second gold medal at London 2012 – and became the most successful British Olympian of all time by overtaking Steve Redgrave's record of five golds. A third gold medal would make me the most decorated British woman Olympian in history.

A less glorious image soon filled the screens above my head. As my bony knees went up and down my heart pumped still harder. The commissaire, once more, stood over a monitor. He scrutinized my victory as if he were determined to deny another British gold medal.

I felt cold as I saw how low Dave Brailsford looked as he listened to the commissaire. My misery came more quickly this time. Within minutes of beating Meares by the width of tyre, it was announced that rider 110, me, had been relegated. My head slumped, along with my normally tenacious fighting spirit, as I realized what that cruel ruling meant.

Despite the fact that Meares had elbowed me, I now had to find the will to come back and win both of the next two races. I had done it in Melbourne and Jan tried to rile me up again. But it was no use. I had lost so much after a second withering blow from the man in a dark blazer. For one crazy moment I thought about sliding off my bike and walking out of the building. I'd had my fill of track cycling. Of course I would never have done that. I needed to end my career properly, on the bike, racing Anna Meares.

In the meantime Laura Trott, aged twenty, had just won the omnium. The brilliant young girl from Cheshunt in Hertfordshire had her second gold of the London Olympics.

It was down to this old girl from Stotfold, in Bedfordshire, just seven weeks from her thirty-second birthday, to overturn the odds yet again. I would try even if my head was in an almighty mess.

Meares led us out in race two. I tracked her slowly and, after half a lap, she headed up the pine banking. Reluctantly, I followed her, only for her to lead me back down. And then, immediately, she went high again. After she had used the tactic against me repeatedly I knew what was coming. Meares forced a standstill. She stood high in her clamped peddles, her legs looking strong as her stationary bike quivered. I brought my own bike to a halt but the slope was steep and my feet were turned the wrong way.

As if I could not bear the toying cat-and-mouse torture of the match sprint any longer, I rolled down the banking and assumed the more unwanted lead-out role. The crowd bellowed, as if I had gained an advantage, but the reality was more tangled. Meares had my wheel to aim at as she began to pressure me.

I could not hold her off as we came down the back straight one last time. She went around on the outside and hurtled past me. It was over. Meares had won our last race. She celebrated even before she crossed the line. Meares pumped her right fist in disbelief.

I caught her down the home straight and, reaching out, clutched her left hand and lifted it high. Meares cried, as she held my hand, and her head dropped. Anna's face crumpled as we parted. She covered her visor with a hand, as if she could not quite fathom that she had won, while I applauded her.

And then I lifted my arms in salute to the crowd. 'Thank you,' I said, knowing that, amid the bedlam, everyone would have to lip-read my words.

My tears fell as I climbed off the bike for the last time at 5.45 on that fevered Tuesday evening. I reeled from one embrace to another, crying hardest with Luc de Wilde and Mark Ingham. And then, at last, I slipped one arm behind my back and tucked the other in front of my tummy. I bowed to the crowd – in gratitude.

Jill Douglas caught up with me. I managed to get the words out of my twitching mouth. 'I'm so relieved right now,' I said, 'but I'm overwhelmed with emotion. I would've loved to have won my final race but I'm just so glad it's over and I can move on.'

Anna Meares, Guo Shuang and I had to wait downstairs for a long time before the medal ceremony. We were together, just the three of us, for twenty minutes in the sapping heat. Anna, who was still crying, gave me a heartfelt hug. I hugged her back. We then spoke as girls rather than cyclists. Obviously Anna and I, sharing a language and a similar culture, did most of the talking. She asked me about wedding plans for Scott and me. She also told us about her own big day.

I laughed when she said that, after her wedding, she had gone straight to a club and kept on her white dress. She figured that you only get to wear your wedding dress once so she had danced in it all night.

Anna then cackled when she saw my horrified expression after she revealed that her father had picked out her wedding dress. It seemed to sum up an essential difference between us. There is simply no chance I would ever allow my dad to choose my wedding dress.

Guo and I had our own history together. She had been with me during my turbulent stint in Aigle. I had been inspired and distressed at the sprint academy in Switzerland and, even though she was five-and-a-half years younger than me, there had been times when I'd doubted I would ever match Guo's strength. But, now, so much had changed.

'So Shuang,' I said, 'what about you? When are you getting married?'

I knew how embarrassed Guo became whenever we spoke personally; but I was not trying to tease her. She had a boyfriend, a rather handsome cyclist on the Chinese team, and I was genuinely interested.

'Maybe when I'm thirty,' Guo blushed. 'Your age …'

Guo was twenty-six and I would soon be thirty-two. Anna would turn twenty-eight three days before me in September 2012. They were not done yet in cycling. But, for me, it really had ended.

I looked across at Anna and smiled. She nodded and smiled back at me. We were two champion fighters saying goodbye. We had been serious rivals, and contrasting riders, but I had never hated Anna. I just wanted to beat her cleanly every time. And she wanted to win just as much as I did. As silence finally settled over us I reflected how much we had needed each other. I doubted I would have achieved so much if I had not had her pushing me every time. I hoped Anna would say the same.

Anna and I had split four Olympic gold medals right down the middle. It was time, at last, for her to receive her second gleaming gold.

On the podium it felt touching and even graceful to link arms with my old rivals. We ducked heads and smiled together – after Anna and I each had cried some more. I then wrapped my arm around Anna's waist and congratulated the new Olympic champion again as I guided her off the podium.

I turned to face the cycling press in a final exchange. 'I was a bit pissed off about the relegation,' I shrugged. 'I didn't see it coming. *C'est la vie.*' And then I told them the truth, as I always did. 'If you paid me a million billion pounds I still couldn't go through that again. I'm so ready to do something else.'

A day later, Jan van Eijden and Iain Dyer had both left Stratford to return to their families. They either could not find me or simply chose not to say goodbye. Our last four years at the velodrome had been painful for each of us. Shane Sutton, meanwhile, still appeared to be seething with both Scott and me. So maybe three gold medals, or even two, as lovely as they'd have been at the end of London 2012, would have provided too illusory an end to my bruising history at British Cycling.

Shane and Dave Brailsford, and Jan and Iain, are champions of celebration. They had been elated when Chris Hoy won the keirin – which meant we had won seven out of ten events at the Olympic Velodrome. Besides my sprint silver, Ed Clancy followed his gold in the team pursuit with bronze in the omnium. Only Jess and I had failed to win a medal after our guaranteed silver was ripped away from us. British Cycling was, again, on an Olympic high. We had matched the incredible achievements of Beijing; while Dave and Shane were also celebrated for Team Sky and Brad Wiggins's Tour de France triumph.

Yet, exactly twenty-four hours after I had stepped off the Olympic podium, I knew why I'd gathered my friends at British Cycling, rather than my coaches and superiors, around me at Team GB's headquarters in Stratford. Each of my mechanics and *soigneurs*, my physiotherapists and performance analysts, are anonymous to the wider public – but I know how hard each of them works and how much they have contributed to everything I've achieved in cycling.

I went to each of them in turn, spending time with Luc de Wilde and Hanlie Fouché, and with Ernie Feargrieve and Mark

Ingham – and also with Richard Freeman, our doctor, Phil Burt, the physiotherapist, and Keith Reynolds, our team manager. They knew how much I'd endured in the lonely velodrome and amid the brutality of racing. I would've felt far lonelier without them.

Before I say goodbye, I retreat to a small room. The walls are very white and the space is cramped. Feeling strangely reflective, I sit in a plastic chair and look at my right arm. My inky tattoo appears dark against my skin. Today is the greatest day I've ever known.

It is not the most apt message for the day I have just spent. I woke up, having not drunk at all, feeling like I had a terrible hangover. There had not been much sleep after my relegation and loss to Anna Meares.

I thought a lot about all that happened to me and Scott over the last four years. I also mulled over so many of the words Shane Sutton had said to me during that time. 'You've got to be more of a bitch, Victoria,' he had advised me in defence of my Olympic title. 'Get more c-u-n-t in you.'

Even spelling out that word did not make it seem right to me. I know that my tenacity and strength of character have helped me achieve most of my goals. I would rather be remembered for being clean and honest, no matter how vulnerable, than being a male coaching archetype. If nothing else, on this tumultuous ride, I have remained true to myself.

I look down again at my arm, recalling the equivalent night four years ago. In Beijing, my world seemed to go awry. The accusations of treachery and betrayal marked me far more deeply than the faint scar I can still see on my right arm. I remember how poignant it felt that my tattoo did not cover it. The scar was meant to remain as a reminder of whom I had once been.

I touch it again, my finger running lightly along the thin line that looks whiter than my pale skin. I'm glad I can still see it. The scar makes me understand how much I have achieved both on and off my bike. It also helps me remember the girl on the hill. I can still see myself on a drizzly Sunday morning in Bedfordshire, chasing my dad's wheel, hoping he will look back to let me know he really does love me. I see myself turning up in a very short skirt and ridiculously sparkly sandals at the velodrome as the world champion boys roll their eyes. I see myself as a lost and confused girl in Aigle. I see myself on the rollers in Beijing, bent on shocking my doubters and annihilating Anna Meares in my first Olympic final. I see Scott and me happy together in Wilmslow and isolated at the velodrome. I see myself wanting to quit cycling but accumulating more World Championships. I see myself at London 2012, crying and smiling, being disqualified and relegated and yet still winning races.

I can hear Scott's words in my head, now, the words he said after I won gold in the keirin.

I'd met him again at the barrier of the track. We had been through so much to finally reach our point of release and freedom. I'd felt happier than I had ever done on my bike. He'd kissed me and then, stepping back to look at me with wonder, he said, 'We've done it, beautiful, we've done it.'

As I handed him the gold medal I answered him. 'Yeah, we've done it,' I said huskily. 'We really have done it.'

Five nights later I stand up and leave the empty white room. I go back inside to say a last farewell to the people who have looked after me best on my bike. I do not cry as I murmur my thanks and goodbyes. Instead, I manage to hug each of them with a smile.

I need to go and get dressed up for dinner with Scott – and my first night out, as a retired athlete, with my fiancé. It's calm and quiet, especially when, twenty-four hours earlier, I had heard the crowd chant my name at the Olympic Velodrome. I had just lost my last race but my name echoed around a heaving arena.

'*Vicky ... Vicky ... Vicky ...*'

I could not quite believe that thousands of strangers would join together in a chant for me.

Now, with a little surge of pride, I put my medals away. They're only two chunks of metal on a ribbon, silver and gold, but I will always keep them. Alongside the scars and the memories, they help tell the story of me.

I feel lighter now, knowing that it really is over. I feel ready for my night out with Scott – and the start of another life. And then, with a little wave, I am on my way.

I am no longer on a bike, going nowhere fast. Instead, I am on my own two feet, walking slowly, even happily, towards somewhere different and new. I push open the door and step out into the real world.

ACKNOWLEDGEMENTS

I would like to thank my father, Max, for teaching me to be competitive, for encouraging and supporting me in the world of cycling, and for the character building.

Secondly, to my mother, Pauline, for being the calming and caring influence on my life – for loving me no matter what and constantly reminding me that you can only do your best.

To my twin brother, Alex, and my sister, Nicola, for their love and support, despite seeing more of their sibling in the media than in person.

To Marshall Thomas and Peter Keen for giving me a chance at sprinting, despite the general consensus that I was too slight to make it.

For my support team (troop), thanks in no particular order to: Matt Parker, Christian Cook, Mark Simpson, Paul Barratt, Jonathan Leeder, Ernie Feargrieve, Mark Ingham, Luc de Wilde, Hanlie Fouché, Phil Burt, Richard Freeman and Diane at reception.

To Steve Peters – without whom I would never had reached the top level of elite sport; my chimp would have sabotaged my journey undoubtedly. Steve is like family to me. He is compassionate, intellectual and determined – qualities that make the world a better place.

To Chris Evans-Pollard: my one and only agent, a rare find in this industry. I am so grateful to him for giving me opportunities that I could only have dreamt of (including this book), but most of all being a dear friend and ally.

For Don McRae who, after our meeting post-Beijing, captured me honestly and truthfully. Reading his article I felt that they were my sentiments, and not the writer's, but far more eloquent. I would not have entered into writing this book with anyone else. I am, however, slightly embarrassed about a writer of Don's calibre and experience being such a great supporter of mine.

Granddad Alf, with whom I wish I could have spent more time, was a confident sportsman. I will always remember him saying: 'Call me Champ – I want to get used to it.'

Finally, to Scott, for being the most tremendous support, and for his patience and commitment on this arduous journey. I am forever in his debt. He is an inspiration to me.

Victoria Pendleton

It's such a solitary old business, being a writer, that one of the many pleasures of this book was rooted in my collaboration with the star of the show – Victoria Pendleton. We met for the first time in October 2008, when I interviewed Vicky for the *Guardian*, and she struck me then as being extraordinarily honest, brave and interesting. Her Olympic gold medal, which she had won a couple of months previously, almost seemed a mere incidental compared with her character. In the three years we've worked together, her candour and courage have become even more striking. I would like to thank Vicky for always talking so openly and rivetingly. She has been an unflinching and an inspiring witness to her own life, and I just hope I have done some justice to everything she has shared with me. I also loved watching her ride, and compete so tenaciously, at different velodromes.

Along the way, she and Scott Gardner looked after me beautifully on the many times I was with them in Wilmslow. They fed me delicious food, gave me lots of coffee and red wine, and ferried me to and from the station time and again. Scott was an invaluable reader and adviser – and thanks to him for all the race footage that helped us write the sporting sections of this book.

Chris Evans-Pollard, Vicky's agent, became a good friend and, together, we shared in some memorable nights as, like a mini-Team Pendleton, we watched so many races – right up until the very last at the Olympic Games. Chris was incredibly supportive of this book and his belief in it helped us get over the line – just in time.

Rory Scarfe and Steve Burdett at HarperCollins have shown great patience while watching an Olympic champion and a less-than-Olympian writer miss more than a few deadlines. Thanks to them – and to Rory, in particular, for both his editing and his understanding over jackets and titles, headaches and re-writes.

His predecessors in the role, Jonathan Taylor and Nick Canham, were both genuine supporters of the book and the way we wanted to write it. I'd also like to thank Caroline March and Tom Whiting.

Dan Gordon and I shared a great deal as we became immersed in the unfolding Victoria Pendleton story. Having read my first interview with Vicky, Dan eventually made a compelling documentary for the BBC, to which I contributed a minimal amount, and our friendship was forged in a shared passion for this story. We learnt a little about track cycling along the way but, far more than that, Dan was always a trusted ally, an insightful interviewer and a remarkable director. He's also, disturbingly, a zealous fan of Sheffield Wednesday but we did teach him that Vicky's granddad, Alf Viney, was much smarter in supporting Arsenal.

Tom Jenkins, apart from being the best sports photographer in the business, was also a real friend and a brilliant documenter of so many moments both on and off the track. It meant a lot to me to be able to include some of his work in the book and I still wish there could have been more from Tom. We also had a few laughs along the way and I'll always remember introducing Tom to the wonders of Arseblog while we watched European track cycling in Apeldoorn.

I wrote a lot about Victoria in the *Guardian* – and thanks to Ian Prior, Steve McMillan and Matthew Hancock for always giving me so much space. Thanks also to Jonny Geller, my agent.

My wife, Alison, as always, read these words before anyone else. She's up to seven books with me now and, each new time, she helps me a little bit more. Thanks go to her for putting up with me being away so much, and with my spending the last year doing little else but work and write. And yet she was never less than generous towards me and this book.

Bella, our eldest daughter, rescued me from various technical nightmares and I'll never forget how she spent one whole

Sunday afternoon helping us with photos and captions. Thanks to her and, of course, to Jack, Emma and Alison for making me laugh and keeping me going right until the very last word.

Donald McRae

PHOTO CREDITS

Photographs courtesy of Victoria Pendleton, with the exception of:

Pages 6 (top), 9 (top left & right), 11, 12 (top left), 14 (top), 15 (bottom), 16 (top left & right, bottom left) © Tom Jenkins

Pages 4 (top), 5 (bottom), 6 (bottom), 8 (top right & bottom), 9 (bottom), 10 (bottom), 12 (top right & bottom), 14 (bottom), 15 (top), 16 (bottom right) © Getty Images

Pages 4 (bottom), 7 (top), 13 (top left) © AFP/Getty Images

Page 5 (top) © Alan Mahon

Page 6 (bottom) © Rex Features